'Kohut's new book provides a comprehensive and focused treatment of empathy as a way of knowing generally and a way of knowing the past in particular ... Kohut's admirably informed and strongly argued book makes a valuable contribution to social-scientific and humanistic disciplines as well as to the public sphere.'

Dominick LaCapra, *Cornell University*

'This book envisions and tracks a new and exciting encounter between history/ historiography and psychoanalysis... Thomas Kohut shows us how the practice of psychoanalysis – as a treatment and in relation to human subjectivity and motivation – enlivens and transforms the practice of historical analysis.'

Adrienne Harris, *Sandor Ferenczi Center, New School*

'... an enjoyable read. It constitutes a very important contribution to historical methodology and to the literature concerned with how to evaluate empathy as an epistemic means for knowing other minds.'

Karsten R. Stueber, *College of the Holy Cross*

'Kohut has combed through an extraordinarily wide range of thinking pertinent to this topic, added his own very trenchant insights, and created what amounts to a master synthesis.'

John Demos, *Yale University*

'This book is a superb introduction to the study of empathy. Kohut's crystal clear analysis of this concept's philosophical capacities, the debates surrounding it and its historiographical uses are brilliant and eye-opening.'

Amos Goldberg, *The Hebrew University of Jerusalem*

'History comes to life in this superb interdisciplinary account, intermixing historical, psychoanalytic, and philosophical questions about the nature and functioning of empathy.'

Donna M. Orange, *New York University Postdoctoral Program in Psychoanalysis and Psychotherapy*

Empathy and the Historical Understanding of the Human Past

Empathy and the Historical Understanding of the Human Past is a comprehensive consideration of the role of empathy in historical knowledge, informed by the literature on empathy in fields including history, psychoanalysis, psychology, neuroscience, philosophy, and sociology.

The book seeks to raise the consciousness of historians about empathy by introducing them to the history of the concept and to its status in fields outside of history. It also seeks to raise the self-consciousness of historians about their use of empathy to know and understand past people. Defining empathy as thinking and feeling, as *imagining*, one's way inside the experience of others in order to know and understand them, Thomas A. Kohut distinguishes between the external and the empathic observational position, the position of the historical subject. He argues that historians need to be aware of their observational position, of when they are empathizing and when they are not. Indeed, Kohut advocates for the deliberate, self-reflective use of empathy as a legitimate and important mode of historical inquiry.

Insightful, cogent, and interdisciplinary, the book will be essential for historians, students of history, and psychoanalysts, as well as those in other fields who seek to know and understand human beings.

Thomas A. Kohut is the Sue and Edgar Wachenheim III Professor of History at Williams College, USA. A historian with psychoanalytic training, Kohut has published on topics in German history and on the relationship between history and psychoanalysis.

Empathy and the Historical Understanding of the Human Past

Thomas A. Kohut

Routledge
Taylor & Francis Group

LONDON AND NEW YORK

First published 2020
by Routledge
2 Park Square, Milton Park, Abingdon, Oxon OX14 4RN

and by Routledge
52 Vanderbilt Avenue, New York, NY 10017

Routledge is an imprint of the Taylor & Francis Group, an informa business

British Library Cataloguing in Publication Data
A catalogue record for this book is available from the British Library

Library of Congress Cataloging-in-Publication Data
A catalog record has been requested for this book

ISBN: 978-0-367-42577-7 (hbk)
ISBN: 978-0-367-42578-4 (pbk)
ISBN: 978-0-367-85364-8 (ebk)

Typeset in Times New Roman
by Taylor & Francis Books

You never really understand a person until you consider things from his point of view ... until you climb into his skin and walk around in it.

Harper Lee, *To Kill a Mockingbird*

For Sophie and Alexander

Contents

Acknowledgments

This book is personally important to me for a number of reasons. First, it engages with the work of my father, Heinz Kohut, the psychoanalyst who perhaps more than any other emphasized the centrality of empathy in psychoanalysis, seeing it in fact as defining psychoanalysis, both clinically and theoretically, as a field of inquiry into the inner life of human beings. Second, it allows me to bring my dual graduate training, in history at the University of Minnesota and in psychoanalysis at the Cincinnati Psychoanalytic Institute, into conversation with one another about the use of empathy to know and understand human beings. Indeed, throughout the manuscript, I draw on my knowledge of psychoanalytic clinical work, enhanced by my very brief career as a psychotherapist while a research candidate at the Institute, to shed light on the use of empathy in history. Finally, my previous scholarship and my teaching are characterized by the attempt to empathize with past people. Thus, in my first book, *Wilhelm II and the Germans: A Study in Leadership* (1991), I sought to empathize with the last German emperor, particularly in his relationship with his subjects. In my second, *A German Generation: An Experiential History of the Twentieth Century* (2012), I sought to empathize with the generation of Germans whose lives spanned the course of the twentieth century, including with their enthusiasm for National Socialism during the Third Reich. In all of my courses, students are encouraged to think and to imagine their way inside the experience of the people of the past, whether those were the authors of childrearing manuals in my course "Victorian Psychology from the Phrenologists to Freud," committed Nazis in my course "National-Socialist Germany," or Bosnian Serbs besieging Sarajevo during the Balkan War in my survey "Europe in the Twentieth Century." Nevertheless, until I began working on this project, I had never systematically studied or thought deeply about the empathic approach that defines me as a historian. This book seeks to raise the consciousness of historians about their use of empathy to know and understand the human past. In the process of working on it, I raised my own.

Therefore, although it can be said that in a sense I grew up with empathy and that taking an empathic approach to the past characterizes my scholarship and my teaching, working on this project brought me into unfamiliar territory. I had to learn about the history of the concept. I had to study assi-duously the way empathy has been understood and used by historians and psychoanalysts. Although the literature on empathy in those two fields was not altogether unfamiliar to me, I had to read the vast literature on empathy in fields that were more or less new to me, including philosophy (the philo-sophy of mind and phenomenology), neuroscience (primarily as it relates to philosophical accounts of the use of empathy to know the minds and mental states of others), psychology (above all cognitive, developmental, and social psychology), sociology and anthropology, and literary and cultural studies.

Friends and colleagues played a crucial role in giving me the intellectual competence and self-confidence to venture into that, for me, uncharted territory. This book could not have been written without their help. Their willingness to engage in discussion about empathy, to read manuscript drafts, to critique what I had written and make suggestions for its improvement reflected not only friend-ship and/or colleagueship but also the fact that empathy as a way of knowing and understanding human beings appears to be such an engaging and important contemporary topic. Where I could, I have tried to acknowledge specific intel-lectual debts in the notes, including to Alexandra Garbarini, Bojana Mlade-novic, Mark Roseman, Jane Tillman, and Armin Vodopuitz. I am so grateful to those who read manuscript drafts carefully and constructively and whose sug-gestions led to its significant improvement, including Ute Daniel, John Demos, Georges Dreyfus, Amos Goldberg, Harald Halbhuber, Eric Knibbs, Thomas Kühne, Bojana Mladenovic, Keith Moxey, and Karsten Stueber. In addition, I would like to acknowledge those whose contributions to this book took the form of general advice and thoughts about the role of empathy in historical knowledge along with simple encouragement. These include Thomas Aichhorn, Steven Aschheim, Kenneth Barish, Alexander Bevilacqua, Marcus Carney, Alon Con-fino, Christina de Bellaigue, Elizabeth Friend-Smith, Gerard Fromm, Friedl Früh, Jeffrey Halpern, Laurie Heatherington, Michael Ann Holly, Richard Honig, Irene Kacandes, Jan-Werner Müller, Diane O'Donoghue, Francis Oakley, Claudia Olk, Anna Ornstein, Sharone Ornstein, Alfred Pfabigan, Magda Pfabigan, Eric Plakun, Lisa Raskin, Karen Remmler, Jürgen Reulecke, Ileene Smith, Matthias Siebeck, Yana Skorobogatov, Christian Thorne, Jane Tillman, Dorothee Wierling, and James Wilk.

Two groups of psychoanalysts, one in the United States and the other in Austria, read parts or nearly all of the manuscript. I am deeply grateful for their willingness to read and engage with my work. In November 2018, members of the Ferenczi Center of the New School for Social Research, the Erikson Institute for Education and Research of the Austen Riggs Center, and the Psychology and the Other of Boston College Study Group met to discuss my manuscript. Although, reflecting its name, the group was too large, about thirty people, for me to able to thank its members individually, I would like to single out Adrienne Harris and Edward Shapiro for their helpful comments during and particularly after the meeting. I am even more deeply indebted to the group of Austrian psychoanalysts who, as part of the series "Psychoanalytische Abende," met with me seven times, each session lasting well over two hours, to discuss chapters of the book manuscript: Erwin Bartosch, Andrea Harms, Peter Hohenbalken, Maria Lindner, Christa Paulinz, Armin Vodopiutz, and Karoline Windhager. Those discussions, characterized by intelligence, thoughtfulness, insight, and warmth, were a highlight of my work on this project. And I would like to thank Jennifer French, Jeffrey Israel, Bojana Mladenovic, Gail Newman, and Jana Sawicki, all members of the reading group on psychoanalytic attachment theory at Williams College, for their thoughtful and helpful discussion of several chapters of the manuscript in the fall of 2018.

I would like to express my gratitude to two people whom I have only come to know over the last several years but who have, in that relatively short time, become close colleagues and friends, Roger Frie and Donna Orange. Although Roger and Donna both played important roles in the publication of this book by Routledge, their contributions to this project, my work in general, and my intellectual and personal life far outweigh that.

I would like to thank Lori Dubois, reference librarian at Williams College, for her patience, good will, and intelligent advice. Teaching me to use End-Note on this project was not an easy task, but her contributions to this book go beyond that. I would like to thank my editor at Routledge, Susannah Frearson, not only for acquiring my manuscript but also for her sensible and intelligent advice, encouragement, and good will throughout the acquisition process. It has been a pleasure working with her. The same can be said about my collaboration with Heather Evans, senior editorial assistant at Routledge during the production process. Efficient, diligent, intelligent, and sensible, Heather has helped make the production of the book a thoroughly enjoyable experience. And I would like to thank Maria Anson for her rigorous and thoughtful copyediting of the manuscript.

I would like to acknowledge the president, dean of faculty, associate dean of faculty, and board of trustees at Williams College for the sabbatical and general financial support I received over the course of the two periods of leave I used to research and write this book. The support I received from the college testifies to the importance that Williams places on having a faculty of active and productive scholars.

I want to single out for special thanks my colleague and friend, Alexandra Garbarini. There is nothing I write that Ali does not read. There is no thorny intellectual issue that I do not talk through with her. Every sentence in this book Ali has read at least once, and frequently more often than that. This book would not have been written without her support, advice, and intelligence. I am fully aware of how lucky I am to have Ali as a friend and colleague. That she is actually my colleague in the History Department at Williams College sometimes seems to me to be nothing short of miraculous.

And, finally, I want to thank my wife Susan who, as in all my intellectual and personal endeavors, is my lifelong friend and partner.

Introduction

Historians' Use of Empathy and Their Discomfort with the Concept

Empathy in history—most or at least very many historians use it, but they do not like to acknowledge that they do.[1] Empathy makes them uneasy. It is a squishy and capacious concept. It lacks rigor. Its precise meaning is unclear.[2] Empathy connotes softness, feeling, something gendered feminine perhaps.[3] It implies forgiveness or sympathy or even love for the people of the past. As opposed to hard evidence, cold reason, and rigorous logic, empathy suggests qualities difficult to reconcile with a "discipline" that still may conceive of itself as rationalistic, empirical, and objective, a social *science*.[4]

The word itself, empathy, is only of relatively recent vintage, having been coined in 1909 by the psychologist Edward Titchener as his translation of the German word *Einfühlung*, meaning "feeling into" or perhaps "feeling one's way inside," first used in a systematic, rigorous way by the German philosopher Robert Vischer in his 1873 doctoral dissertation on aesthetics.[5] Indeed, given empathy's ambiguity, a number of scholars have engaged in etymological analyses of the term going back to the Greek *empatheia* hoping to find the key to unlock the concept's true meaning, seemingly unaware that the word's origins probably go back barely 100 years to one man's idiosyncratic translation of *Einfühlung*.[6] Adding to the confusion is the fact that what we call empathy has frequently been called "sympathy" going back to the philosopher David Hume and continuing on well into the twentieth century, connoting not compassion but "sympathetic understanding." In German, not only Einfühlung but *sich hineinversetzen, nachbilden,* and *nacherleben*—"putting oneself in the place of," "reproducing or reconstructing," and "re-experiencing," respectively—also convey empathy. Indeed, discomfort with Einfühlung has led scholars in Germany, some in history and literary studies, most in psychoanalysis, to use the English translation translated back into German as *Empathie*. A number of the most theoretically sophisticated and thoughtful proponents of the use of empathy in history and some of the most sensitive and empathic historians never actually use the word. Thus, it is striking that Reinhart Koselleck, whose account of empathic understanding will figure prominently in these reflections, never to the best of my knowledge used or explicitly considered the concept in his writings. In avoiding the term Einfühlung, historians and other scholars perhaps wish to deny or disguise the fact that "feeling" may play a role in knowing.

Indeed, historians' uneasiness with empathy as a way to know and understand the human past may not simply derive from its conceptual murkiness or from stereotypical and inaccurate assumptions about the concept. While it relies on evidence, logic, reason, and other uncontroversial ways of knowing in history, empathy also involves imagination, insight, sensitivity to people, emotional intelligence, even emotional resonance. Although these features of empathy may make hardheaded empiricists uncomfortable, they are the qualities that ultimately make the practice of history a fascinating, creative, and fully human enterprise. Without those qualities, there could be no understanding of the human motivation of past events, and no understanding of the way past people experienced themselves or the worlds they inhabited. As a result, most historians use empathy in knowing the past even if they almost never acknowledge their reliance on empathy to their readers—or to themselves. As the historian Barbara Taylor puts it, "our interpretations of past subjectivities draw on our imaginative identifications, conscious and unconscious, with the people we study. This empathic experience, I have proposed, is not optional; without it history writing is impossible."[7] Neither general reluctance to reflect systematically on how they know the past nor possible embarrassment about the imaginative and emotional dimensions of knowing should prevent historians from facing up to and, indeed, embracing their use of empathy in history. Historians need to acknowledge empathy's role in historical knowledge, to be self-aware in their use of empathy, and to think systematically and rigorously about empathy's meaning, applications, implications, and limitations.[8]

Empathy as the Focus of Contemporary Attention—Although Not in History

Although historians and philosophers of history, with a few notable exceptions, have not in recent decades focused systematic attention on empathy, even as they use it, empathy is currently the focus of considerable contemporary attention, the subject of a vast and growing literature in neuroscience, zoology, ethology, the philosophy of mind and phenomenology, cognitive, developmental, and social psychology, psychoanalysis, and more.[9] It is striking that the philosopher Amy Coplan recently listed thirteen areas where empathy has been the focus of recent attention—none of them history.[10] One of the principal reasons for the current attention paid to such a venerable concept is that in the last decades empathy appears to have been "naturalized." Neuroscience research suggests that human beings are neurobiologically able, in the words of Georg Vielmetter, "to *automatically identify and empathetically understand the (expressive) situation of conspecifics.*"[11] As a result of neuroscientific findings over the last two or three decades, empathy, a concept held in ill-repute for most of the latter half of the twentieth century, is now seen as a fundamental attribute enabling human beings to recognize and to understand one another.

The fact that empathy is currently the subject of so much attention confirms its importance, but the burgeoning research and literature in so many different fields also renders the concept even more confusing. Scholars in various disciplines have developed numerous definitions of empathy, some complementary and some mutually exclusive. Indeed, one social psychologist, C. Daniel Batson, listed eight related but distinct definitions of empathy.[12] Part of the confusion about the concept can be traced to the fact that the various disciplines in which empathy is currently so important have different concerns and different priorities. Some, above all philosophy of mind and phenomenology, focus primarily on empathy's cognitive dimension. Others, above all developmental psychology, focus on its emotional or affective dimension. Still others, above all zoology and ethology, focus on its "prosocial" or altruistic dimension. And some, above all cognitive neuroscience, philosophy, social psychology, and psychoanalysis, seek to bring two or even three of these dimensions together. Despite these differences, current discussions of empathy tend to relate to the question of how we know the minds and mental states of others encountered *directly*, face-to-face, in the here and now. Empathy's role in knowing the minds and mental states of the people of the past, whom we encounter only *indirectly* through their expressions and creations, is only occasionally considered in these debates, and then principally because philosophers of history like Wilhelm Dilthey and R. G. Collingwood were prominent theorizers of empathy. Thus, the consideration of empathy's role in historical knowledge tends to be subordinated to knowing others in the present.

Aims of the Book

This book then is not about empathy as a *subject* of historical knowledge, about the role that empathy and its absence has played in human history. That is a legitimate and important subject of historical inquiry. Instead, this is a book about empathy *as a way to know and understand* the people of the past historically. The book presents some of the concept's history and the principal accounts of the concept in a variety of disciplines (including philosophy, psychology, sociology, and psychoanalysis) to lay the foundation for a consideration of the use of empathy in historical knowledge. A primary aim of this book is to inspire and contribute to a knowledgeable and rigorous discussion on the part of historians about the role of empathy in historical knowledge. In the process, the book seeks to overcome the skepticism with which some historians regard the concept, and advocates for the deliberate, self-conscious, and self-critical use of empathy by historians as a legitimate and important mode of historical inquiry.

Given that there are numerous, frequently incompatible, definitions of empathy, it is incumbent upon historians employing empathy to have an articulated definition of the concept that is clear to readers and, even more, to themselves and that is employed consistently throughout their work. In keeping with that prescription, empathy as it is presented here is a way of knowing, a mode of observation and an observational vantage point. The book seeks to establish empathy as a way to know and understand the people of the past by imagining, thinking, and perhaps even feeling one's way inside their experience. Although empathizing with past people is to no small degree a rational enterprise, the book seeks to emphasize the vital role that imagination plays in historical knowledge, enabling historians to know and understand past human beings and past experiences that they have not had themselves. In the eternal struggle over whether the present dominates the past or the past dominates the present in historical writing, an empathic historical approach shifts the balance of power in favor of the past, ceding more authority to the people of the past, their perceptions, experiences, and feelings, than historians have traditionally been wont to do. Indeed, the people of the past are better thought of less as the passive subjects of our investigation, and more as our collaborators, with whom we are in an affective and cognitive relationship that profoundly influences what we know and write about them. By reading the historical subject less from the perspective of the present and more from the perspective of the historical subject, empathy enables historians to approach the past non-deterministically. By taking seriously the experiences that past people took seriously themselves, empathic history illuminates possibility and contingency, not what ultimately happened but what might have occurred. Given the fact that the position of the observer determines what he or she is able to see, the book seeks to demonstrate that history written from an empathic vantage point, written, that is, from the perspective of the historical subject, is different from history written with the benefit of hindsight—and of equal value.

Throughout the book, I distinguish between the external and the empathic observational positions. The historian occupying the external observational position views historical phenomena from his or her own perspective, with all the benefit of hindsight, distance, and scope that the external observational position affords. The historian occupying the internal or empathic observational position seeks to view historical phenomena from the perspective of the people of the past, to view and understand their world as they themselves viewed and understood it. Although some historians occupy the external observational position more or less exclusively (economic and many social historians, for example), those interested in human experience (many cultural historians, for example) often occupy the empathic observational position in order to know and understand the feelings, thoughts, and actions of their historical subjects. Nevertheless, empathizing historians also occupy the external observational position, before, after, and even while empathizing with past people. Because, even while empathizing, historians never step out of their own skins completely and on some basic level *must* remain themselves, empathy is always attenuated and partial. Even as it seeks to know and understand difference, empathy affirms alterity.

The book insists, then, that the historian's effort to adopt the perspective of the historical subject be self-aware and self-reflective. Although exceedingly difficult, it is critical that historians try to be aware of which observational position they are adopting at any given moment, not least because, as noted above, the external and the empathic observational positions yield different histories. In part perhaps because of the difficulty, it is my impression that historians are only rarely aware of when they are empathizing and when they are not. One of this book's take-home messages is that they need to be.

Finally, the book has a personal dimension. It draws on the fact that I am a historian who has had psychoanalytic training, with a brief career as a psychotherapist, and it engages with the work of my father, Heinz Kohut, who prominently theorized empathy and saw introspection and empathy as defining psychoanalysis as a field of inquiry into the inner life of human beings. Indeed, perhaps the central claim of the book—namely, that historians adopt two different observational positions in seeking to know the past—can be traced back to my father's distinction between what he called the "extrospective" and the "empathic" observational positions. For Kohut, we observe and seek to understand the external world from the extrospective position using our sense organs, at times aided by the instruments we use to enhance them (telescopes or microscopes, for example). By contrast, we observe and seek to understand the internal world of human beings through introspection, through the observation of our own inner life, and through empathy, which Kohut at times defined as "vicarious introspection" or "the application of the introspective mode of observation to another person."[13] To the extent that they rely on empathy, psychoanalysts and historians seek to think, feel, and imagine their way inside the experience of other people.[14] Throughout the book, I draw parallels and define differences between the way psychoanalysts use empathy to understand human beings in the present and the way historians use empathy to understand human beings in the past.

Notes

1 Peter Loewenberg and Barbara Taylor have considered the largely unacknowledged use of empathy by historians in understanding the people of the past. Peter Loewenberg, "Cultural History and Psychoanalysis," *Psychoanalysis and History* 9, no. 1(2007): 19; Barbara Taylor, "Historical Subjectivity," in *Psyche and History*, ed. Sally Alexander and Barbara Taylor (Basingstoke: Palgrave Macmillan, 2012), 199. See also the recent book by Tyson Retz, *Empathy and History: Historical Understanding in Re-Enactment, Hermeneutics and Education*, ed. Stefan Berger, Making Sense of History (New York and Oxford: Berghahn, 2018), 2–3. Helpful throughout my research into empathy was Frederic William Lieber's

unpublished dissertation, the product of prodigious effort, intelligence, and thought. Frederic William Lieber, "The Legacy of Empathy: History of a Psychological Concept" (Indiana University, 1995).

2 Not just historians but psychoanalysts, for whom empathy is a much more openly acknowledged central concept, frequently complain about the cavalier, undisciplined application of the term, about its vagueness and capaciousness. See, for example, Stefano Bolognini, "Empathy and 'Empathism'," *International Journal of Psycho-Analysis* 78(1997); Warren Poland, "Clinician's Corner: The Limits of Empathy," *American Imago* 64(2007).

3 Personal communication from the psychoanalyst Jane Tillman.

4 Dominick LaCapra, *Writing History, Writing Trauma* (Baltimore: Johns Hopkins University Press, 2001), 38; "Tropisms of Intellectual History," *Rethinking History* 8, no. 4(2004): 503.

5 Karsten Stueber, "Empathy," in *Stanford Encyclopedia of Philosophy*, ed. Edward Zalta (Palo Alto: Stanford University Press, 2014); Jay Winter, "From Sympathy to Empathy: Trajectories of Rights in the Twentieth Century," in *Empathy and Its Limits*, ed. Aleida Assmann and Ines Detmers (London and New York: Palgrave Macmillan, 2016), 101. For a succinct account of the role of Einfühlung in Vischer's theory of aesthetics, see Retz, *Empathy and History*, 75. Although not using the precise term, what it seeks to convey was already articulated by the philosopher Wilhelm Gottfried Herder 100 years before Vischer. Laura Hyatt Edwards, "A Brief Conceptual History of Einfühlung: 18th-Century Germany to Post-World War II U. S. Psychology," *History of Psychology* 16, no. 4(2013): 272–273.

6 George Pigman notes that "empathy" actually has nothing at all to do with the Greek *empatheia*. George W. Pigman, "Freud and the History of Empathy," *International Journal of Psycho-Analysis* 76(1995): 243. Etymologically, it makes more sense to go back to the roots of Einfühlung, as Laura Hyatt Edwards has done. Emerging out of Old High German, *fühlen* "meant to grasp, comprehend, or know with certainty through touch," "'the way to look at what we cannot see' … via all the senses combined holistically." Edwards, "Brief Conceptual History of Einfühlung," 271.

7 Taylor, "Historical Subjectivity," 205–206.

8 Ibid.

9 The philosopher of history Dominick LaCapra is one notable exception. Very recently, Tyson Retz published a book that focuses on the status of empathy in historical knowledge in relation to the history of historicism, the thought of R. G. Collingwood and Hans-Georg Gadamer, and particularly the education of secondary-school teachers in Great Britain, Canada, and Australia. In the end, Retz appears to prefer bringing Collingwood and Gadamer together in a way that offers "a better alternative to empathy" in understanding events and ideas historically. Retz, *Empathy and History*, 11; also 114, 122, 127, 128, 131, 153, (154), 157, 166, 215.

10 Amy Coplan, "Understanding Empathy: Its Features and Effects," in *Empathy: Philosophical and Psychological Perspectives*, ed. Amy Coplan and Peter Goldie (Oxford: Oxford University Press, 2011), 2.

11 Georg Vielmetter, "The Theory of Holistic Simulation: Beyond Interpretivism and Postempiricism," in *Empathy and Agency: The Problem of Understanding in the Social Sciences*, ed. Hans Herbert Kögler and Karsten Stueber (Boulder: Westview, 2000), 87 (emphasis in original).

12 C. Daniel Batson, "These Things Called Empathy: Eight Related but Distinct Phenomena," in *The Social Neuroscience of Empathy*, ed. Jean Decety and William John Ickes (Cambridge, MA: MIT Press, 2009).

13 Lotte Köhler, "Von der Freud'schen Psychoanalyse zur Selbstpsychologie Heinz Kohuts: Eine Einführung," in *Von der Selbsterhaltung zur Selbstachtung: Der*

geschichtlich bedingte Wandel psychoanalytischer Theorien und ihr Beitrag zum Verständnis historischer Entwicklungen, ed. Hans Kilian and Lotte Köhler (Giessen: Psychosozial-Verlag, 2013), 39. Heinz Kohut spelled out his view that introspection and empathy defined psychoanalysis as a field of inquiry in two important essays, the first published in 1959 and the second in 1982, following his death the previous year: Heinz Kohut, "Introspection, Empathy, and Psychoanalysis: An Examination of the Relationship between Mode of Observation and Theory," in *The Search for the Self: Selected Writings of Heinz Kohut: 1950–1978,* ed. Paul H. Ornstein (London: Karnac, 2011); Heinz Kohut, "Introspection, Empathy, and the Semicircle of Mental Health," in *The Search for the Self: Selected Writings of Heinz Kohut: 1978–1981,* ed. Paul H. Ornstein (London: Karnac, 2011).

14 Thomas A. Kohut, "Psychohistory as History," *American Historical Review* 91, no. 2 (1986).

Chapter 1

Historical Excursus

Empathy in the Debates over Knowing in
the Natural and in the Human Sciences

Although empathy's role in historical knowledge has not been the focus of much recent attention, empathy—or what the term seeks to convey—was implicitly and frequently explicitly considered within the larger debate that dominated much of the nineteenth and part of the twentieth century about the relationship between knowing in the natural sciences (*Naturwissenschaften*) and knowing in the human sciences (*Geisteswissenschaften*). Indeed, it was frequently asserted that empathy is at the very heart of the unique mode of "understanding" (*Verstehen*) that constitutes our knowledge of the human world.[1] Empathy as a way of knowing was the subject of considerable attention in two disciplines that emerged over the course of the nineteenth century to study the human world: first history, as the study of human beings and their societies in the past; and then sociology, as the study of human beings and their societies in the present.[2]

The Status of Empathy in the Emerging Discipline of History

The role played by empathy in knowing the human world generally and the human past in particular can be traced back at least as far as the early eighteenth-century philosopher and historian Giambattista Vico. Vico's philosophy of history came in reaction to the view articulated by his younger contemporary, David Hume, that the aim of history, like any other science,

> is only to discover the constant and universal principles of human nature, by showing men in all varieties of circumstances and situations ... These records of wars, intrigues, factions, and revolutions, are so many collections of experiments, by which the politician or moral philosopher fixes the principles of his science, in the same manner as the physician or natural philosopher becomes acquainted with the nature of plants, minerals, and other external objects, by the experiments which he forms concerning them.[3]

In contrast to Hume, Vico denied that the human world could be known in the way we know the world of nature. In his famous *verum factum* maxim that the "true" (verum) and the "made" or "created" (factum) are inter-changeable, Vico set forth both the distinction between the world of nature and the human world and the justification for our uniquely privileged access to the latter in a way that can readily be connected with empathy.[4] The *truth* of the natural world can only be known by God, according to Vico, since it is His *creation*. We can only observe the physical world from without or through experiments where we in effect seek to imitate God's creation of the natural world in the laboratory. By contrast, we can know the *truth* of the human world from within since we ourselves have made or *created* it, and "its prin-ciples are therefore to be found within the modifications of our own human mind."[5] According to Isaiah Berlin, Vico argued that because the human world is the creation of human beings like ourselves, whose thoughts and actions we can share, we are able to "re-experience the process" of creation "in our imagination" to achieve a "true" knowledge of the human past.[6]

In reacting against the Enlightenment rationalism of philosophers like David Hume, various nineteenth-century German philosophers, oft unawares, drew Vico's distinction between knowledge in the natural sciences as a form of external knowing and knowledge in the human sciences as a form of internal knowing based on Verstehen or "understanding," a process identical or at least closely related to what we would today call empathy. Indeed, Johann Gottfried Herder actually used the phrase *sich hinein fühlen* in claiming that to know human beings and their creations one needs to "feel oneself" into them. The connection between knowledge and feeling was not restricted to the human world for Herder but applied to knowledge of the world in general. Nevertheless, his claim that each culture has its own unique spirit and value, and that to know and appreciate the spirit and value of another culture one must feel one's way inside it, made Einfühlung the means by which one comprehends the time, place, and history of a people.[7]

Following Herder, "sich hinein fühlen" played a central role in most sub-sequent attempts to define and articulate the form of knowledge unique to the human sciences, history par excellence.[8] In the 1830s, Leopold von Ranke, gen-erally thought of as the founder of modern source-based history, echoed Vico in arguing that the "essence" or "content" of every historical phenomenon is "spiritual," and hence can only be known "through spiritual apperception." Historical "apperception" of this spiritual essence was, according to Ranke, based upon the congruence between the operation of the "observing" spirit of the historian and that of the spirit emerging from the historical phenomenon itself.[9] Although Ranke's contemporary, the historian Gustav Droysen, criticized Ranke for going "little beyond collecting facts," he followed his older colleague in seeing historical knowledge as "spiritual apperception."[10] Droysen regarded this way of knowing to be characteristic not merely of history, however, but of all the human sciences. Indeed, what distinguished the human from the natural sci-ences, for Droysen, was the fact that the latter explain (*erklären*) the physical world of nature, whereas the former understand (*verstehen*) the spiritual world of human beings. The natural sciences *explain* by constructing formal general-izations that take the form of universal laws about "repetitive causal chains"; history and the other human sciences *understand* "the unique inner world of spirit" through Einfühlung.[11] Like Vico, Droysen believed that our knowledge of the natural world is superficial, since those things which belong to it "have for us no individual, at least no personal, existence," whereas traces left by the people of the past speak "to us and we can understand" them as a result of the "kinship of our nature with that of the utterances lying before us as historical material."[12] In history we are able to relive the inner states of the people of the past through the expressions they have left behind because we ourselves are the product of history and what we seek to know is therefore already contained within us, "the result," as Droysen put it, "of the entire mental content [of the past] that we have unconsciously collected within ourselves and transformed into our own sub-jective world." In the end, for Droysen, it is our very historicity that makes it possible for us to know the past.[13]

The philosopher with whom the distinction between the human sciences and the natural sciences is most often associated is Wilhelm Dilthey, and history was for him the paradigmatic discipline in the human sciences. In a voluminous series of works characterized by rich imagination and deep insight, along with shifting views and some lack of intellectual rigor, Dilthey sought, following Kant, to produce a "critique of historical reason" that would, in his words, lay the "epistemological foundation for the human sci-ences."[14] Whereas the Naturwissenschaften are concerned with the physical world of nature, the Geisteswissenschaften are concerned with the spiritual and/or mental world of human beings. While the physical world, for Dilthey (as for Vico and for Droysen), is "a mere shadow cast by a hidden reality," in the human world "we possess reality as it really is" "in the form of the facts of consciousness given in inner experience."[15] For Dilthey, the Natur- and the Geisteswissenschaften were distinguished less by their objects of study and more by how they know those objects, specifically by the perspective adopted by the observer.[16] In the natural sciences, we can only know the physical world from without, through sense perception. In the human sciences, we can know the world of thought and feeling by experiencing it from within.[17] Following Droysen, Dilthey asserted that the natural sciences only explain, for we are not able to "understand the processes of nature ... It is different in the domain of the moral [human] world. Here I understand everything."[18] Knowledge in the human sciences for Dilthey, then, was rooted "in lived experience and understanding, both of which lead the human sciences to differ radically from the natural sciences and give the formation of the human sciences a character of its own."[19]

Dilthey believed that objective knowledge was possible in the Geis-teswissenschaften because the subject and the object of knowledge are the same.[20] In the case of history, the primary condition for the possibility of historical science is contained in the fact that I am myself a historical being and that the one who investigates history is the same as the one who makes history ... Lived experience contains the totality of our being. It is this that we re-create in understanding.[21]

That is to say, objective knowledge is possible in the human sciences generally and in history in particular, according to Dilthey, because the means and ends of knowledge are the same. Experience is at once what we seek to know and how we know it. Specifically, Dilthey saw historical understanding as coming through the historian's re-experience of past experience. Although never using the word "Einfühlung," Dilthey, in words and phrases including *sich hinein-versetzen, nacherleben,* and *nachbilden,* suggested that we know the "inner experience," "the facts of consciousness" that constitute the human world, "through a kind of transposition," by putting ourselves in the place of the other to re-experience the other's experience.[22]

Scholars have generally distinguished between an early Dilthey, of the *Intro-duction to the Human Sciences* (1883), and a later Dilthey, of *The Formation of the Historical World in the Human Sciences* (1910). The early Dilthey believed that objective knowledge in the human sciences was possible because we and the people we study are fundamentally similar psychologically. In history, we can know past experience because the historian and the people of the past "are not opposed to each other like two incomparable facts. Rather, both have been formed upon the substratum of a general human nature." It is that shared human nature which makes human understanding in general and historical understanding in particular possible.[23] Past experiences are "intelligible to us from within" because "we can, up to a certain point, reproduce them in ourselves on the basis of the perception of our own states."[24] In knowing the human world we engage in a process of experience, expression, and under-standing (*Erlebnis, Ausdruck, und Verstehen*). Our empathic imagination, our common humanity, and our own lived experiences enable us to recreate past experience within our psyche.[25] Through introspection, we are then able to observe what we have re-experienced, to identify, articulate, understand, and interpret it.

The later Dilthey moved away from the idea that a universal human psychology enabled us to know past experience, adopting instead the more Hegelian notion that historical understanding was possible because the historian and the past both partake of some ill-defined "objective spirit," which he called "life philosophy," whereby "the past is continuously an enduring present for us."[26] Now, following Droysen, a shared historicity enabled us to know past experience; or, as Dilthey put it, "individuals can understand history because they themselves are historical beings."[27] Various scholars see him moving away from empathy here and seeking to ground historical understanding in a universal hermeneutics, in "a commonly shared and understood historical world."[28] For the early Dilthey, we know past experience by transposing ourselves into the people of the past and reviving past experiences of our own that are the same as those of the past people. The content of past experience and of our re-experience was the same. By contrast, the later Dilthey believed that we know past experience, including experience very different from our own, because we and the people of the past engage in the same universal process of objectifying experience. In the words of the sociologist Jürgen Habermas, for the later Dilthey "the knowing subject is simultaneously part of the process in which the cultural world originates."[29] Returning to the triad of "experience, expression, and understanding," the early Dilthey placed primary emphasis on our empathic imagination, our common humanity, and our own lived experiences that enable us to recreate past experience within us. The later Dilthey placed primary emphasis on the *process* whereby we observe, conceptualize, understand, and interpret what we have re-experienced.[30] To the best of my understanding, experience that has been conceptualized, understood, and given the form of interpretation has been "objectified" for Dilthey. That is, it has been freed from the constraints of the time and place that gave rise to it in order to be able to assume the status of objective knowledge, indeed perhaps of historical truth.[31]

Before the outbreak of the First World War, the philosopher, humanist, and sometime politician, Benedetto Croce, followed his idol, Vico, as well as Dilthey in emphasizing the profound epistemological difference between the study of nature and the study of history. According to Croce, if we view the human past "from the outside," and thereby fail to attend to its spiritual essence, history is transformed into a "mummified and mechanicized [*sic*]" form of natural history.[32] He contrasted chronicle (a mere account of events) with living, present-day history.[33] It was the historian who breathed life into the dead facts of the past by reanimating past thought in his or her imagination.[34] Anticipating R. G. Collingwood (who would translate Croce's work into English), Croce saw the historian rethinking past thought and recreating past experience.[35] But, unlike his successor Collingwood, who focused on causation in history, Croce basically rejected causal history as reducing the historical particular to a means to an end. Instead, he saw the particular, in the form of past ideas and experiences, as the end of historical knowledge in itself.[36] And, unlike his predecessor Dilthey, Croce was concerned less with establishing that objective knowledge of the past was possible and more with establishing that for the past to come to life it must matter in the present, a view captured in his well-known aphorism that all "history is contemporary history."[37]

The Status of Empathy in the Emerging Discipline of Sociology

As in the developing discipline of history during the nineteenth century, so too for sociology, which emerged as a "social science" at century's end, the status and nature of knowledge of the human world and of human society were issues of central importance. As with their historian counterparts, sociologists in Germany and the United States during the last decade of the nineteenth and the first decades of the twentieth century emphasized the distinctiveness of the human sciences and considered the role of empathy in knowing the human world generally and human societies in particular, including past human societies.

Like Vico, Droysen, and Dilthey, Georg Simmel saw us unable to "penetrate the inner processes of nature" but able "to reproduce the contents of another mind with complete adequacy."[38] As in the present so in history to know and understand a historical person, "we must be able to 'occupy or inhabit the mind'" of that person.[39] Given that in history we seek to reconstruct and understand not merely conscious and articulated thought "but also what has been wished for and felt," we must therefore employ "some mode of mental transposition or translation" so that we ourselves can wish for and feel what had been wished for and felt.[40] As for the early Dilthey, at times Simmel believed that a shared psychology or shared psychological experiences made this transposition possible, even going so far as to call history "a form of applied psychology."[41] At other times, some unconscious or latent inheritance, "organic modifications" of mental processes "transmitted" across the generations, apparently allowed us to know the experience of past people objectively.[42] Despite his need to maintain the possibility of objective knowledge in the human sciences, Simmel, like Croce, appreciated the active role played by the historian in generating historical knowledge, and that "historical knowledge represents a transformation of experienced reality." As a result of the fact that in history "one mind speaks to another," historical understanding is not simply the subjective experience of the past person as taken in by the historian or the subjective experience of the historian as projected onto the past person; historical understanding represents an amalgam of both.[43]

Simmel's contemporary, Max Weber, also upheld the autonomy of the human sciences, seeing them as having different aims and objects of study and employing somewhat different methodologies than the natural sciences. The natural sciences are concerned with physical objects and their movements, which we know by applying formulated causal uniformities, i.e., universal laws, to them. But we cannot "understand" the natural world. By the same token, the natural science approach cannot comprehend the "subjective meanings," and in particular the subjective meanings of complex human actions (their motivations and the experience of their effects) that are the focus of the human sciences.[44] General laws therefore have no place in the human sciences.[45] Nevertheless, the Geisteswissenschaften were still to be empirical and scientific for Weber. To be sure, he accepted that the human sciences are centrally concerned with understanding. And he even allowed for the possibility that some understanding could be, in his words, "emotionally empathic" and involve "sympathetic participation."[46] But the empathic "recapturing" of "experience," was not, for him, "an absolute precondition for its interpretation."[47] Moreover, even though Einfühlung might help the social scientist arrive at an understanding of the subjective meaning of action, understanding (whether arrived at empathically or not) needed to be supplemented by rigorous empirical, causal analysis—needed, that is, to be objectified.[48] Our understanding of subjective meaning in the human world can be scientific, can be objectively valid, as long as our conceptualization is logical and coherent, our interpretation is confirmed by empirically derived evidence, and our findings are consistent with the established findings of other social scientists.[49] Simply because investigators study subjective meaning in the human world does not imply that "research in the cultural sciences can have results which are 'subjective' in the sense that they are *valid* for one person and not for others."[50] Hence, for Weber, it was possible in the human sciences to have objective, scientific knowledge of subjective human meaning.[51]

On the other side of the Atlantic, seven years before the psychologist Edward Titchener coined the term "empathy" in 1909, the sociologist Charles Cooley made the crucial distinction between the external and what I call here the empathic observational position. It is the latter, according to Cooley, that characterized the emerging science of sociology. From the external observational position, we can know the physical aspects of the human world, but these Cooley regarded to be of secondary importance. As an external observer, one can know the human world only superficially. Instead, for Cooley imagination was crucial in sociology, both in *how* and in *what* one studied. On the one hand, "persons and society must ... be studied primarily in the imagination." On the other hand, the aim of sociology was to study "the imaginations which people have of one another."[52] Cooley defined what he called "sympathy" as "entering into and sharing the minds of other persons," what we would call empathy today. Cooley explicitly distinguished "sympathy" from compassion.[53] In contrast to those who presume that empathy is somehow reserved for people with whom we can identify, Cooley believed one could have sympathy—empathy—for a criminal: "If one man strikes down another to rob him, or in revenge, we can imagine the offender's state of mind ... Indeed, to understand an act *is* to think of doing it ourselves."[54]

In his presidential address to the Michigan Academy of Science, Arts, and Letters in 1926, Cooley drew the by now familiar epistemological distinction between the natural and the human sciences, with the former investigating a world that can only be observed and known externally and the latter investigating a world accessible only through "sympathetic knowledge" (i.e., through empathy).[55] In knowing the material world, we use our senses and the instruments we have invented to extend them to gather data that our mind transforms into measurable and verifiable knowledge. In knowing the human world, the role of our senses is "ancillary." They merely initiate the process of knowing which involves our "vast and obscure outfit of human susceptibilities" that we use to transform what we have observed into "sympathetic" "personal or social knowledge."[56] In ways that echoed Theodor Lipps and that anticipated today's "simulation theory" (both of which will be considered in the following chapter), Cooley thought that personal knowledge of another is gained by reading his expressions; but it "also consists of inner sentiments which you yourself feel in some degree when you think of him in these situations, ascribing them to him."[57] Cooley believed that we rely on "sympathy" and "introspection" to acquire "social knowledge," as we first share the sentiments of others and then understand those sentiments by looking within ourselves.[58] Our knowledge of others was not personal or idiosyncratic but socially conditioned, not least through the language we use to understand others and ourselves and that we use to communicate our understanding.[59] All of the human sciences, then, "rest in great part upon sympathetic introspection, or the understanding of another's consciousness by the aid of your own, and give full play to the mental-social complex."[60]

Finally, the sociologist, philosopher, and psychologist George Herbert Mead, in a series of lectures over decades at the University of Chicago compiled by his students and published in 1934, defined empathy, which he unfortunately conflated with "sympathy," as "the capacity to take the role of the other and to adopt alternative perspectives vis-à-vis oneself."[61] Like Cooley (and, as we shall see, Lipps and contemporary simulation theorists), Mead defined sympathy as calling "out in ourselves the attitude" of the other: "We feel with him and we are able so to feel ourselves into the other because we have, by our own attitude, aroused in ourselves the attitude of the person whom we are assisting."[62] Indeed, for Mead, empathy was an essential aspect of social life:

> Human society endows the human individual with a mind; and the very social nature of that mind requires him to put himself to some degree in the experiential places of, or to take the attitudes of, the other individuals belonging to that society.[63]

Already in childhood, we are socialized to empathize, to engage in role playing as an essential way to know and understand the other: "The common term for this is 'putting yourself in his place'."[64] Indeed, as I shall argue throughout this book, it is our capacity to imagine ourselves in the place of the other that makes empathic knowledge of the people of the past possible.

The Status of Empathy in the Debates over Covering Laws in History and R. G. Collingwood's Philosophy of History

During most of the twentieth century, with the notable exception of Collingwood and a handful of others, philosophers of history focused relatively little attention on the epistemological status of empathy within historical knowledge. In the 1940s, 1950s, and 1960s, however, during the heyday of science, logical positivism, and social science, empathy re-emerged as a focus of interest within the context of renewed debate over the question of whether there was one world of scientific knowledge or, as had been contended during most of the nineteenth century, two. History became a focus of attention because it seemed a legitimate scholarly, even scientific, discipline; yet its approach seemed very different from that taken in the natural sciences. Most philosophers arguing for the unity of knowledge sought less to discredit history as an illegitimate branch of knowledge and more to show that, despite appearances, historians actually approach their subject in much the same way as natural scientists do.[65] Specifically, it was claimed that, like natural scientists, historians rely on universal "covering" laws, albeit implicitly, in making historical explanations.[66] According to some positivist philosophers, for history to achieve full scientific status, those laws needed to be made explicit in historical explanation. Thus, Carl Hempel in his famous article of 1942, "The Function of General Laws in History," compared historical explanations with the scientific account of the cracking of an automobile radiator on a cold night, purporting to show that every historical explanation relied upon at least one and frequently more than one testable "universal explanatory hypothesis" comparable to the universal laws that water freezes at 32 degrees Fahrenheit; that, as water temperature decreases, water pressure increases; and that, when water freezes, pressure again increases.[67] Because in history these universal hypotheses, these "covering laws," were mostly only implicit, historical explanations based on them were merely "explanation sketches," according to Hempel. His aim was to convince historians to make the universal explanatory hypotheses their explanations employed explicit, and thereby produce full-fledged scientific explanations.[68]

Hempel himself thought that "empathetic understanding" could be employed in history, but he denied that empathy distinguished history from natural science epistemologically. Empathy for Hempel was not an indispensable tool of the historian, and he denied that it had any evidentiary value. At best, it sometimes had heuristic value in suggesting certain explanatory possibilities, "but its use does not guarantee the soundness of the historical explanation to which it leads. The latter rather depends upon the factual correctness of the empirical generalizations which the method of understanding may have suggested." Empathic understanding for Hempel:

> must clearly be separated from scientific understanding. In history as anywhere else in empirical science, the explanation of a phenomenon consists in subsuming it under general empirical laws; and the criterion of its soundness is not whether it appeals to our imagination, whether it is presented in suggestive analogies, or is otherwise made to appear plausible—all this may occur in pseudo-explanations as well—but exclusively whether it rests on empirically well confirmed assumptions concerning initial conditions and general laws.[69]

In response to Hempel, philosophers of history like William H. Walsh, Patrick Gardiner, and particularly William Dray to a greater or lesser degree sought to defend empathy's scientific status in history and, in the process, drew attention to Collingwood's notion that the historian, in arriving at historical understanding, adopts the perspective of the historical actor and rethinks the historical actor's past thought.[70] Collingwood had strongly argued for the difference between knowledge in the natural and in the human sciences. According to Collingwood, truth is discovered though observation and experimentation in science, whereas in history we seek to know that which has "vanished" and hence cannot be directly observed, reproduced, or confirmed in the same way "as we verify our scientific hypotheses."[71] Natural science analyzes and classifies, comparing phenomena and bringing them under "a general formula or law of nature," whereas history, as the study of change, can never become a frozen compendium of abstract, unchanging, universal laws. The natural scientist can only know physical bodies and their movement from "an external point of view," whereas the historian can know individual historical phenomena from within.[72]

Writing during the heyday of high intellectual and political history, Collingwood was primarily interested in historically significant ideas, like those expressed in Plato's *Dialogues* or in the Theodosian Code, or historically significant events, like Caesar's crossing of the Rubicon or the building of Hadrian's Wall. To know and understand a great past creation of the mind, the historian needs to rethink the thoughts that gave rise to it. Thus, to understand Plato's *Dialogues*, the historian must rethink Plato's thought in writing them. Similarly, to know and understand historical events, the historian needs to rethink the past thought that had produced them.[73] Historical events were merely embodied thought for Collingwood: "the thought in the mind of the person by whose agency the event came about" is nothing "other than the event" itself; "it is the inside of the event."[74] Thus, for Collingwood, "all history is the history of thought." And "how does the historian discern the thoughts which he is trying to discover? There is only one way in which it can be done: by re-thinking them in his own mind."[75] Collingwood's emphasis on thought, his view that the historical exterior invariably reflected and expressed its interior, his contention that the historian is concerned with events "only by the way, in so far as these reveal to him the thoughts of which he is in search," meant that there was little room for the study of human activity independent of the thoughts that produced it in the historical repertoire.[76]

Collingwood's was a philosophy of history perfectly suited to high intellectual and political history, to understanding the ideas of great thinkers and the actions of great leaders. Rational "purposive action" was the subject matter of history for Collingwood, and there was little room for the irrational in his approach.[77] His historian rethought the thoughts of rational actors and/or reenacted the rationale that led to their decisions, perhaps even what the logic of the situation demanded of the historical actor.[78] History as the history of thought could only be known from within the mind of the person of the past. Nothing apprehended from the outside counted as history.[79] Hence, there was little room in Collingwood's philosophy of history for the behavior of groups or economic and social activity.

The Status of Empathy in the Shift from Political History through Social History to Cultural History and the History of Experience

Collingwood's philosophy, then, was incompatible with social history, which came on the scene with a vengeance in the 1960s and 1970s. The earlier intense discussion of empathy—both those who questioned empathy's epistemological value in knowing the past, like Hempel, Abel, Nagel, Danto, or White, and those who upheld it, like Walsh, Gardiner, and Dray—reflects the heyday of political history, with historians attempting to explain the historically significant actions of great leaders, whether by uncovering universal laws of political behavior or by rethinking the thoughts of historical actors. With the rise of social history and the rejection of high political history, there was a move away from empathy as a way to know the past in favor of the conceptualization of the impersonal processes and structures that influenced human beings regardless of consciousness. Indeed, for many social historians, past people were frequently wholly unaware of the forces that shaped their lives. Those forces could generally be viewed and defined only from without, by the social scientist observer who, with the benefit of hindsight and historical distance, could discern the processes and structures that shaped history in ways the people of the past could not. As social history, the discipline of history became a full-fledged social science.

To the extent that social historians focused on people, it was generally on those who until then had been ignored by political historians, women, the working classes, peasants, ethnic and racial minorities, gay people, and other marginalized groups. At the same time, European and American historians came increasingly to study the world beyond the West, to investigate indigenous peoples' experiences of imperialism and colonialism and, indeed, the history of non-Western people more generally. For these historians empathy was firmly associated with high political history, with the study of white male leaders in Europe and America, who had left behind written sources documenting their motives and whose essential cultural, psychological, and intellectual similarity to the investigating historian had generally been assumed. Empathic knowing of women, workers, peasants, minorities, gays, other marginalized groups, and non-Western people appeared to founder on the lack of available written sources spelling out their motives and/or on the presumed cultural, psychological, and intellectual differences separating the investigating historian from the historical subject. Hence, empathy, along with high political history with which it was so firmly associated, was either dismissed or more often ignored by the new generation of social historians who came to dominate the historical profession.

The 1980s witnessed two challenges to social history conceived of as a social science. The first challenge was the influence of postmodernism on historians; the second and related challenge was the emergence of cultural history. In some ways, empathy as a way of knowing the past might seem compatible with these two developments, since they turned historians away from the study of abstract historical forces and structures, deemphasized causation in favor of meaning and its creation, called into question the demand for and the possibility of historical objectivity, and recognized the central role in historical knowledge played by the subjectivity of the historian, who was now seen not as a social scientist but as closer to a literary scholar and writer in the case of postmodernism and to a cultural anthropologist in the case of cultural history. Nevertheless, empathy was often explicitly rejected by historians influenced by postmodernism, and was generally ignored or only vaguely considered by cultural historians even as they used it to know and understand the human past.

The questioning of the ideal of historical objectivity as either achievable or desirable by historians influenced by postmodernism might have opened up space for empathy as a way of knowing the past. As we shall see, given its attenuated nature and the fact that empathizing historians enter into a subjective relationship with the people they are seeking to know and understand, empathy is difficult to reconcile with historical objectivity. Indeed, as we have already seen, the accounts of historians like Droysen, philosophers like Dilthey, and sociologists like Simmel were considerably complicated and effectively compromised by their need to combine empathy with objective historical knowledge. Nevertheless, historians influenced by postmodernism were and frequently remain skeptical of empathy because it seems to deny difference and overlook its creation, to posit the possibility of knowledge of a more or less fixed historical reality (instead of seeing the past as an infinite series of re-presentations), fails to appreciate the constructed nature of the self and of its experience (both that of the historical subject and of the observing historian), and to presume a capacity to transcend one's historical moment and historicity that is simply naïve. Empathy, at best, is seen as innocent self-projection and, at worst, as hegemonic, when applied to non-Western peoples, a form of intellectual colonialism.[80] As the literary theorist Hans Ulrich Gumbrecht put it to a gathering of his former students and colleagues at the University of Siegen in the mid-1990s, "*no one* believes in empathy anymore."[81] To a degree, the postmodern critique of empathy in historical knowledge is based on empathy's association with high political and intellectual history and with the epistemological assumptions on which that history was based. As I shall argue here throughout, the postmodernist critique fails to recognize that the experience of alterity, of otherness, is essential to the empathizing process, fails to grasp that the empathizing historian is in a reciprocal cognitive and even emotional relationship with the people of the past, overestimates the historian's authority over the past and underestimates the authority of the past over the historian, and fails to appreciate the power of the human imagination.[82]

Around the time that postmodernism began to influence historical thinking in the 1980s, cultural history emerged out of social history to join the postmodernist challenge to the conception of history as an objective social science.

Sharing social history's focus on previously overlooked and marginalized groups, cultural historians were now increasingly interested in the everyday life of these groups, and oral history emerged as a way to recover everyday experiences. Instead of focusing on objective social reality, on the impersonal forces and structures that social historians had seen moving history and shaping consciousness, many cultural historians concerned themselves with subjective experience—with how past people experienced themselves and their world, their past, their present, and their expectations for the future. Thus, cultural historians returned to a focus on people; now not the great political leaders and intellectual figures studied by the historians of Collingwood's era but ordinary human beings, their perceptions, emotions, memories, and subjective experiences more generally. Beyond the individual, cultural historians focused on culture understood in an anthropological sense, on moral values, identities, mentalities, on past life worlds. These historians were concerned less with historical events, their causes and consequences. Instead, many were concerned more with how the people of the past experienced those events; with their subjective understanding of why those events occurred and with their subjective understanding of the consequences of those events; with their memories and with how those memories influenced their actions and sense of themselves.[83] Cultural history, then, was concerned with meaning, its creation, its acceptance, its appropriation, and its effects. According to the historian Ute Daniel, virtually any historical phenomenon can be the subject of cultural history, so long as it is "understood, described and explained" within its "cultural context of meaning and belief, fears and knowledge, the ways in which that phenomenon made sense" to the people of the past.[84]

Cultural history then studies past subjective experience. And, in contrast to the objective social scientific observer, the subjectivity of the observing cultural historian is seen as thoroughly engaged in knowing past subjective experience. The subjectivity of the historian affects what he or she knows and understands about the historical subject, and the historical subject in turn affects the subjectivity of the historian. Again quoting Daniel, this circularity

> is not an obstacle to scholarly understanding but its precondition, for without it there would be no questions to ask of the past. It is the task of methodological self-reflection to thematize the mutual interaction between the "knowing subject" and the "known objects" in historical writing ... To wish to learn something about history is not to be separated from the wish to learn something about oneself. That this is so makes historical knowledge not problematic but essential.[85]

Given that they study past human subjectivity (perceptions, feelings, experience, memory, and meaning), cultural historians use empathy all the time.[86] Nevertheless, they only rarely acknowledge that they do and often employ empathy unknowingly and uncritically. Indeed, a cultural historian like Daniel who demands methodological self-consciousness views empathy with skepticism because of its unacknowledged and unreflective use by historians.[87] Therefore, promoting critical self-consciousness on the part of historians about the use of empathy in historical knowledge is a primary purpose of this book.

The emergence of cultural history over the last two or three decades, particularly as it focuses on experience, brings empathy as a way of knowing the human past back into play, now in a wholly different context from that of the political and intellectual history of Collingwood's day.[88] We have moved away from the largely depopulated historical world of social history, where people and their experiences play at best a secondary role. We are once again interested in people, not so much in political leaders as in ordinary human beings. And we conceive of those people less as rational actors and more as complex, contradictory, and emotional human beings shaped by and also in often small and subtle ways shaping history. Now the subjective experiences of past people are a focus of historical attention, not merely historically consequential political events and ideas or historically determinative structures and processes.

To be sure, historians are still concerned with causation in history, and empathy can play a role in helping us to understand the motivations behind historically significant events, as, following Collingwood and his adherents, we rethink the thoughts of historical actors or re-enact the rationale of historical events from the perspective of those actors. Causal explanations in history do not *require* empathy, however. As Collingwood's positivist critics were at pains to point out, and as most economic and much social history make clear, causal sequences can be known from an external observational position without historians having to adopt the observational position of the historical actors.[89] Now the whole question of whether history is a way of knowing identical or at least related to knowing in the natural sciences is off the table. Now most or at least very many historians no longer conceive of history as an objective social science. Now subjectivity becomes not something to be overcome in the historian in order to achieve objective knowledge of the past. Now the historian's subjectivity is seen as thoroughly engaged in historical knowing, with the historian's personality, interests, life experiences, feelings, and historical and cultural moment potentially not only interfering with knowledge of the past but also facilitating it. Empathy as a way of knowing that focuses on past subjective experience and that engages the subjectivity of the historian in knowing that experience is in tune with these new historical interests and approaches.[90]

Notes

1 Karsten Stueber, *Rediscovering Empathy: Agency, Folk Psychology, and the Human Sciences* (Cambridge, MA: MIT Press, 2006), 15.
2 The following historical excursus focuses for the most part on historians and sociologists sympathetic to empathy and not on empathy's critics.
3 David Hume, *Enquiries Concerning Human Understanding and Concerning the Principles of Morals*, 3rd edition (Oxford: Clarendon, 1975), 83–84. See, also, Hume's claim that politics can be reduced to principles as universally valid "as any

which the mathematical sciences afford us." "That Politics May Be Reduced to a Science," in *Essays: Moral, Political, and Literary*, ed. Eugene F. Miller (Indianapolis: Liberty Fund, 1987), 16.

4 Roger Hausheer, "Three Major Originators of the Concept of Verstehen: Vico, Herder, Schleiermacher," in *Verstehen and Humane Understanding*, ed. Anthony O'Hear, Royal Institute of Philosophy Supplements 41 (Cambridge: Cambridge University Press, 1996), 49; Retz, *Empathy and History*, 85–86.

5 Hausheer quoting Vico in Hausheer, "Three Major Originators of the Concept of Verstehen," 49; Giambattista Vico, *On the Most Ancient Wisdom of the Italians: Drawn out from the Origins of the Latin Language*, trans. Jason Taylor (New Haven and London: Yale University Press, 2010), 17, 27, 51; *The New Science of Giambattista Vico*, Abridged translation of the 3rd edition (1744), ed. Thomas Goddard Bergin and Max Harold Fisch (Ithaca, NY: Cornell University Press, 1970), 53, 62–63.

6 Isaiah Berlin, *Vico and Herder: Two Studies in the History of Ideas* (London: Hogarth, 1976), 112. Hausheer spells out Vico's view that we understand the human world using what we would call empathy in "Three Major Originators of the Concept of Verstehen," 50–51.

7 Berlin, *Vico and Herder*, 186–187; Edwards, "A Brief Conceptual History of Einfühlung," 271–272; Hausheer, "Three Major Originators of the Concept of Verstehen," 53, 55; Retz, *Empathy and History*, 87–88.

8 Any survey of the history of empathy should consider the work of Friedrich Schleiermacher. Because his emphasis was on empathy's role in understanding and interpreting texts, particularly religious texts, I shall not consider him here. For a summary of Schleiermacher's use of empathy in understanding see Hausheer, "Three Major Originators of the Concept of Verstehen," 56–70. Hans-Georg Gadamer gives a thoughtful, if critical, account of Schleiermacher's empathic hermeneutics in Hans-Georg Gadamer, *Truth and Method*, trans. Joel Weinsheimer and Donald G. Marshall, Revised 2nd edition 2004 (London: Bloomsbury, 2014), 191–202.

9 Eberhard Kessel, "Rankes Idee der Universalhistorie," *Historische Zeitschrift* 178, no. 2(1954): 296; Leopold von Ranke, "On the Character of Historical Science (a Manuscript of the 1830s)," in *The Theory and Practice of History*, ed. Georg G. Iggers and Konrad von Moltke (Indianapolis: Bobbs-Merrill, 1973), 39. The language in the original unpublished manuscript as in the translation by Iggers and Moltke is cumbersome. The German text reads as follows: "Diese [die geistige Apperzeption] beruht auf der Übereinstimmung der Gesetze, nach welchen der betrachtende Geist verfährt, mit denen, welche das betrachtete Objekt hervortritt."

10 Georg G. Iggers, *The German Conception of History: The National Tradition of Historical Thought from Herder to the Present* (Middletown, CT: Wesleyan University Press, 1968), 105.

11 Jacques Bos, "Individuality and Interpretation in Nineteenth-Century German Historicism," in *Perspectives on Erklären and Verstehen*, ed. Uljana Feest (Dordrecht: Springer, 2010), 216; Michael J. Maclean, "Johann Gustav Droysen and the Development of Historical Hermeneutics," *History and Theory* 21, no. 3(1982): 348; Karl-Otto Apel, "The Erklären–Verstehen Controversy in the Philosophy of the Natural and Human Sciences," in *Contemporary Philosophy: A New Survey*, ed. Guttorm Fløistad (The Hague: Martinus Nijhoff, 1982), 21–22. For a succinct account of nineteenth-century historicism and the role played by Verstehen in the Geisteswissenschaften, see Retz, *Empathy and History*, 91–105.

12 Johann Gustav Droysen, *Outline of the Principles of History (Grundriss der Geschichte)* (Boston: Ginn and Company, 1893), 12–13.

13 Maclean, "Droysen and the Development of Historical Hermeneutics," 355; Philipp Müller, "Understanding History: Hermeneutics and Source-Criticism in Historical Scholarship," in *Reading Primary Sources: The Interpretation of Texts from Nineteenth- and Twentieth-Century History*, ed. Miriam Dobson and Benjamin Ziemann (London and New York: Routledge, 2008), 28. For an account of the role played by the historian, his or her interests, methods, goals, and culture, in knowing the past for Droysen, see Retz, *Empathy and History*, 97–98.

14 Wilhelm Dilthey, *Introduction to the Human Sciences*, trans. Michael Neville, Wilhelm Dilthey: Selected Works, vol. 1 (Princeton: Princeton University Press, 1989), 49.

15 Ibid., 50.

16 Wilhelm, Dilthey, *Introduction to the Human Sciences: An Attempt to Lay a Foundation for the Study of Society and History*, ed. Ramon J. Betanzos (London: Harvester, Wheatsheaf, 1988), 327.

17 Wilhelm, Dilthey, *The Formation of the Historical World in the Human Sciences*, ed. Rudolf A. Makkreel and Frithjof Rodi, Wilhelm Dilthey: Selected Works, vol. 3 (Princeton: Princeton University Press, 2002), 164.

18 Wilhelm, Dilthey, *Hermeneutics and the Study of History*, ed. Rudolf A. Makkreel and Frithjof Rodi, Wilhelm Dilthey: Selected Works, vol. 4 (Princeton: Princeton University Press, 1996), 229.

19 Dilthey, *Formation of the Historical World*, 3, 160.

20 Mark Bevir, "Introduction: Historical Understanding and the Human Sciences," *Journal of the Philosophy of History* 1 (2007): 262. See, also, Müller, "Understanding History," 31.

21 Dilthey quoted in Bevir, "Introduction," 262.

22 Dilthey, *Introduction to the Human Sciences*, 1, 50. Michael Ermarth, *Wilhelm Dilthey: The Critique of Historical Reason* (Chicago: University of Chicago Press, 1978), 250, 256; Rudolf A. Makkreel, "How Is Empathy Related to Understanding?," in *Issues in Husserl's Ideas II*, ed. Thomas Nenon and Lester Embree, Contributions to Phenomenology (Dordrecht: Springer, 1996), 205; Wilhelm Dilthey, *Understanding the Human World*, ed. Rudolf A. Makkreel and Frithjof Rodi, Wilhelm Dilthey: Selected Works, vol. 2 (Princeton: Princeton University Press, 2010), 235. Given his restricted definition of empathy as Einfühlung and his sense that empathy is at heart a projection of the observing self onto the observed other, Rudolf Makkreel attempts to disassociate Dilthey from empathy. Wrongly in my view, Makkreel rejects "empathy" as a translation of *nacherleben* ("re-experience") or of *sich hineinversetzen* ("putting oneself in the place of"), phrases Dilthey frequently used that are the essence of empathy as presented here. Rudolf A. Makkreel, *Dilthey: Philosopher of the Human Sciences* (Princeton, NJ: Princeton University Press, 1992), 6–7 and 252; "How Is Empathy Related to Understanding?," 205, 212.

23 Dilthey, *Hermeneutics and the Study of History*, 249.

24 Dilthey, *Introduction to the Human Sciences*, 1, 88; see also 89.

25 Dilthey, *Hermeneutics and the Study of History*, 229.

26 Rudolf A. Makkreel and Frithjof Rodi, "Introduction to Volume III," in *Wilhelm Dilthey: The Formation of the Historical World in the Human Sciences*, ed. Rudolf A. Makkreel and Frithjof Rodi, Wilhelm Dilthey: Selected Works, vol. 3 (Princeton: Princeton University Press, 2002), 1; Dilthey, *Formation of the Historical World*, 3, 229. See also Retz, *Empathy and History*, 102.

27 Dilthey, *Formation of the Historical World*, 3, 173; see here also 141–142, 154–155, 164, 236.

28 Hans Herbert Kögler and Karsten R. Stueber, "Introduction: Empathy, Simulation, and Interpretation in the Philosophy of Social Science," in *Empathy and*

Agency: The Problem of Understanding in the Social Sciences, ed. Hans Herbert Kögler and Karsten R. Stueber (Boulder, CO: Westview, 2000), 27.

29 Jürgen Habermas, *Knowledge and Human Interests*, trans. J. Shapiro (London: Heinemann, 1973), 146, 148–149. Habermas rejected Dilthey's later account as "completely unsatisfactory for a logic of the sciences." The identity of what we know and how we know renders Dilthey's epistemology circular, holding a mirror up to a mirror, according to Habermas. Ibid., 149–150.

30 Ermarth, *Wilhelm Dilthey*, 259–260, 264.

31 Makkreel, *Dilthey*, 213, 251; Dilthey, *Formation of the Historical World*, 3, 163. Hans-Georg Gadamer's efforts "to uphold Dilthey's claims with regard to the distinctiveness of the historical and cultural sciences while providing a different rationale" for knowledge in the Geisteswissenschaften will be considered in Chapter 6. Dieter Misgeld, "On Gadamer's Hermeneutics," *Philosophy of the Social Sciences* 9, no. 2(1979): 224.

32 Benedetto Croce, *History: Its Theory and Practice*, trans. Douglas Ainslie (New York: Russell and Russell, 1960), 134–135.

33 Ibid., 24.

34 Ibid., 76.

35 Ibid., 73. For the relationship between the philosophies of history of Croce and Collingwood, see Retz, *Empathy and History*, 107–108.

36 Croce, *History*, 76.

37 For example, ibid., 19. This phrase appears frequently in Croce's writing.

38 Georg Simmel, *The Problems of the Philosophy of History*, trans. Guy Oakes (New York: Free Press, 1977), 66.

39 Ibid., 64.

40 Ibid., 65.

41 Ibid., 39–40.

42 Ibid., 95.

43 Ibid., 87, 67–68.

44 Max Weber, *Economy and Society: An Outline of Interpretive Sociology*, ed. Guenther Roth and Claus Wittich, vol. 1 (Berkeley: University of California Press, 1978), 13, 15.

45 Guy Oakes, "Introductory Essay," in Max Weber, *Roscher and Knies: The Logical Problems of Historical Economics*, trans. Guy Oakes (New York: Free Press, 1975), 32–33.

46 Weber, *Economy and Society*, 1, 5. See, also, *Roscher and Knies*, 125, 129, 170, 175, 177–178.

47 Although we use logic and reason to know the rational context of an action, according to Weber we may need to use empathy to know its emotional context. *Economy and Society*, 1, 5.

48 Weber, *Roscher and Knies*, 147–148, 170, 184.

49 Max Weber, "Critical Studies in the Logic of the Cultural Sciences," in *The Methodology of the Social Sciences*, ed. Edward A. Shils and Henry A. Finch (New York: Free Press, 1977), 176.

50 Max Weber, "'Objectivity' in Social Science and Social Policy," in *The Methodology of the Social Sciences*, ed. Edward A. Shils and Henry A. Finch (New York: Free Press, 1977), 84, 129.

51 Weber, *Roscher and Knies*, 185–186. Following Weber, Jürgen Habermas sought to bridge the gap between the human and the natural sciences by bringing subjective understanding and objective social analysis together. He regarded psychoanalysis as an apt model for this integration since it applies a theoretically objectifying approach to subjective meaning. Theory is required to detach "the [observing] self from its embeddedness into situated and interpretive contexts." Nonetheless, we are interested in "a historically and culturally understood world" and we belong to

a historical and cultural world that influences "the very identification of the meaning to be explained." Hence, objectified theory is surrounded on both sides by subjectivity. Habermas seems close to Weber here, with Weber's objectified ideal type replaced by Habermas' objectified theory. Jürgen Habermas, *On the Logic of the Social Sciences*, trans. S. Nicholsen and J. Stark (Cambridge, MA: MIT Press, 1988), 1; Kögler and Stueber, "Introduction," 41–42.

52 Charles H. Cooley, *Human Nature and the Social Order* (New York: Schocken, 1964), 120–121.

53 Ibid., 136 and particularly the footnote on 137.

54 Ibid., 417–418.

55 Charles H. Cooley, "The Roots of Social Knowledge," *American Journal of Sociology* 32, no. 1(1926): 59.

56 Ibid., 60.

57 Ibid., 65. Here is Cooley's definition of "sympathy" from his book *Social Theory and Social Research* (New York: Holt, 1930), 293–94: "As you see another man do these things you repeat, sympathetically, your own inner response on former occasions and ascribe it to him. A new reach of human experience is opened to you and you enlarge your understanding of men." Quoted in Gerald A. Gladstein, "The Historical Roots of Contemporary Empathy Research," *Journal of the History of the Behavioral Sciences* 20, no. 1(1984): 44.

58 Cooley, "Roots of Social Knowledge," 68–69.

59 Ibid., 69.

60 Ibid., 70.

61 George H. Mead, *Mind, Self, and Society: From the Standpoint of a Social Behaviorist* (Chicago: University of Chicago Press, 1967), 219.

62 Ibid., 299.

63 Ibid., 300.

64 Ibid., 366.

65 Theodore Abel, "The Operation Called Verstehen," *American Journal of Sociology* 54(1948); Morton White, *Foundations of Historical Knowledge* (New York: Harper, 1965); Ernest Nagel, *The Structure of Science: Problems in the Logic of Scientific Explanation* (New York: Routledge and Kegan Paul, 1961); Arthur C. Danto, *Analytical Philosophy of History* (Cambridge: Cambridge University Press, 1965).

66 Abel, "Operation Called Verstehen," 216–218; White, *Foundations of Historical Knowledge*, 7, 148, 216; Karl R. Popper, *The Open Society and Its Enemies*, vol. 2 (London: Routledge, 1945), 251–252.

67 Carl G. Hempel, "The Function of General Laws in History," *Journal of Philosophy* 39, no. 2(1942): 37.

68 Hempel contended that all scientifically legitimate explanations have the same structure: They all present the determining conditions for the event to be explained and one or more general laws setting forth that, when such conditions are present, events like the one to be explained will occur. Both the determining conditions and the general laws can be or have been confirmed empirically. All scientifically legitimate explanations have the same structure and essentially the same status as predictions, and could effectively function as predictions. Thus, in the case of the event of the cracking automobile radiator, the determining conditions were that the car was left out overnight, that the radiator was completely filled with water, that the temperature overnight dropped well below 32 degrees Fahrenheit, etc., and the general laws were that water freezes below 32 degrees, that when the temperature drops water expands and expands especially when water freezes, that metal cracks under so and so much pressure, etc. These determining conditions and these general laws are empirically provable. They explain the cracking of the radiator

and, formulated differently, could have predicted that the radiator would in fact crack. Hempel believed that explanations in history have the same essential structure, with empirically demonstrable determining conditions and general laws or at least general hypotheses. He cites in his article the statement that "the Dust Bowl farmers migrate to California 'because' continual drought and sandstorms render their existence increasingly precarious, and because California seems to offer them so much better living conditions." This explanation of the Dust Bowl migration contains determining conditions (drought, sandstorms, a precarious existence, the appearance of better living conditions in California) and also "rests on some such universal hypothesis as that populations will tend to migrate to regions which offer better living conditions." Hempel acknowledged that it would be difficult to prove this universal hypothesis so as to give it the status of a general law; but he argued that all explanations, including explanations in history, "rest on the assumption of universal hypotheses," which are often only "tacitly assumed." Ibid., 36–41. For a lucid, if critical, account of Hempel's covering law theory by a philosophically sophisticated historian, see Saul Friedländer, *History and Psychoanalysis: An Inquiry into the Possibilities and Limits of Psychohistory*, trans. Susan Suleiman (New York: Holmes and Meier, 1978), 3.

69 Hempel, "General Laws in History," 44–45. See also, Abel, "Operation Called Verstehen," 217; Rolf Gruner, "Understanding in the Social Sciences and History," *Inquiry* 10, no. 1–4(1967): 160–162; Nagel, *Structure of Science*, 483–485. Although coming from the philosophical tradition to which Hempel, Abel, and White belonged, Maurice Mandelbaum recognized history's distinctiveness and downplayed the significance of universal laws in historical explanation. Nevertheless, he rejected empathy for potentially introducing relativism into historical science. Maurice Mandelbaum, *The Problem of Historical Knowledge: An Answer to Relativism* (New York: Liveright, 1938), 94; *The Anatomy of Historical Knowledge* (Baltimore: Johns Hopkins University Press, 1977), 8 and 15. Arthur Danto also denied empathy any role in historical understanding. Danto, *Analytical Philosophy of History*, 232.

70 William Henry Walsh, *An Introduction to Philosophy of History* (London: Hutchinson's University Library, 1951); Patrick Gardiner, *The Nature of Historical Explanation* (Oxford: Oxford University Press, 1961); "Interpretation in History: Collingwood and Historical Understanding," in O'Hear, *Verstehen and Humane Understanding*; William Dray, *Laws and Explanation in History* (Oxford: Clarendon, 1957); *History as Re-Enactment: R. G. Collingwood's Idea of History* (Oxford: Clarendon, 1999). See, also, Alan Donagan, "The Verification of Historical Theses," *Philosophical Quarterly* 6, no. 24(1956); Louis O. Mink, "The Autonomy of Historical Understanding," *History and Theory* 5, no. 1(1966).

71 R. G. Collingwood, *The Idea of History* (Oxford: Oxford University Press, 1956), 5.

72 Ibid., 199, 214.

73 Ibid., 213–214.

74 Ibid., 215.

75 Ibid. Although Collingwood's notion that in knowing the past the historian re-enacts or rethinks past thought is often seen as a form of historical empathy, Tyson Retz rejects the connection between empathy and re-enactment in Collingwood's philosophy of history as a "misconception." Indeed, Retz sees Collingwood's concepts of "re-enactment and question-and-answer logic" as preferable to empathy, understood by Retz as the "unification of subject and object." Retz, *Empathy and History*, 122, 128; see also 114, 127, 131, 157, 166, 215.

76 Collingwood, *Idea of History*, 217.

77 Ibid., 231.
78 Walsh, *Philosophy of History*, 52–58; Gardiner, "Interpretation in History," 114; Dray, *History as Re-Enactment*, 56, 75, 116; Giuseppina D'Oro, "Re-Enactment and Radical Interpretation," *History and Theory* 43(2004); Dale Jacquette, "Collingwood on Historical Authority and Historical Imagination," *Journal of the Philosophy of History* 3, no. 1(2009): 60–63.
79 Collingwood, *Idea of History*, 309.
80 See, for example, William V. Harris, "History, Empathy and Emotions," *Antike und Abendland* 56(2010); Keith Jenkins, *Re-Thinking History* (London: Routledge, 2003); Joan W. Scott, "The Evidence of Experience," *Critical Inquiry* 17, no. 4(1991).
81 I was in attendance at the gathering.
82 A philosopher of history who brings empathy and a postmodern sensibility together in productive and thought-provoking ways is Dominick LaCapra.
83 Alon Confino, "From Psychohistory to Memory Studies: Or, How Some Germans Became Jews and Some Jews Nazis," in *History Flows through Us: Germany, the Holocaust, and the Importance of Empathy*, ed. Roger Frie (London and New York: Routledge, 2018), 19.
84 Ute Daniel, *Kompendium Kulturgeschichte: Theorien, Praxis, Schlüsselwörter* (Frankfurt: Suhrkamp, 2006), 17.
85 Ibid., 17, 19. The historian Tyson Retz makes a similar claim: "The so-called lessons we take from history should emerge from history itself, from a preparedness to treat the historical subject matter as a potential beacon into some important element of our lives." Retz, *Empathy and History*, 12; also 65, 166.
86 Confino, "From Psychohistory to Memory Studies," 21.
87 For that reason, Daniel does not discuss "Einfühlung" or "Empathie" in her introduction to cultural history, and neither term is considered in the chapter "Keywords" in cultural history. Daniel, *Kompendium Kulturgeschichte*, 380–466. Nor does she use the term in a body of historical work that is characterized by historical empathy.
88 Magdalena Nowak, "The Complicated History of Einfühlung," *Argument* 1, no. 2 (2011): 315. Frank Ankersmit connects the history of experience with the history of everyday life and with cultural history. "In these variants of historical writing the emphasis is on how people in the past experienced their world and in what way this experience may differ from how we relate to our own world ... So, in both history and philosophy we may observe an effort to rehabilitate the almost forgotten and thoroughly marginalized category of experience, a category that, if noticed at all, was regarded with so much contempt and disdain in most of the twentieth century's philosophy of language." Frank R. Ankersmit, *Sublime Historical Experience* (Stanford, CA: Stanford University Press, 2005), 3–4, 7.
89 Danto, *Analytical Philosophy of History*, 232.
90 Nowak, "Complicated History of Einfühlung," 315.

Chapter 2

The Principal Contemporary Definitions of Empathy

Throughout the nineteenth century and at the beginning and middle of the twentieth century, then, empathy figured prominently in debates about knowledge in the natural and in the human sciences, about whether there were two worlds of knowledge or only one. History, as the paradigmatic human science, was at the center of these debates, as was the role of empathy in historical knowledge. Since then, despite its (largely unacknowledged) presence in recent historical work, empathy as a way of knowing in history has received little attention. Instead, the lively contemporary debates about empathy in a variety of disciplines other than history relate less to the question of how we know human beings and their creations in the past and more to the fundamental philosophical and psychological question of how we know the minds and mental states of others primarily in the here and now.

Three principal positions have emerged in response to the question of how we know the minds and mental states of others. The first two belong to what is called the philosophy of mind. Of these, the first position, espoused by analytic philosophers, is called "theory theory." Since theory theory rejects empathy as a way of knowing the minds and mental states of others, I will only consider it briefly here.

Theory theory basically contends that knowing in history or sociology or in the natural sciences or in everyday life is fundamentally the same. We approach what we wish to know, be it a society, a planet, or a person, in the same way—namely we approach our subject matter with a theory and set of hypotheses. In the case of understanding other people, we approach them with a general, largely implicit, theory of human psychology and with a set of hypotheses, based in part upon that theory, about what those other people are experiencing. Through empirical observation we confirm, reject, or modify our hypotheses. This process of testing and revising our hypotheses continues until we think that one or more of our hypotheses about the other person have been confirmed by our empirical observations, by the evidence we have collected about that person's state of mind. As we mature, we develop ever more sophisticated theories about how the world works, including the inner world of other people. Thus the older we get and the more we learn, the more sophisticated we will be in applying theories to explain the world generally and other people in particular.[1] As suggested above, there would be no distinction between the way we know a person in the here and now or in the past and in the way we know a person and any other phenomenon in the human or natural world.

Theory theory has no place for empathy, for feeling one's way, imagining one's way, or thinking one's way inside the unique experience of another. One never seeks to nor really can adopt the perspective of the person one wishes to know. As in natural science, we know others from without, as outside observers, applying theoretical hypotheses about their mind and mental state to them and revising those hypotheses based on the acquisition of new evidence (including the others' responses to our hypotheses). Our understanding of others is based on our having a theory of human psychology. In everyday life, that theory is largely implicit and is called "folk psychology"; in academic psychology that theory is largely explicit.

In contrast to theory theory, the second paradigm in contemporary philosophy of mind, "simulation theory," rejects the centrality of theory, generally an implicit psychological theory, in our ability to know others in everyday life. It appears to have been anticipated by David Hume when he claimed "that the minds of men are mirrors to one another."[2] As one of simulation theory's principal advocates, the philosopher Karsten Stueber, defines it, empathy is "a form of inner or mental imitation for the purpose of gaining knowledge of other minds."[3] For the philosopher Alvin I. Goldman and Vittorio Gallese, the cognitive neuroscientist who discovered "mirror neurons":

> the core difference between TT [theory theory] and ST [simulation theory], in our view, is that TT depicts mindreading as a thoroughly "detached" theoretical activity, whereas ST depicts mindreading as incorporating an attempt to replicate, mimic, or impersonate the mental life of the target agent.[4]

The roots of simulation theory can be traced back to Theodor Lipps, who in the first decade of the twentieth century developed first a theory of aesthetics and, then, based on his account of how we relate to works of art, an account of how we know others using "Einfühlung."[5] According to Lipps, when we perceive a work of art, we experience it physiologically in that we physically imitate what we see. Our physical experience, the muscle movements we make in response to the work of art, generates feelings and sensations in us. Those feelings and sensations we then attribute to the work of art, projecting our own inner state and our characterization of that state onto the aesthetic object. Lipps' account then remains very much internal to us: we see, we imitate, we feel, we project. Much the same process occurs in knowing other minds and mental states according to Lipps. When we perceive another's facial expressions, gestures, and posture, we imitate those expressions and gestures and that posture ourselves. This imitation gives rise to certain feelings and experiences of our own. We observe or introspect these feelings and experiences, connecting them with the same or similar experiences we have had in the past, and based on that comparison label those experiences or feelings. Finally, we project those experiences and feelings now named back onto the other, ascribing them to the other. Here again knowing another is an internal process consisting of perception, imitation, introspection, and projection.[6]

Following Lipps, contemporary "simulation theory" is based upon the notion that "processes of 'inner imitation'" underlie our ability to know the minds and mental states of others.[7] Indeed, these processes of inner imitation are what constitute empathy. As far-fetched as this account of knowing other minds through inner imitation may seem, simulation theory appeared to have been confirmed by research in neuroscience, specifically by the discovery of "mirror neurons" at the end of the twentieth century.[8] Based predominantly on primate studies, neuroscientists discovered that when a "subject" observes a "target" engaging in a particular action, neurons fire in the observing subject that mirror the neuronal activity in the observed acting target. Although some cognitive scientists have in the last few years raised doubts about the central role played by mirror neurons in cognition and understanding, seeing it instead as the product of a complex and sophisticated process of sensorimotor learning, the discovery of mirror neurons appeared to confirm Lipps' original notion of motor mimicry now not on the muscular but on the neurophysiological level.[9] Simulation theory generally breaks "mindreading" down into three phases. First, we observe the actions of another and imitate the actions of the other on a neurological, emotional, and ideational level. Second, we observe or introspect the feelings, experiences, and thoughts that our observation of the other has triggered within us, knowing and identifying them. And, finally, we attribute what we are feeling, experiencing, and/or thinking back onto the other person, reading the other's mind based on the knowledge we have gained through introspection.[10]

Empathy in the third contemporary account of how we know other minds is, if possible, even more central than in simulation theory but comes from a very different philosophical tradition, namely phenomenology. Indeed, this account is called the "phenomenological position." The phenomenological position, in contrast to theory theory or simulation theory, contends that we do not know others indirectly (either through the application of theory or through mimicry and inference by analogy with ourselves), but that we can experience and know others directly, in an unmediated way, through empathy. Going back first to Edmund Husserl, his student Edith Stein, and Max Scheler, empathy as a way of knowing other minds in spontaneous acts of imaginative self-transposition (*sich hineinphantasieren*) is primordial, not acquired or learned but a fundamental intrinsic human capacity to recognize and to know other human beings.[11] In the words of Scheler, "nothing is more certain than that we can think the thoughts of others as well as our own, and can feel their feelings (in sympathy [empathy]) as we do our own."[12] Indeed, we can empathize with the experiences of others without ever having had those experiences ourselves.

Empathy according to the phenomenological position is not self-projection but self-transcendence.[13] According to the phenomenologists, theory theory and simulation theory are based upon a Cartesian conception of the mind, which falsely assumes that all we can ever really know is ourselves, "that the minds of others are hidden," that "the only emotions we have experiential access to are our own," that the only true knowledge is introspective knowledge (simulation theory), or that we apply empirically derived theories to others from a position of complete cognitive autonomy (theory theory).[14] These assumptions are simply wrong according to the phenomenological position since they ignore the fact that human consciousness is socially and culturally constructed and that knowing is an intersubjective process. When we know another, we know *with* another, according to Scheler: "What occurs, rather, is an immediate flow of experiences, undifferentiated as between mine and thine, which actually contains both our own and others' experiences intermingled and without distinction from one another."[15]

Influenced by sociologists, phenomenologists frequently emphasize the social relationship involved in people knowing one another, a relationship that breaks down the false distinction between the knower and the known, and sees knowledge as a social and communicative process engaging and affecting both parties to it. Influenced by Wittgenstein and post-structural philosophy, phenomenologists also emphasize that the language and concepts we use to make sense of ourselves and of others are provided for us and shared with others through the culture, the "life world" (our system of norms, meanings, and beliefs) to which we belong, the language games that we play—all of which render the notion of an autonomous knowing self naïve and misguided. In the words of Scheler, "a man tends, in the first instance, to live more in *others* than in himself; more in the community than in his own individual self."[16] Not least Freud demonstrated that self-knowledge is limited and distorted, and that we can frequently know others better than we know ourselves. Although more an advocate for simulation theory than the phenomenological position, the philosopher Jane Heal notes that:

> one has no more access to the intrinsic nature of one's own thoughts than one does to the intrinsic nature of those of others. Thinking about my own thoughts is not ... direct and intimate confrontation with something about whose nature I cannot be deceived.[17]

Indeed, the knowledge that others have about us profoundly influences what we know about ourselves. It is true that we know others through ourselves, but we also know ourselves through others. Those who argue that we can *only* know others through ourselves have, according to Scheler, "an inveterate tendency to under-estimate the difficulty of self-knowledge, just as they over-estimate the difficulty of knowing other people."[18]

In sum, the phenomenological position presents a thoroughly social, cultural, and intersubjective view of empathic knowledge of other human beings. Many historians may well be attracted to the account of empathy presented in the phenomenological position, given its emphasis on social relationships and on the embeddedness of human beings in a cultural and social environment, in a historical "life world." Unfortunately, phenomenologists tend to restrict the primordial capacity to know others through empathy to face-to-face human interaction, to distinguish empathy from the "more cognitively demanding form of imaginative perspective taking," and to deny that empathy provides "us with an understanding of why" another feels, thinks, or acts as he does.[19] It is therefore difficult to reconcile the use of empathy in the phenomenological position, which on the face of it seems so congenial to historical thinking, with the use of empathy in historical knowledge. The relevance of the phenomenological position to the use of empathy in history shall be considered below.

Of these three philosophical positions, simulation theory in one of its various permutations seems currently to dominate the discussion of empathy in psychology, cognitive neuroscience, and even philosophy, although there are forceful and effective contemporary proponents of the phenomenological account of empathy such as Shaun Gallagher, Kathleen Haney, and Dan Zahavi. Buttressed by neuroscience research, simulation theory emphasizes our ability to read another's mind by putting ourselves in the other's shoes, seeing the world from the other's perspective, and understanding why the other has the experiences he does. According to Karsten Stueber, "empathy is epistemologically central to our folk-psychological ability to understand other agents." Indeed, it is the "default method of gaining knowledge of the minds of other individual agents."[20]

In considering empathy as a way of knowing the minds and mental states of others, philosophers and more recently psychologists and cognitive neuroscientists have distinguished between two forms of empathy, a distinction that shall prove relevant in our subsequent consideration of empathy as a way of knowing in history. Perhaps the first to do so was the phenomenologist Max Scheler. Scheler distinguished between basic empathy, which, according to Dan Zahavi, was the focus of Scheler's interest, and "a more advanced cognitive type which might involve perspective-shifting, imaginative projection or inferential attribution."[21] Simulation theorists like Stueber have followed Scheler in distinguishing these two forms of empathy as employed in everyday life.[22] The first, called "basic empathy" by Stueber and "mirroring empathy" by Alvin Goldman, is understood to be a process of affective sharing through simulation that we use instinctively and unconsciously to know or "pick up on" the minds and mental states of others.[23] The second—called "reenactive empathy" by Stueber, "reconstructive empathy" by Alvin Goldman and Frederique de

Vignemont, and "imaginative empathy" by Aleida Assmann and Ines Detmers—is less affective and automatic and more "cognitive and deliberative" than basic or mirroring empathy. Here we reflect on the other's situation and consciously seek to put ourselves in his place to imagine both "how things are (were or will be) playing out for him" and how we would "feel" if we "were in his shoes."[24] In this form of empathy as a deliberate "process of perspective taking," we use "our own motivational and emotional resources" along with our reasoning capacity in order to see the world "as it appears from" the other's "point of view" and then deliberating and reasoning from the other's perspective.[25]

The cognitive neuroscientist Jean Decety and his colleagues, as well as other neuroscience researchers, have presented the neurophysiological and psychological evidence confirming the existence of both forms of empathy.[26] Although Decety sees re-enactive or reconstructive empathy to be true empathy, most simulation theorists follow Stueber in arguing that we employ both basic and re-enactive empathy in understanding others, the former perhaps a lower-order, more affective and unconscious form of empathy and the latter a higher-order, more cognitive and self-conscious form of empathy.[27] I shall return to this distinction in considering the role of empathy in historical knowledge.

Notes

1 See, here, Hume, *Enquiries Concerning Human Understanding*, 84–85.
2 David Hume, *A Treatise of Human Nature*, ed. L. A. Selby-Bigge, 2nd edition (Oxford: Clarendon, 1978), 365, see, also, 575–576.
3 Stueber, *Rediscovering Empathy*, 28.
4 Vittorio Gallese and Alvin I. Goldman, "Mirror Neurons and the Simulation Theory of Mind-Reading," *Trends in Cognitive Sciences* 12(1998): 497.
5 Indeed, according to Tyson Retz, Lipps' account of the role of empathy in aesthetic appreciation, which formed the basis for his account of how we know the minds and mental states of others, was already anticipated by Robert Vischer in his 1873 doctoral dissertation, "On the Optical Feeling of Form: A Contribution to Aesthetics." Vischer saw Einfühlung as producing a state of harmony or union between observing subject and aesthetic object. Retz, *Empathy and History*, 75.
6 It is striking and significant that Sigmund Freud's two models of the mind developed around this same time, the topographical and the structural, depicted the psyche as an autonomous world nearly complete unto itself, with the role of the environment restricted to the gratification or the frustration of instinctual wishes. It was only later with the elaboration of the structural model of the mind and the development of ego psychology that the environment came to play a somewhat greater role in psychological life for Freud.
7 Stueber, *Rediscovering Empathy*, 115. See also Retz, *Empathy and History*, 77.
8 Vittorio Gallese, Christian Keysers, and Giacomo Rizzolatti, "A Unifying View of the Basis of Social Cognition," *Trends in Cognitive Sciences* 8(2004).
9 Gregory Hickok and Marc Hauser, "(Mis)Understanding Mirror Neurons," *Current Biology* 20, no. 14(2010): R593–594; Gregory Hickok, *The Myth of Mirror Neurons: The Real Neuroscience of Communication and Cognition* (New York: Norton, 2014), particularly 240–241; Karsten Stueber, "Empathy," in *Stanford Encyclopedia of Philosophy*, ed. Edward Zalta (Palo Alto: Stanford University Press, 2019).

10 Stueber, *Rediscovering Empathy*, 120 and 124–125. For a psychoanalytic version of the empathizing process following simulation theory, see Köhler, "Von der Freud'schen Psychoanalyse zur Selbstpsychologie Heinz Kohuts," 40.

11 Peter Shum, "Avoiding Circularities on the Empathic Path to Transcendental Intersubjectivity," *Topoi* 33, no. 1(2014): 150; Natalie Depraz and Diego Cosmelli, "Empathy and Openness: Practices of Intersubjectivity at the Core of the Science of Consciousness," in *The Problem of Consciousness: New Essays in Phenomenological Philosophy of Mind*, ed. Evan Thompson (Calgary: University of Calgary Press, 2003), 173. For lucid accounts of Husserl's view of empathy, see Dan Zahavi, "Empathy and Mirroring: Husserl and Gallese," in *Life, Subjectivity, and Art: Essays in Honor of Rudolf Bernet*, ed. Roland Breeur and Ullrich Melle (Dordrecht: Springer, 2012); Makkreel, "How Is Empathy Related to Understanding?"

12 Max Scheler, *The Nature of Sympathy*, trans. Peter Heath (London: Routledge and Kegan Paul, 1954), 242.

13 Dan Zahavi, "Empathy and Other-Directed Intentionality," *Topoi* 33, no. 1(2014): 133.

14 Dan Zahavi, "Simulation, Projection, and Empathy," *Conscious Cognition* 17 (2008): 519; "Empathy and Other-Directed Intentionality," 130.

15 Scheler, *Nature of Sympathy*, 246.

16 Ibid., 247.

17 Jane Heal, *Mind, Reason, and Imagination* (Cambridge: Cambridge University Press, 2003), 26.

18 Scheler, *Nature of Sympathy*, 251.

19 Zahavi, "Empathy and Other-Directed Intentionality," 139 and 140; also 135. See, also, Zahavi, "Simulation, Projection, and Empathy," 522.

20 Stueber, *Rediscovering Empathy*, ix, 19.

21 Zahavi, "Simulation, Projection, and Empathy," 517.

22 Stueber, *Rediscovering Empathy*, 131–171.

23 This form of "mental mimicry" appeared to have been confirmed with the discovery of mirror neurons. Amy Coplan and Peter Goldie, "Introduction," in *Empathy: Philosophical and Psychological Perspectives*, ed. Amy Coplan and Peter Goldie (Oxford: Oxford University Press, 2011), xxxiii; Alvin I. Goldman, "Two Routes to Empathy: Insights from Cognitive Neuroscience," in Coplan and Goldie, *Empathy*, 33. See also Rick B. van Baaren et al., "Being Imitated: Consequences of Nonconsciously Showing Empathy," in *The Social Neuroscience of Empathy*, ed. Jean Decety and William John Ickes (Cambridge, MA: MIT Press, 2009).

24 Goldman, "Two Routes to Empathy," 36; Aleida Assmann and Ines Detmers, "Introduction," in *Empathy and Its Limits*, ed. Aleida Assmann and Ines Detmers (London and New York: Palgrave Macmillan, 2016), 5. See also Margarethe Bruun Vaage, "Fiction Film and the Varieties of Empathic Engagement," *Midwest Studies in Philosophy* 34(2010).

25 Stueber (in part quoting Gordon and Heal), *Rediscovering Empathy*, 21 and 111. Most contemporary theorists of empathy like Stueber follow Collingwood in tending to focus on empathy as a way to explain the motives and causes of human action and in tending to overlook empathy as a way to understand lived experience. Ibid., 42–59.

26 Jean Decety, Philip L. Jackson, and Eric Brunet, "The Cognitive Neuropsychology of Empathy," in *Empathy in Mental Illness*, ed. Tom F. D. Farrow and Peter W. R. Woodruff (Cambridge: Cambridge University Press, 2007), 247, 254; Jean Decety and Andrew N. Metzoff, "Empathy, Imitation, and the Social Brain," in *Empathy: Philosophical and Psychological Perspectives*, ed. Amy Coplan and Peter Goldie (Oxford: Oxford University Press, 2011), 72–75; Jean Decety and Claus Lamm, "Empathy versus Personal Distress: Recent Evidence from Social Neuroscience,"

in *The Social Neuroscience of Empathy*, ed. Jean Decety and William John Ickes (Cambridge, MA: MIT Press, 2009), 206, 209; Claus Lamm, C. Daniel Batson, and Jean Decety, "The Neural Substrate of Human Empathy: Effect of Perspective Taking and Cognitive Appraisal," *Journal of Cognitive Neuroscience* 19, no. 1 (2007): 43, 56; Henrik Walter, "Social Cognitive Neuroscience of Empathy: Concepts, Circuits, and Genes," *Emotion Review* 4, no. 1(2012): 13–14; van Baaren et al., "Being Imitated." See, also, Karen E. Gerdes, "Empathy, Sympathy, and Pity: 21st-Century Definitions and Implications for Practice and Research," *Journal of Social Service Research* 37, no. 3(2011); Frederique De Vignemont and Tania Singer, "The Empathic Brain: How, When, Why?," *Trends in Cognitive Neuroscience* 10, no. 10(2006). Zaki and Ochsner present the neuroscience research confirming both affective sharing and what they call "mentalizing," which is basically re-enactive or complex empathy. Both forms of empathy are neurophysiologically based but employ altogether different neural systems. Jamil Zaki and Kevin Ochsner, "The Neuroscience of Empathy: Progress, Pitfalls and Promise," *Nature Neuroscience* 15, no. 5(2012): 675. Indeed, neuroscience research suggests that empathy is "hardwired." Jeanne C. Watson and Leslie S. Greenberg, "Empathic Resonance: A Neuroscience Perspective," in *The Social Neuroscience of Empathy*, ed. Jean Decety and William John Ickes (Cambridge, MA: MIT Press, 2009), 127.

27 Coplan and Goldie, "Introduction," xxxiii.

Chapter 3

Narrower Definitions of Empathy and their Relation to Historical Inquiry

Below the three main approaches to knowing the minds and mental states of others—theory theory, simulation theory, and the phenomenological position, two of which rely primarily or exclusively on empathy—there are various narrower contemporary definitions of empathy not directly associated with these well-elaborated philosophical positions (the philosophy of mind and phenomenology). Some, usually in psychology, emphasize empathy's affective dimension. Some, usually in philosophy, emphasize its cognitive dimension. Without going into detail or the subtle variations, empathy has generally been defined in one of the following ways: as role playing or perspective-taking (imagining oneself in the shoes of the other); as affective sharing or emotional contagion (feeling oneself what is felt by the other); as merger (losing one's self in the other); as identification (experiencing oneself as the same as the other); and as sympathy (feeling distress at the suffering of the other).

For the purposes of historical knowledge, the first of these narrower definitions, empathy as role playing or perspective-taking, appears most relevant to the attempt of historians to know and understand the thoughts, feelings, and experiences of the people of the past. This definition focuses on empathy's cognitive dimension. Here, empathy is a mode of observation, a way of knowing. Empathy as affective sharing—if *not* as contagion—would seem to play a secondary, although perhaps not insignificant, role in historical knowledge and understanding. Certainly, empathy as merger and identification seems problematic, and not just in historical work. Indeed, I shall argue that merger and identification are incompatible with the disciplined use of empathy to know and understand human beings—whether in the past or in the present. Finally, although empathy may give rise to sympathy, to altruism, and to a pro-social attitude, it does not necessarily lead to these attitudes, and it can be and often is used for hostile purposes. As I shall make clear, empathy and sympathy are not at all the same and can be characterized perhaps as being something like polar opposites.

Imagination and Perspective-Taking in Empathy

Empathy in historical knowledge, as it is defined here, represents our attempt to know and understand the people of the past by adopting their perspective, by imagining our way inside their experience. Already Adam Smith defined what he called "sympathy" as imaginative perspective-taking. "As we have no immediate experience of what other men feel, we can form no idea of the manner in which they are affected, but by conceiving what we ourselves should feel in the like situation," Smith wrote in 1759. "It is by the imagination only that we can form any conceptions" of what another is experiencing:

> By the imagination we place ourselves in his situation ... we enter as it were into his own body, and become in some measure the same person with him, and thence form some idea of his sensations, and even feel something which, though weaker in degree, is not altogether unlike them.[1]

Nearly 150 years later, R. G. Collingwood also emphasized the centrality of imagination and perspective-taking in knowing human beings, set now within the specific context of history. Historians, according to Collingwood, do not use their imagination simply to represent the past in writing; historical imagination is "indispensable" in how they know the past in the first place.[2] It is the imagination that allows us to know a historical phenomenon "by thinking oneself into it, making its life one's own."[3]

Another English historian of Collingwood's era, Herbert Butterfield, also emphasized the importance of "sympathetic imagination for the purposes of getting inside human beings," "feeling with them ... thinking their thoughts over again and sitting in the position not of the observer but of the doer of the action." Butterfield recognized and appreciated the attenuated nature of empathy, that complete empathy with another can never be achieved. Nevertheless, he argued that attempting to adopt the position of the historical subject prevented the historian from adopting a "merely casual or stand-offish attitude towards the personalities of the past." Empathic history:

> does not treat [the people of the past] as mere things, or just measure such features of them as the scientist might measure; and it does not content itself with merely reporting about them in the way an external observer would do. It insists that the story cannot be told correctly unless we see the personalities from the inside.[4]

Fifty years later, the philosopher of history Dominick LaCapra echoed Butterfield's claim that empathy humanizes "historical understanding," making it, in LaCapra's words, "responsive."[5] It is empathy, according to LaCapra, that prevents historians from objectifying history, transforming past people and past experiences into "objects" of study. Without empathy, historians are detached from their human historical subjects, aloof, in the ethically untenable position of being a "bystander" to history.[6]

Numerous scholars in various disciplines have defined empathy in ways similar to Smith, Collingwood, and Butterfield, if generally more prosaically. Although many of these scholars' definitions of empathy will be quoted over the course of this book, a few will have to suffice here.[7] Thus, for the philosopher Martha Nussbaum, empathy is

> [the] imaginative reconstruction of another person's experience.[8]

For the literary scholar Fritz Breithaupt, it is "co-experience" (*Mit-Erleben*):

> adopting in one's imagination the position of the other and sharing his or her reaction to that situation. One slips into the skin of the other at that point where it encounters its environment ... Co-experience means that one transports oneself into the cognitive, emotional, and physical situation of the other.[9]

For the cultural studies scholar Alison Landsberg,

> the experience of empathy requires an act of imagination—one must leave oneself and attempt to imagine what it was like for that other person given what he or she went through.[10]

And, finally, for Dominick LaCapra, empathy is

> an imaginative, intellectual and emotional rapport with the other as other that does not imply an ability to take the place of, or speak for, the other. It might rather be understood as putting oneself in the other's position without taking the other's place—a distinction that recognizes difference.[11]

A number of scholars have conceptualized perspective-taking empathy as a form of narrative. Thus, Breithaupt presents empathy as developed through and expressed in storytelling, for "when we understand, we narrate." We are able to empathize "when we think in stories, and we feel ourselves into narratives thereby developing empathy with others and with fictional characters."[12] In this account, the empathizing observer adopts the perspective of the observed in order to tell his or her story from his or her perspective as he or she would tell it.[13] The philosopher Shaun Gallagher, a critic of simulation theory, argues that "understanding the other's situation is ... facilitated more by narrative than by simulation abilities."[14] In order to understand another empathically one needs to "narratively frame the other person's experience."[15] Gallagher concludes that "understanding persons in the context of their situation—having a sense of what their story is—is essential to forming an empathic attitude toward them."[16] We grow up learning stories, which "give interpretive insights into the actions of others," and, as we get older, we develop increasing narrative competency that helps us to understand ourselves and others, to know "what to expect from people and how to deal with them."[17] We can empathize not only with people in the here and now but also with people living in different times and places. "This is possible, however, only when we know their stories—only when we can frame their behavior in a narrative that informs us about their history or their situation."[18] Indeed, according to Gallagher, we know the experiences of people who are like us better than those who are different (a problematic claim that will be considered in "The Role of Subjective Experience in Empathy" in Chapter 5), less because we share specific experiences with them and more because we are familiar with their stories and "have an easier time placing" those stories "in a narrative framework."[19] Empathy conceptualized as narration appears to mean telling the stories that others, in the present and in the past, *might* have told about themselves.[20] Certainly, we should follow the historian Alon Confino who in his book *A World without Jews* focused on the stories that past people *actually* told about themselves. Specifically, Confino sought to reconstruct and understand the "story the Nazis told themselves to justify and legitimize the persecution and extermination of the Jews."[21]

Two concepts developed by the historian and philosopher of history Reinhart Koselleck seem particularly applicable to empathy conceived of as imaginative perspective-taking. In adopting the perspective of past people in our imagination, we reconstruct what Koselleck called their "space of experience" and their "horizon of expectation." By "space of experience," Koselleck meant the historical subjects' past as it was alive in them at any given moment. It is, in Koselleck's words, "present past" (*gegenwärtige Vergangenheit*). By "horizon of expectation," Koselleck meant the historical subjects' hopes, fears, and sense of what will be as it was alive in them at any given moment. In his words, it is "present future" (*vergegenwärtigte Zukunft*). Since our space of experience and our horizon of expectation are not only uniquely personal but also socially and culturally shared and constructed, we are not always entirely conscious of our experience or of our expectations. Furthermore, experience and expectation exist only in the moment and are constantly changing. With each new moment, our experience of the past changes and, with it, our expectations for the future. The always changing interplay between experience and expectation constituted historical time for Koselleck, generating, that is to say, change in history.[22] As mentioned at the outset, Koselleck never characterized the process of reconstructing the space of experience and horizon of expectation of past people as "empathy." Nevertheless, imagining one's way, thinking one's way, feeling one's way inside the "space of experience" and "horizon of expectation" of past people is precisely how empathy as a way of knowing and understanding in history is defined here.

Thus, empathy as a mode of observation in history not only seeks to know and understand past experience; it is also an experiential way of knowing and understanding. In empathy, we know experience through experience: empathy is an experience *in* the observer of the experience *of* the observed.[23] Investigators who see themselves as social scientists generally adopt an external observational position, viewing phenomena, their movements, and their relationships from without. Historians interested in demographics, economic developments, institutions, and causal sequences, who are concerned with events and activity, or who engage in comparative history, often view the past largely from the external observational position. By contrast, historians interested in the experience of the people of the past often adopt the internal, the empathic position, the vantage point of their historical subjects, imagining their way, thinking their way, feeling their way inside their subjects' "space of experience" and "horizon of expectation."[24]

The History of Emotions and Empathy

On the surface, the developing subfield of the history of emotions seems related to empathic history, where the historian adopts in his or her imagination the position of the historical subject. Empathic history certainly focuses on emotions, particularly as they were experienced by emoting historical subjects, although empathic history is also concerned with experiences that were not emotional, or at least not centrally emotional. Nevertheless, what principally distinguishes empathic history from the history of emotions is that the latter, emerging from social history, views emotional life more from the position of the outside observer than from that of the emoting historical subject. The history of emotions, as best I understand it, is concerned less with how emoting subjects experienced their own feelings and more with how specific societies defined, processed, repressed, and expressed emotions—that is, with the cultural function of emotions in specific societies. The historian of ancient Rome, William V. Harris, argues that the use of empathy in history "either in an intellectual or an emotional sense" is impossible, and advocates instead for the history of emotions.[25] He appeals for the study of what the medievalist Barbara Rosenwein calls "emotional communities" and for a "descriptive historiography, consisting of attempts to work out how particular emotions functioned in historical societies."[26] Harris' claim that we do not need empathy to know the emotional lives of the people of the past is of course true if we are satisfied with restricting our knowledge of past emotional life to the observation of its social and cultural manifestations and functions.[27] If we are interested in knowing how past people subjectively experienced and made sense of emotional life, their own and others', then we need to adopt the internal, empathic perspective. The external observational stance generally adopted by historians of emotions alone will not do.

Empathy versus Contagion, Merger, and Identification

Although empathy as a way of knowing in history means adopting the subjective position of the people of the past, the empathizing historian does not occupy the empathic position either completely or all the time. Empathy, whether in history or everyday life, is *always* partial and temporary, a fact confirmed by both empirical psychological studies and neuroscience research.[28] We simulate neurologically only some but not all aspects of another's experience. When we observe a person in pain, for example, parts of the brain "associated with the emotional content of the pain" are activated, but we do not experience actual pain ourselves.[29] Thus, in empathy we simultaneously adopt the perspective of the other while maintaining our own independent sense of self; we both imagine "being in the other's shoes" and recognize "where the self ends and the other begins."[30] Or, as the psychoanalyst Lotte Köhler put it, empathy "means to put oneself in the place of another while at the same time remaining oneself."[31]

It is the awareness of the distinction between self and other that distinguishes empathy from affective contagion, where the emotional state of others "infects" the self to become one's own emotional experience (as at a bar, sporting event, or mass rally); from psychological merger, where the self of the observer becomes absorbed by the self of the observed; and from identification, where one experiences oneself as being the same as the other. In all three cases, the psychological boundary between self and other is erased and the observer loses his or her own independent sense of self.[32] There is no loss of self in empathy. Edith Stein put it neatly: empathy is "Einfühlung," feeling into the other, not "Einsfühlung," becoming "one with" the other.[33]

The fact that empathy has often been mistakenly conceived as merger or identification may have contributed to the skepticism with which historians view the concept. Particularly in relation to the victims of historical trauma, empathy conceived as identification has resulted in the "idealization or even sacralization of the victim," according to Dominick LaCapra, "as well as an often histrionic self-image [of the historian] as surrogate victim undergoing vicarious experience."[34] Empathy conceived as identification, then, can lead to the erasure of the victim's experience in favor of the pathos of the identifying historian. When employed self-consciously and critically, however, empathy, according to LaCapra, works not to promote but to counteract both the reduction of past people to the status of victim and experiences of second-hand victimization on the part of the historian.[35]

Merger and identification assume that observer and observed are the same; empathy, by contrast, recognizes and appreciates difference, even while attempting to know and understand it.[36] To the extent that empathy involves merger, it is only a partial and a self-conscious merger; to the extent that empathy involves identification, it is what the psychoanalyst Robert Fliess called "trial identification." Indeed, he compared it to "tea tasting."[37] Nonetheless, even the notion of empathy as "trial identification" is misleading for, as Lotte Köhler points out, in trial identification "one's own identity is temporarily relinquished, which is precisely what does not happen in empathy."[38] "Empathy," the historian Mark Roseman notes, "involves the very maintenance of the observing self. Its loss is identification, not empathy."[39] Closely related to the need to maintain a clear self–other distinction in empathy is the awareness of what the psychologist Carl Rogers called its "as if," imaginary nature. One seeks to feel and think one's way inside the other person's experience "as if" one were the other person, while recognizing that the other is not oneself and that the other's emotional response is not one's own.[40]

Given that empathy is not merely experiencing what the other is experiencing but a way of *knowing* the other's experience, contagion, merger, and identification preclude empathy as a form of cognition. The philosopher Austin Harrington makes the essential point that "self-extinction culminates only in self-projection."[41] While empathizing, one needs a clear sense of the distinction between self and other in order to recognize that the other's experiences belong not to oneself and, conversely, that one's own experiences do not belong to the other.[42] Even when we experience the feelings of another in empathy, as for example happens in psychoanalytic treatment, we need to be aware of the difference between feelings that belong to the other and one's own feelings.[43] It is the awareness of the difference between self and other that allows us, in the words of Carl Rogers, "for the time being" to "lay aside [our] views and values in order to enter another world without prejudice."[44] Not only do we need temporarily to "quarantine" our own beliefs in order to know the beliefs of another, but, as we adopt the "perspective of the other person," it is self-awareness that, according to Karsten Stueber, allows us to "quarantine [empathized] pretend-beliefs from [our] own cognitive grasp of the world."[45] For the psychoanalyst Heinz Kohut empathy meant dipping a toe into the pool of the patient's experience, not jumping in.[46] Just as we can understand another's argument without agreeing with it, so too can we experience another's affect without it becoming our own emotional response.[47]

Empathy as a form of cognition, then, is a deliberate and self-conscious activity in which we use our "self" as the "vehicle for understanding" others without ever losing our own self-identity.[48] In history, even as we adopt in our imagination the position of the historical subject, another part observes ourselves in the place of that subject. According to the intellectual historian Michael Ermarth, already Dilthey recognized that knowledge in the human sciences consisted of "'inside' understanding and critical judgment."[49] R. G. Collingwood too emphasized that in empathy we do not "become" the person of the past whose thought we are rethinking. Instead, our rethinking must be self-conscious and critical. While empathizing, we are simultaneously subjectively and objectively engaged with past thought. We are both rethinking that thought and thinking about that thought.[50] Empathy, then, involves a kind of splitting on the part of the historian, who occupies both the empathic and the external observational positions simultaneously.[51] We imagine our way inside the experience of the historical subject, while at the same time we observe the historical subject and ourselves in its place from our own observational vantage point. According to the Russian philosopher, literary critic, and semiotician Mikhail Bakhtin, we need both empathy and what he called "extopy": while empathizing we also need to occupy the external observational position in order to have a full aesthetic experience and to be able to take ethical action. Bakhtin contended that not only in relation to art but also in relation to other people, in the present as in the past, the self–other distinction needs to be maintained throughout the empathizing process.[52]

Thus, even as we empathize, we need to maintain critical distance from our subject's experience, to remain self-reflective, attuned to the uniqueness of the subject, and aware of the attenuated nature of our empathy.[53] The self-consciousness and self-critical application of empathy leads to what LaCapra calls "empathic unsettlement." Although LaCapra acknowledges that the term resists precise definition, in my reading of his work, essential to empathic unsettlement is the historian's pervasive experience of difference even while attempting to know and understand it.[54] Empathic unsettlement prompts historians to scrutinize their own subjective and empathic responses to insure that empathy does not become contagion, merger, or identification; that empathy does not lead to pathos, to the instrumentalization of past people, or to simplifying and satisfying closure, but to an understanding that opens up as much as it closes off.[55] As Herbert Butterfield pointed out, empathy is always partial and always incomplete.[56] It is the attenuated nature of empathy, in fact, that enables us to recognize difference, to appreciate that our empathized experience can never fully capture the experience of the other, which in elusive and important ways ultimately always escapes our empathic grasp.[57]

Not only do historians need to be objectively engaged during the subjective process of empathizing, they also occupy the position of the outside observer in knowing when to adopt the empathic position. It is when something does not make sense from our external observational position, or perhaps when normal intuitive understanding breaks down, that we deliberately and consciously adopt the perspective of the historical subject. Not only in history but in everyday life, we deliberately adopt the empathic observational position when, in the language of simulation theory, mirror or basic empathy cannot do the job or when, in the language of the phenomenological position, "our shared engagement" in a "common world," our normal intersubjective understanding is insufficient to enable us to understand another.[58] That is to say, historians deliberately and self-consciously engage in what philosophers and psychologists call perspective-shifting or in what literary and film scholars call "imaginative empathy" to re-enact or reconstruct a historical subject's experience when they are confronted with an explanatory puzzle.[59] To solve that puzzle, historians self-consciously adopt the empathic position to understand why the feeling, thought, or behavior that does not make sense when viewed from without or with basic empathy makes sense from within the experience of the historical subject. And historians return to the position of the outside observer in interpreting the understanding they have gained through empathy, for our interpretations—by employing logic, comparison, and knowledge only indirectly related to that of the historical subject—transcend the subject's experience and view of the world.[60]

Empathy versus Sympathy

Empathy is decidedly *not* sympathy, a distinction that should make historians more sympathetic to empathy as a way to know and understand the people of the past.[61] The notion that empathy and sympathy are synonymous or that empathy inevitably engenders sympathy threatens to make empathic history a maudlin enterprise or even more problematic if, say, empathizing with Nazis also means sympathizing with them. The equation of empathy and sympathy is obviously misplaced for, as Alon Confino elegantly put it: "One can understand without forgiving and forgive without understanding."[62] That is, one can empathize with people for whom one feels no sympathy, and one can sympathize with people in whose place one could never imagine oneself being.

Part of the confusion of empathy and sympathy can be traced to the way these terms have been used in the past. As we have seen, David Hume, Adam Smith, Charles H. Cooley, George Herbert Mead, and Herbert Butterfield all used the term "sympathy" to designate what we would call empathy today. Contemporary definitions of empathy produced by philosophers, psychologists, neuroscientists, primatologists, and ethologists have occasionally included sympathy as one of empathy's permutations and connect empathy with an altruistic or "pro-social" attitude. Despite the difference between empathy and sympathy, the terms continue to be conflated in popular usage, and even within the academic community. Thus, the thoughtful and perceptive literary scholar Johannes von Moltke criticizes the 2004 film *Der Untergang*, in English *Downfall*, which portrays the final days of Adolf Hitler in his Berlin bunker, for its "empathetic" treatment of Hitler. According to Moltke, the film, by engendering empathy for Hitler, creates sympathy for him on the part of viewers, causing them even to develop an "allegiance" to the Führer. Moltke and, it would seem from his article, many other literary scholars equate empathy and sympathy, emotional alignment and allegiance. Thus, what is problematic about *Der Untergang* for Moltke is that the film, by emotionally aligning the viewer with Hitler, causes the viewer to develop an allegiance to him.[63] These are two distinct processes, however. Emotional or cognitive "alignment" is empathy; "allegiance" is not.

To avoid the problem apparently posed by applying empathy to a historical figure like Adolf Hitler, most historians who write about empathy consider it mainly in relation to victims and not to perpetrators in history, presuming or implying that we can only think or feel our way inside the experience of people who are sympathetic to us. That association is the result of the fact that many scholars tend—wrongly—to see empathy as identification, to share Jonathan Boyarin's view, speaking of empathy in relation to Holocaust memory, that "we can only empathize with, feel ourselves into, those we can imagine as ourselves."[64] Empathy in historical knowledge is not about imagining the people of the past as being like *ourselves*, however; empathy in historical knowledge is about recognizing that the people of the past are different from us and then trying to imagine being like *them*.

By linking empathy to identification, the historian Carolyn Dean brings empathy and sympathy uncomfortably close to one another. Indeed, she is critical of historians who indulge in the attempt to restore dignity to victims in history, above all to the Jewish victims of the Nazi genocide, through redemptive empathic identification with them.[65] Given the link Dean sees between empathy and identification, empathy with perpetrators would be problematic since empathizing with the perpetrators would mean identifying with them. As we have seen, Dominick LaCapra rejects "the conflation of empathy with identification."[66] Nevertheless, because he links empathy with compassion, he too tends to focus on empathy in relation to the victims of historical trauma, and asks whether certain perpetrators "have earned or deserve mourning (even empathy) but instead warrant modes of understanding insistently related to critique?"[67] Despite his profound sympathy for Collingwood, the philosopher Dale Jacquette sees a limit to empathy in trying to enter into "Hitler's warped way of thinking" in his final days in Berlin in his bunker, asking "must I as a historian of these events myself actually believe and desire what Hitler believed and desired?"[68] The historian William V. Harris, a critic of the use of empathy in history, deems empathy for perpetrators, such as members of the SS, to be simply "impossible."[69] Indeed, for the historian Charles Maier, the "extremes of twentieth-century history" make clear the impossibility of historical empathy.[70]

In empathy, we do not need to share someone's beliefs to understand them, however. The philosopher Jane Heal put it this way: "given the person's beliefs it follows that he will believe X. I may not share those beliefs, but if I did, I would believe X."[71] One can and should attempt to empathize with beliefs one finds abhorrent. In relation to contemporary political conflict, such as the one between Palestinians and Israeli Jews, the historian Steven Aschheim calls for a politically relevant empathy that "demands access to other selves, even, indeed, to those with whom we may be locked in conflict."[72] Similarly, it seems crucial that we attempt to empathize with Nazis. As Christopher Browning wrote in relation to his history of Reserve Police Battalion 101, which carried out mass killings of Jews during World War II:

the men who carried out these massacres ... were human beings ... This recognition does indeed mean an attempt to empathize. What I do not accept, however, are the old clichés that to explain is to excuse, that to understand is to forgive. Explaining is not excusing; understanding is not forgiving. The notion that one must simply reject the acts of the perpetrators and not try to understand them would make impossible not only my history but any perpetrator history that sought to go beyond one-dimensional caricature.[73]

Certainly, in my own historical work, I have used empathy to understand not victims but perpetrators of, or at least bystanders to, genocide. As discussed in the previous section, we consciously and deliberately adopt the empathic position, the position of the historical subject, in order to understand feelings, thoughts, and actions of the historical subject that do not seem to make sense, that puzzle us. The attitudes and behavior of those who carried out or enabled genocide present me at least with an explanatory puzzle. To cite one example, I wish to understand how a man ordered to shoot men, women, and children lying naked in a trench could think that order made sense. Although perhaps at the current limit of our empathic capacities, attempting to understand the man with the gun before the trench is not only possible, it is morally and intellectually imperative.[74] Although in my book *A German Generation* I did not deal with those who actually carried out genocide, I did seek to empathize with Nazis and their supporters and to engender empathy for them on the part of readers, without my having any sympathy for them and without, I think, making them at all sympathetic to readers. Thus, despite my abhorrence of National Socialism, I sought to understand its appeal to the generation of Germans that was the focus of my book. Specifically, I sought to empathize with their attraction to what I regard to be National Socialism's central ideological tenet, the racial collective of the *Volksgemeinschaft*.[75]

Just as we can empathize with people for whom we have no sympathy, empathy can be used for unsympathetic purposes. Empathy is not simply and inevitably a force for good, the basis of altruism, and the source of compassionate human understanding. In Martha Nussbaum's words, "empathy is limited, fallible, and value neutral."[76] It can be used to harm, manipulate, defeat, and destroy people.[77] Countless examples of the use of empathy for harmful, manipulative, or aggressive purposes might be cited here, ranging from the calculated dig that targets another person's most vulnerable emotional spot, through sophisticated advertising campaigns, to the interrogator who uses empathy to extract information from a suspect.[78] The psychoanalyst Heinz Kohut cited the attempt by the Luftwaffe during the Second World War "to create disintegrating panic in those they were about to attack" by attaching sirens to the wings of dive bombers as an example of "fiendish empathy," empathy used for a hostile purpose. "It was empathy (vicarious introspection) that allowed them to predict how those exposed to the mysterious noise from the skies would react."[79] Indeed, one can even see empathy at work in the Nazi extermination project where the SS authorities designed a genocidal process "based on a sensitivity and access to the experience of the intended victims" designed to reduce their resistance leading up to the moment the doors closed on them in the gas chambers of Auschwitz.[80] As Martha Nussbaum puts it, "enemies often become adept at reading the purposes of their foes and manipulating them for their own ends."[81] Along similar lines, the anthropologist Nils Bubandt argues that "sometimes empathy is at the heart of violence." As an example of what he calls "hostile empathy," he cites forged letters produced by Muslims in Indonesia at the end of the twentieth century which mimicked the voices of their Christian enemies in order to provoke the Muslim community to engage in violence against Christians. Producing letters that would enrage the Muslim community required the forgers to "make an imaginary leap into the mind and emotions" of their Christian enemies, "entailed, in short, an act of *empathy*."[82] As the psychoanalyst Warren Poland put it:

> the con man, the demagogue, the exploiter, and the sadist all function best when their empathic skills are sharp. Indeed, the effectiveness of a sadist's cruelty is directly related to the capacity for empathy, to the ability to sense what will hurt the most.[83]

Empathy, then, is not sympathy. In the words of Lauren Wispé:

> sympathy refers to the heightened awareness of another's plight as something to be alleviated. Empathy refers to the attempt of one self-aware self to understand the subjective experiences of another self. Sympathy is a way of relating. Empathy is a way of knowing.[84]

For Alison Landsberg,

> Empathy, unlike sympathy, requires mental, cognitive activity, it entails an intellectual engagement with the plight of the other; when one talks about empathy one is not talking simply about emotion, but about contemplation as well. Contemplation and distance, two elements central to empathy, are not present in sympathy.[85]

In empathy, I leave my own subjective position in order to attempt to adopt the subjective position of the other in my imagination. I seek to align myself with the other mentally, in that I try to see the world from the other's perspective, and emotionally, in that I try to feel something of what the other feels. Mental or emotional alignment means adopting the empathic position, the subjective position of the other. When I experience sympathy, I maintain my own subjective position—I do not adopt the position of the person with whom I sympathize. The other person may feel sorrow or anger; I feel sympathy, an emotion entirely different from the sorrow or anger that the other is experiencing.[86] My feelings of sympathy are *my* feelings for someone else; they are not the feelings experienced by the person for whom I experience sympathy.[87] Being clear about one's observational position lifts the fog of confusion surrounding empathy and sympathy.[88] When I empathize, I seek to adopt in my imagination the position of the other; when I sympathize, I regard and react to the other from my own autonomous position. In a nutshell, empathy is feeling *with*; sympathy is feeling *for*.[89]

Although empathy and sympathy are demonstrably different, perhaps there is something humanizing that may *result* from empathy that we, as in the case of Hitler, may wish to resist. And perhaps, as the philosopher Giuseppina D'Oro contends, there is something to the claim that:

> to explain an action rationally is *ipso facto* to justify it. If one accepts that the concept of rational explanation is closely linked to that of justification or, as the point is sometimes put, that all reasons are good reasons, a conflict may arise between the requirement to understand why agents act as they do, and the requirement to evaluate whether they should have so acted.[90]

Although this problem seems related less to empathy and more to rational explanation in general, keeping straight which observational position one occupies in knowing the people of the past helps resolve the problem of understanding and judgment in relation to empathy. Initially the historian occupies the position of the external observer who judges which past feelings, thoughts, and actions require empathic understanding. Then, the historian occupies the internal, empathic position in an attempt to understand those feelings, thoughts, and actions in the terms and experience of the historical subject—without endorsing those feelings, thoughts, and actions in any way. And, finally, the historian returns to the position of the external observer to assess—perhaps to condemn—the feelings, thoughts, and actions of the historical subject that have been empathically understood. Conceptualized as perspective-taking, historical empathy, then, is fully compatible with historical critique.[91] Perhaps, as a result of empathically derived understanding, one may regard past people more sympathetically; but that increased sympathy is the result of empathy, not empathy itself.[92] And, it is demonstrable that sympathy is not the inevitable product of empathy, although it may sometimes be.

That said, although empathy is "morally neutral," as Martha Nussbaum points out,

> it does involve a very basic recognition of another world of experience, and to that extent it is not altogether neutral. If I allow my mind to be formed into the shape of your experience … I am still in a very basic way acknowledging your reality and humanity.[93]

Even when empathy is used for hostile purposes, it brings the empathizer closer to the empathized as a human being, temporarily overcoming the friend/foe, you/me distinction.[94] Indeed, the historian Lynn Hunt has argued that consciousness of empathy was at the heart of the development in Europe between 1689 and 1776 of the notion of human rights: namely, the idea that all people, not just members of a particular group, have universal, natural, and equal rights, rights, which in the latter half of the eighteenth century were seen to be "self-evident." "Everyone would have rights if everyone could be seen as in some fundamental way alike"; and it was empathy, according to Hunt, that enabled people to recognize "that others feel and think as we do, that our inner feelings are alike in some fundamental fashion."[95] "Learning to empathize," Hunt concludes, "opened the path to human rights."[96] Jay Winter makes a similar argument, although sharply distinguishing between empathy and sympathy. For him, the shift from humanitarianism to human rights represented "a change in optics, a move from the verticality of sympathy to the horizontality of empathy ... from the sympathy of humanitarian law to the empathy of human rights law."[97]

Notes

1   Adam Smith, *The Theory of Moral Sentiments*, ed. Knud Haakonssen (Cambridge: Cambridge University Press, 2002), 11–12; see also 374. Smith distinguishes "sympathy," which we would call empathy, from "compassion."

2   Collingwood, *The Idea of History*, 241. See, also, Jacquette, "Collingwood on Historical Authority and Historical Imagination," 58–59.

3   Collingwood, *The Idea of History*, 199. To be sure, Collingwood's account of empathy in history as rethinking the past thought of the artists and intellectuals who created canonical works and of the rational actors who produced historically significant events now seems dated. Although I do not conceive of empathy in history solely as rethinking the past thought of past people, we do at times rethink the thought of another as part of the process of understanding. Whether in reading a complex written text or in listening to a complex verbal account, we frequently think along with the writer or the speaker in trying to understand what is being communicated. Thus, when I was a Visiting Fellow at Exeter College in Oxford, I engaged in a conversation with a Classicist who sought to explain his scholarship on late-Roman poetry to me. I found him difficult to follow. As he spoke, I was aware that, in seeking to understand his account of his work, I was thinking along with him, thinking his thoughts in my own mind and in my own words. I recall listening to one long sentence with a number of subordinate clauses. And I recall hoping that he would conclude the sentence with a particular phrase that I had in my mind. I was anticipating that phrase because if he in fact used that phrase or something like it, it meant that I was understanding him. When he in fact uttered that phrase at the end of the long sentence, I experienced relief: I had understood him more or less.

4   Herbert Butterfield, *History and Human Relations* (London: Collins, 1951), 145–146. Butterfield also considers the limits of empathy, ibid., 116–117.

5   LaCapra, "Tropisms of Intellectual History," 503.

6   Dominick LaCapra, *History in Transit: Experience, Identity, Critical Theory* (Ithaca: Cornell University Press, 2004), 70. See, also, 5.

7 These include Rosalind F. Dymond, "A Scale for the Measurement of Empathic Ability," *Journal of Consulting Psychology* 13, no. 2(1949): 127; for Gordon Allport's nearly identical definition, see Lauren Wispé, "History of the Concept of Empathy," in *Empathy and Its Development*, ed. Nancy Eisenberg and Janet Strayer, Cambridge Studies in Social and Emotional Development (New York: Cambridge University Press, 1987), 26; Evan Thompson, *Mind in Life: Biology, Phenomenology, and the Sciences of Mind* (Cambridge, MA: Belknap Press of Harvard University Press, 2007), 396–397; C. Jason Throop, "On the Problem of Empathy: The Case of Yap, Federated States of Micronesia," *Ethos* 36, no. 4 (2008): 405; Coplan, "Understanding Empathy," 17–18. Imagination and perspective-taking are also central to Husserl's conception of empathy according to Peter Shum, "Avoiding Circularities."

8 Martha C. Nussbaum, *Upheavals of Thought: The Intelligence of Emotions* (Cambridge: Cambridge University Press, 2001), 301–302; see also Assmann and Detmers, "Introduction," 4.

9 Fritz Breithaupt, *Die dunklen Seiten der Empathie* (Frankfurt: Suhrkamp, 2017), 16, also 15. See also Fritz Breithaupt, "Empathy for Empathy's Sake: Aesthetics and Everyday Empathic Sadism," in *Empathy and Its Limits*, ed. Aleida Assmann and Ines Detmers (London and New York: Palgrave Macmillan, 2016), 152; Fritz Breithaupt, *Kulturen der Empathie* (Frankfurt: Suhrkamp, 2012), 8.

10 Alison Landsberg, "Memory, Empathy, and the Politics of Identification," *International Journal of Politics, Culture, and Society* 22, no. 2(2009): 223.

11 Dominick LaCapra, *Understanding Others: Peoples, Animals, Pasts* (Ithaca and London: Cornell University Press, 2018), 47.

12 Breithaupt, *Kulturen der Empathie*, 10, 114. Breithaupt is particularly concerned with the role that empathy can play in conflict resolution. His view of empathy fits well with Lynn Hunt's argument that the concept of universal human rights was based on empathy, on being able to imagine that "someone else is like you." Empathy in turn developed in European culture, in her view, out of eighteenth-century novels whereby readers learned to imagine their way inside the life stories and experiences of the novels' characters. The novels, in Hunt's words, allowed readers "to extend the purview of empathy … As a consequence, they came to see others—people they did not know personally—as like them, as having the same kind of inner emotions. Without this learning process, 'equality' could have no deep meaning and in particular no political consequence." Lynn Hunt, *Inventing Human Rights: A History* (New York: Norton, 2007), 32, 40, and in general Chapter 1.

13 Shelley Berlowitz, "Unequal Equals: How Politics Can Block Empathy," in Assmann and Detmers, *Empathy and Its Limits*, 42. Berlowitz advocates for "narrative empathy." Like Breithaupt, she is primarily interested in empathy in relation to conflict resolution.

14 Shaun Gallagher, "Empathy, Simulation, and Narrative," *Scientific Context* 25, no. 3(2011): 369. See also Retz, *Empathy and History*, 159.

15 Gallagher, "Empathy, Simulation, and Narrative," 370.

16 Ibid., 374.

17 Ibid., 371.

18 Ibid., 370. See also Shaun Gallagher and Somogy Varga, "Social Constraints on the Direct Perception of Emotions and Intentions," *Topoi* 33, no. 1(2014): 196. Indeed, the philosopher David Carr prefers narrative to empathy, which, in his view, focuses on individuals and on their intentions. By contrast, "a story seems capable of encompassing multiple actions and events, as well as longer-term actions, sub-actions, and reactions to events." David Carr, "Narrative Explanation and Its Malcontents," *History and Theory* 47(2008): 24–25.

19 Gallagher, "Empathy, Simulation, and Narrative," 370.
20 See, for example, Berlowitz, "Unequal Equals," 42. My understanding of Breithaupt and Gallagher is that they too see the empathizing narrative as constructed by the observer who imagines the story that the observed might have told about him- or herself.
21 Confino, "From Psychohistory to Memory Studies," 27; Alon Confino *A World without Jews: The Nazi Imagination from Persecution to Genocide* (New Haven, CT: Yale University Press, 2014). See also LaCapra, *Understanding Others*, 48.
22 Reinhart Koselleck, "'Space of Experience' and 'Horizon of Expectation': Two Historical Categories," in *Futures Past: On the Semantics of Historical Time*, ed. Keith Tribe (New York: Columbia University Press, 2004), particularly 272 and 275; "'Erfahrungsraum' und 'Erwartungshorizont': Zwei historische Kategorien," in *Vergangene Zukunft: Zur Semantik geschichtlicher Zeiten* (Frankfurt: Suhrkamp, 1979), 354–355.
23 Coplan, "Understanding Empathy," 17.
24 The distinction drawn here between the external and the empathic observational standpoints finds a parallel in Karsten Stueber's distinction between what he calls the "detached" and the "engaged perspective." For Stueber, these two observational perspectives form the basis of the epistemological difference between the natural and the human sciences. Karsten Stueber, "Understanding Versus Explanation? How to Think About the Distinction between the Human and the Natural Sciences," *Inquiry: An Interdisciplinary Journal of Philosophy* 55, no. 1(2012): 18.
25 Harris, "History, Empathy and Emotions," 1.
26 Ibid., 15.
27 See, here, Nicole Eustace et al., "AHR Conversation: The Historical Study of Emotions," *American Historical Review* 117, no. 5(2012): 1487-1531.
28 The neurophysiological basis of the distinction between self and other in empathy has been confirmed by behavioral and functional magnetic resonance imaging (fMRI) data. See, for example, Lamm et al., "Neural Substrate of Human Empathy," 56. Empirical psychological studies have demonstrated the centrality of this distinction in empathy as well. See, for example, Martin L. Hoffman, "Interaction of Affect and Cognition in Empathy," in *Emotions, Cognition, Behavior*, ed. C. E. Izard, J. Kagan, and R. B. Zajonc (Cambridge: Cambridge University Press, 1984).
29 Watson and Greenberg, "Empathic Resonance," 127.
30 Coplan, "Understanding Empathy," 5–6, 17; also 15 and 16.
31 Köhler, "Von der Freud'schen Psychoanalyse zur Selbstpsychologie Heinz Kohuts," 39.
32 LaCapra, "Tropisms of Intellectual History," 503; *History in Transit*, 43, 76–77; Breithaupt, *Kulturen der Empathie*, 25–26, 35, 166–167; "Empathy for Empathy's Sake," 152; *Die dunklen Seiten der Empathie*, 22; Nussbaum, *Upheavals of Thought*, 327–328.
33 Coplan and Goldie, "Introduction," xiv.
34 LaCapra, *History in Transit*, 65, 77. See also Dominick LaCapra, *History and Memory after Auschwitz* (Ithaca: Cornell University Press, 1998), 12, 182, 186–187.
35 LaCapra, *Writing History, Writing Trauma*, 40, 78, 219. See also *History and Memory after Auschwitz*, 12, 54.
36 For Dominick LaCapra, what distinguishes empathy from identification is that empathy "requires recognition of the difference of the other," thereby counteracting the tendency in identification "to project or simply incorporate the other in ways that obliterate differences." LaCapra, *Understanding Others*, 123–124. See also 47, 113, 146.
37 Robert Fliess, "The Metapsychology of the Analyst," *Psychoanalytic Quarterly* 11 (1942): 212, 214.

38 Köhler, "Von der Freud'schen Psychoanalyse zur Selbstpsychologie Heinz Kohuts," 49.

39 Personal communication.

40 Wispé, "History of the Concept of Empathy," 28. See also Breithaupt, *Kulturen der Empathie*, 35; Gladstein, "Contemporary Empathy Research," 54; Jodi Halpern, *From Detached Concern to Empathy: Humanizing Medical Practice* (Oxford: Oxford University Press, 2001), 82. Dominick LaCapra describes empathy as "a virtual experience." LaCapra, *Writing History, Writing Trauma*, 40; *History in Transit*, 125.

41 Austin Harrington, "Dilthey, Empathy and Verstehen: A Contemporary Reappraisal," *European Journal of Social Theory* 4, no. 3(2001): 312.

42 Assmann and Detmers, "Introduction," 6.

43 Köhler, "Von der Freud'schen Psychoanalyse zur Selbstpsychologie Heinz Kohuts," 39.

44 Rogers quoted in Wispé, "History of the Concept of Empathy," 28.

45 Stueber, *Rediscovering Empathy*, 114. Or, as the film scholar Margrethe Bruun Vaage puts it, "empathy is always just a partial sharing of someone else's state, and only sharing the same type of state. It is quarantined as the *other's* state, thus not swamping the observer's mental economy completely, but allowing the observer as well to have reactions of his own to the empathic experience. If I empathize with others in real life, this is always from my position as observer of the other's state, which is different from my state." Vaage, "Fiction Film and Empathic Engagement," 167.

46 Personal communication.

47 Constantine Sandis, "A Just Medium: Empathy and Detachment in Historical Understanding," *Journal of the Philosophy of History* 5, no. 2(2011): 198.

48 Lauren Wispé, "The Distinction between Sympathy and Empathy: To Call Forth a Concept, a Word Is Needed," *Journal of Personality and Social Psychology* 50 (1986): 318. See also Assmann and Detmers, "Introduction," 6; Breithaupt, *Kulturen der Empathie*, 8; Nussbaum, *Upheavals of Thought*, 327–328.

49 Ermarth, *Wilhelm Dilthey*, 314.

50 Collingwood, *The Idea of History*, 292. See also Retz, *Empathy and History*, 118, 128, 158.

51 The historian Carlo Ginzburg discusses the need for splitting on the part of the anthropologist-historian in relation to witchcraft persecution. The split he considers, however, is not that the historian needs simultaneously to occupy the empathic and the external observational positions. Rather, Ginzburg sees the historian simultaneously occupying the position of the inquisitor in seeking information about witches, and the position of the victim out of compassion for those accused of witchcraft. Carlo Ginzburg, "The Inquisitor as Anthropologist," in *Clues, Myths, and the Historical Method*, trans. John and Anne C. Tedeschi (Baltimore: Johns Hopkins University Press, 1989), 158.

52 Sophie Oliver, "The Aesth-*Ethics* of Empathy: Bakhtin and the *Return to Self* as an Ethical Act," in *Empathy and Its Limits*, ed. Aleida Assmann and Ines Detmers (London and New York: Palgrave Macmillan, 2016), 166–186, especially 167, 176–177, 182.

53 Austin Harrington, *Hermeneutic Dialogue and Social Science: A Critique of Gadamer and Habermas* (New York: Routledge, 2001), 126.

54 LaCapra, *Understanding Others*, 48.

55 LaCapra, *History in Transit*, 65, 83, 103, and 135; *Writing History, Writing Trauma*, xi.

56 Butterfield, *History and Human Relations*, 116–117, 145–146.

57 Dan Zahavi and Søren Overgaard, "Empathy without Isomorphism: A Phenomenological Account," in *Empathy: From Bench to Bedside*, ed. Jean Decety (Cambridge, MA: MIT Press, 2012), 9. See also Breithaupt, *Kulturen der Empathie*, 64.

58 Dan Zahavi, *Subjectivity and Selfhood* (Cambridge, MA: MIT Press, 2005), 165–
167. The psychoanalyst Lotte Köhler distinguishes between intuition and empathy.
Although empathy may be used unconsciously and automatically, it, in contrast to
intuition, is "a complex affective-cognitive act." Köhler, "Von der Freud'schen
Psychoanalyse zur Selbstpsychologie Heinz Kohuts," 49.

59 I am indebted to the philosopher Bojana Mladenovic for this formulation. See also
Dray, *Laws and Explanation in History*, 125–126. With his emphasis on historical
causation, Dray defined what I have called an "explanatory puzzle" as a moment
when an action and the rationale for that action do not seem to match, when the
logical equilibrium between action and rationale seems upset. By adopting the position of the actor, the historian then adds considerations that make the action and the
rationale match up again, that restore equilibrium. See also Assmann and Detmers,
"Introduction," 5; Köhler, "Von der Freud'schen Psychoanalyse zur Selbstpsychologie
Heinz Kohuts," 51; Vaage, "Fiction Film and Empathic Engagement."

60 LaCapra, *Understanding Others*, 113.

61 In Dominick LaCapra's words, empathy has been often confused with "patronizing
sympathy." *Writing History, Writing Trauma*, 38. Unfortunately, in my view,
LaCapra nevertheless conflates empathy with compassion, particularly in his most
recent book, *Understanding Others*, 4, 22, 47, 113, 121, 123–124, 146, 181.

62 Alon Confino, *Germany as a Culture of Remembrance: Promises and Limits of
Writing History* (Chapel Hill: North Carolina University Press, 2006), 10. See also
Nussbaum, *Upheavals of Thought*, 329.

63 Johannes von Moltke, "Sympathy for the Devil: Cinema, History, and the Politics
of Emotion," *New German Critique* 34 (2007), especially 25–27, 29–30, 32.

64 Quoted in Amos Goldberg, "Empathy, Ethics, and Politics in Holocaust Historiography," in Assmann and Detmers, *Empathy and Its Limits*, 67. Even some scholars who recognize that empathy is not identification tend to associate empathy
with sympathetic victims rather than unsympathetic perpetrators. Steven E. Aschheim, "The (Ambiguous) Political Economy of Empathy," in Assmann and Detmers, *Empathy and Its Limits*, 22, 26–28; LaCapra, *Writing History, Writing
Trauma*, 215; Nussbaum, *Upheavals of Thought*, 327–328. Other scholars seem to
see empathy as identification, and therefore bring empathy and sympathy uncomfortably close together: Ute Frevert, "Empathizing in the Theater of Horrors or
Civilizing the Human Heart," in Assmann and Detmers, *Empathy and Its Limits*,
80, 87, 88, 93–96; Goldberg, "Empathy, Ethics, and Politics in Holocaust Historiography," 52–76, particularly 57, 58, 59, 67; Hunt, *Inventing Human Rights*, 55,
65.

65 Carolyn J. Dean, *The Fragility of Empathy after the Holocaust* (Ithaca: Cornell
University Press, 2004), 6; "History Writing, Numbness, and the Restoration of
Dignity," *History of the Human Sciences* 17, no. 2–3(2004): 57–59, also 67 and 70.

66 LaCapra, *Understanding Others*, 47, 48.

67 LaCapra, *Writing History, Writing Trauma*, 215. See also LaCapra, *History and
Memory after Auschwitz*, 12, 182, 186–187. In a footnote, LaCapra acknowledges
that limited empathic engagement with perpetrators may be "defensible" as long
as it remains "unsettled, inadequate, or even consciously constrained." *History in
Transit*, n. 28, 65. In his most recent book, LaCapra also sees "a role for empathy
with the perpetrator at least in the sense of recognizing the possibility of certain
actions or experiences oneself under certain conditions." *Understanding Others*, 47.
Nevertheless, he questions whether "Trump himself and some of his more cynical

supporters warrant empathy or only the type of understanding that critically investigates their deceptive procedures and attempts to counteract them?" Ibid., 182.

68 Jacquette, "Collingwood on Historical Authority and Historical Imagination," 71.

69 Harris, "History, Empathy and Emotions," 7.

70 It appears that Maier here sees empathy as a "psychological merging of historian and protagonist." If so, he is in fact right that such a shared experience is at the very least ethically "unfeasible" in relation to the horrors of the twentieth century. But empathy is not merger. The historian must maintain critical distance while empathizing. And empathy is not sympathy either. Charles S. Maier, *The Unmasterable Past: History, Holocaust, and German National Identity* (Cambridge, MA: Harvard University Press, 1988), 98.

71 Heal, *Mind, Reason, and Imagination*, 34.

72 Aschheim, "(Ambiguous) Political Economy of Empathy," 29.

73 Christopher R. Browning, "German Memory, Judicial Interrogation, and Historical Reconstruction: Writing Perpetrator History from Postwar Testimony," in *Probing the Limits of Representation: Nazism and the "Final Solution"*, ed. Saul Friedländer (Cambridge, MA: Harvard University Press, 1992), 36.

74 See page 126 below.

75 Thomas A. Kohut, *A German Generation: An Experiential History of the Twentieth Century* (New Haven: Yale University Press, 2012), 17. As Steven Aschheim puts it, "if the historian wants to comprehend the psychology and motivations of Nazi perpetrators or Russian rapists or Rwandan killers this will involve a deliberate act of empathy, but one that hardly entails ethical identification." Aschheim, "(Ambiguous) Political Economy of Empathy," 23.

76 Nussbaum, *Upheavals of Thought*, 331; see also Breithaupt, "Empathy for Empathy's Sake," 151; Köhler, "Von der Freud'schen Psychoanalyse zur Selbstpsychologie Heinz Kohuts," 39.

77 Kohut, *A German Generation*, 16–17; Assmann and Detmers, "Introduction," 5; Breithaupt, *Kulturen der Empathie*, 8; Köhler, "Von der Freud'schen Psychoanalyse zur Selbstpsychologie Heinz Kohuts," 39, 51; Nussbaum, *Upheavals of Thought*, 301–302. Fritz Breithaupt's recent book, *Die dunklen Seiten der Empathie*, is devoted to a consideration of the "dark sides of empathy."

78 Heinz Kohut, "On Empathy," in *The Search for the Self: Selected Writings of Heinz Kohut 1978–1981*, ed. Paul H. Ornstein (London: Karnac, 2011), 529; Assmann and Detmers, "Introduction," 5.

79 Kohut, "On Empathy," 529; Heinz Kohut, "Letter to a Colleague," in *The Search for the Self: Selected Writings of Heinz Kohut 1978–1981*, ed. Paul H. Ornstein (London: Karnac, 2011), 580;

80 Louis Agosta, *Empathy in the Context of Philosophy* (Basingstoke: Palgrave Macmillan, 2010), 71.

81 Nussbaum, *Upheavals of Thought*, 329.

82 Nils Bubandt, "The Enemy's Point of View: Violence, Empathy, and the Ethnography of Fakes," *Cultural Anthropology* 24, no. 3(2009): 565, 567.

83 Poland, "Clinician's Corner," 89. See, also, Assmann and Detmers, "Introduction," 5; Breithaupt, "Empathy for Empathy's Sake," 162; *Die dunklen Seiten der Empathie*, 149–186; Köhler, "Von der Freud'schen Psychoanalyse zur Selbstpsychologie Heinz Kohuts," 39; Nussbaum, *Upheavals of Thoughts*, 329; Zaki and Ochsner, "Neuroscience of Empathy," 6.

84 Wispé, "Distinction between Sympathy and Empathy," 314. See also Assmann and Detmers, "Introduction," 3–4.

85 Landsberg, "Memory, Empathy, and the Politics of Identification," 223.

86 Nancy Eisenberg and Paul Miller, "Empathy, Sympathy, and Altruism: Empirical and Conceptual Links," in *Empathy and Its Development*, ed. Nancy Eisenberg and Janet Strayer (Cambridge: Cambridge University Press, 1987), 292.

87 I have also considered these issues in Thomas A. Kohut, "Reflections on Empathy as a Mode of Observation in History," in *Sinngeschichten: Kulturgeschichtliche Beiträge für Ute Daniel*, ed. Christian Frey et al. (Cologne: Böhlau, 2013), 90–96.

88 According to Shaun Gallagher, empathy and sympathy are distinguished by virtue of the fact that "the intentional structure of the affective state" of each is different. Gallagher, "Empathy, Simulation, and Narrative," 360.

89 According to the historian Jay Winter, already Theodor Lipps made this crucial distinction between empathy and sympathy: "Lipps's usage suggests that empathy enters the other; sympathy remains apart." Or, as Winter puts the distinction in his own words, "empathy is a feeling, which changes the subject position of the person who feels it; sympathy (in this definition) leaves the subject position of the observer intact." Winter, "From Sympathy to Empathy," 101–102.

90 Giuseppina D'Oro, "Collingwood, Psychologism and Internalism," *European Journal of Philosophy* 12(2004): 163.

91 It is here where I differ from LaCapra, who links empathy with compassion and sees a tension between historical empathy and historical judgment. Because of our ability to shift observational positions, we are able both to know and understand empathically and to criticize and even condemn historical subjects.

92 Nussbaum, *Upheavals of Thought*, 331–332. Adam Smith argued that empathy (which he called sympathy) with another will cause one to judge the other less harshly, whereas the absence of empathy for another will cause one to judge the other more harshly. Smith, *Theory of Moral Sentiments*, 20–21. See, also, Hume, *Treatise of Human Nature*, 369, 577–578; Cooley, *Human Nature and Social Order*, 136–137. Empathy has been shown to "mediate" altruism at least in adults. Eisenberg and Miller, "Empathy, Sympathy, and Altruism," 310. See, also, Batson, "These Things Called Empathy"; Mark H. Davis, *Empathy: A Social Psychological Approach*, Social Psychology Series (Boulder, CO: Westview, 1994), 102, also 204; Martin L. Hoffman, "Empathy, Role-Taking, Guilt, and the Development of Altruistic Motives," in *Moral Development and Behavior: Theory, Research, Social Issues*, ed. T. Lickona (New York: Holt, Rinehart, and Winston, 1976); "The Contribution of Empathy to Justice and Moral Judgment," in *Empathy and Its Development*, ed. Nancy Eisenberg and Janet Strayer (Cambridge: Cambridge University Press, 1987); Nancy Sherman, "Empathy and Imagination," *Midwest Studies in Philosophy* 22, no. 1(1998).

93 Nussbaum, *Upheavals of Thought*, 333. As Shelley Berlowitz puts it, "Sharing someone else's feelings or taking another's perspective cognitively does not automatically lead to the acceptance of another's values and aims. Nevertheless, it does lead to the acknowledgement of others' feelings, experiences, emotions, and thoughts as equal to our own, thereby humanizing them." Berlowitz, "Unequal Equals," 41.

94 Köhler, "Von der Freud'schen Psychoanalyse zur Selbstpsychologie Heinz Kohuts," 49–50.

95 Hunt, *Inventing Human Rights*, 21, 26–29, and more generally 26–34.

96 Ibid., 68.

97 Winter, "From Sympathy to Empathy," 104–105, 113–114.

Chapter 4

Three Examples of Empathy in Historical Understanding

This chapter presents three concrete examples of the use of empathy in historical understanding. Reflecting my area of historical expertise, the first two are from the history of modern Germany, and the third relates to the history of the Holocaust. They are meant to bring down to the earth of actual historical work the largely theoretical material that has been presented thus far. They are meant to illustrate the *difference* in what the historian sees, knows, and understands about the past based on the observational position he or she adopts, that of the external or of the empathic observer. They are meant to demonstrate that the historian needs to be aware of the observational position he or she is adopting, the external or the empathic, and, when empathizing, the observational position of which particular historical subject. And, finally, they are meant to reveal not only the value of adopting the empathic observational position, but also some of the complexities and problems that empathizing historians face, particularly how important and yet difficult it is for historians to be aware of their observational position at any given moment.

The Majority Social Democrats and the German Revolution

In recent decades, historical scholarship on Weimar Germany has become less deterministic.[1] Nevertheless, given its fate and knowing what took its place, historians have, to one degree or another, traditionally written the history of Weimar Germany to answer the question: Why did the Weimar Republic fail? Frequently, they have traced the roots of the republic's failure back to its origin and to the conduct of the majority Social Democratic Party of Germany (SPD) between 1918 and 1920 after the end of the First World War. Specifically, historians implicitly or explicitly have criticized the ruling majority Social Democrats for having allied the fledgling republic with the anti-democratic forces of the authoritarian Right against the radical Socialists who threatened it from the revolutionary Left. A number of historical accounts critical of the majority Social Democrats could be cited here.[2] The following paragraph represents a paraphrase of perhaps the most cogent example of that critique, Gordon Craig's chapter, "From Kiel to Kapp: The Aborted Revolution, 1918–1920," in his book *Germany: 1866–1945.*[3]

Rather than actively and aggressively establishing democracy in Germany and laying the economic, social, and cultural foundations for its survival, President Friedrich Ebert and his majority Socialist colleagues contented themselves with establishing a parliamentary political system, albeit with a powerful president who was able to govern through the power of emergency decree granted by Article 48 of the Weimar Constitution. In spite of the revolution and the establishment of parliamentary democracy in Germany, the groups that had dominated state and society in Imperial Germany before the war—who at best looked upon the republic with distaste and at worst awaited their opportunity to reestablish authoritarian, perhaps even monarchical, rule in Germany—maintained much of their bureaucratic, economic, social, and cultural power. The economic strength of the industrialists and large landowners was unbroken. The civil service remained virtually unchanged from the Imperial period, with the result that Germany was administered in an authoritarian undemocratic spirit, and little attempt was made to adapt government to a pluralistic and democratic society. The educational system was controlled from top to bottom by officials appointed during the *Kaiserreich*, whose commitment to democracy was lukewarm at best. As a result, no sustained and forceful effort was made to instill democratic values in young people. Instead, school curricula were openly anti-republican, nationalistic, and revanchist, and universities were seedbeds of ultra-nationalism, conservatism, and fascism throughout the Weimar period. The judiciary was another center of antirepublicanism, with judges meting out draconian sentences to those on the Left and absurdly lenient sentences to those on the Right. Most dangerous of all, the army remained "a state within a state," eager to crush leftwing Socialists but unwilling to defend the republic against its rightwing enemies. The army remained a bastion of traditional nationalistic and conservative values, with officers selected for their loyalty not to the republic but to Prussian military traditions. The majority Socialists hoped that these traditional groups would in time develop loyalty to the republic; instead, these groups used their power to undermine the republic from within. Ultimately, the army high command, the leaders of industry, and members of other anti-democratic elites would play a decisive role in destroying the republic and bringing Adolf Hitler to power in 1933.

This then was, and in some form remains, a standard explanation for the failure of democracy in Weimar Germany.[4] It saw the republic as fatally flawed from the outset as a result of the conduct of the governing majority Socialists in the years immediately after the end of the war. It is an interpretation of the history of Weimar Germany made from the position of the outside observer who knows what the historical participants did not, namely the ultimate consequences of their actions. It is not an empathic account of that history, at least in relation to the conduct of the majority Social

Democrats. In the language of Reinhart Koselleck, this interpretation fails sufficiently to appreciate the "space of experience" and the "horizon of expectation" of the moderate Socialist leaders.[5] Their past experience was of the First World War, which led them to seek to secure peace, order, and stability in Germany and to insure that the demobilized troops returned home to a more or less functioning society. Even more, their past experience and their expectations for the future were dominated by the Russian Revolution. One needs to keep in mind that all of these men subscribed to one degree or another to a Marxist theory of history. They saw history as progressive, moving in a coherent direction from feudalism to capitalism to socialism to communism. The Russian Revolution was an anomaly, from a Marxist perspective, because it had occurred in an industrially backward, largely peasant society. According to Marxist theory, however, industrialized Germany was the logical place for the international proletarian revolution to begin. Moreover, the German revolutionaries, the moderate Socialists, and indeed the representatives of the Old Order had the concrete example of the Russian Revolution before their eyes. History seemed quite literally to be repeating itself. This apparent repetition was no accident, however, since the revolutionary Socialists in Germany actively sought to follow in the footsteps of their Bolshevik exemplars in Russia. As in Russia, military collapse had produced the overthrow of the monarchy and led to the establishment of a provisional government. As in Russia, workers' and soldiers' councils had emerged to challenge the authority of the provisional government. As in Russia, there had been a split between radical and moderate Socialists. In both countries, the moderates initially dominated both the provisional government and the workers' and soldiers' councils; but in Russia, the former had been overthrown and the Bolsheviks had seized power. A repeat of this scenario is what Socialists on the Left hoped for and sought to implement, and what moderate Socialists, and indeed liberals and conservatives in Germany, feared and sought to prevent.

As we have seen, general laws were thought to be an essential part of historical explanation by those who regarded history to be a social science fundamentally similar epistemologically to any of the natural sciences. Indeed, from an external observational position one could, as the historian Crane Brinton once did, compare various revolutions (in his case the English, American, French, and Russian) in order to develop general laws or stages of revolutionary development.[6] From the empathic point of view, the historian seeks to know the laws or stages of revolution not as defined by the observing historian but as defined by the historical participants themselves, based upon the comparisons *they* made—in this case, first by the Bolsheviks in Russia, who looked to the French Revolution, and then by the Spartacists and Social Democrats in Germany, who looked to the Russian Revolution for guidance or in fear. The laws of revolutionary development as identified by the historical participants influenced the way they interpreted the situation in which they found themselves and the way they acted in response, encouraging the radical Socialists to push for socialist revolution and the moderate Socialists to ally with the forces of reaction to prevent it.

Thus, one cannot empathically understand the decisions and actions of the majority Socialists without thinking one's way inside their space of experience and horizon of expectation. Because of the threat of the revolutionary Left, and with the memory of the Bolshevik's October Revolution fresh in their minds and with the spectacle of the Russian civil war right before their eyes, the majority Socialist leaders of the Weimar Republic could not afford to break the power of the forces of reaction. Viewed with hindsight from an external observational perspective, their accommodation of the Old Order—their failure to smash its economic, social, and political power—seems misguided and feckless, a fatal historical mistake. Viewed from an empathic perspective, from the perspective of the majority Socialists between 1918 and 1920, their alliance with the Old Order against the revolutionary Left makes perfect sense.

As this example hopefully makes clear, taking an empathic approach to the people of the past works against the tendency toward determinism on the part of historians. To be sure, hindsight may influence what we wish to know about the past, as when we seek to understand what puzzles us from the perspective of the present or when we seek to find the roots of the present in the past. Nevertheless, while empathizing we must constantly try to keep in mind that, whereas we know the consequences of our historical subjects' actions, they of course did not. As epistemologically challenging as it may be to bracket temporarily our knowledge that transcends the subjective experience of the people of the past, while empathizing we must try as best we can to view the world from their perspective, not from ours.[7] If while adopting the empathic position we are able temporarily to quarantine the knowledge provided by hindsight, we can avoid producing deterministic historical accounts. Determinism focuses historical attention on what is important to us; history written from the empathic perspective focuses historical attention on what was important to the people of the past. It allows us to appreciate that they anticipated very different futures for themselves and for their world than what ultimately came to pass.[8] Empathic history prevents us from producing narratives in which knowledge of how it all turned out transforms past ideas, actions, and experiences into stepping stones to the present and allows us to see and to appreciate ideas, actions, and experiences important to the people of the past that failed to contribute to history's eventual outcome. Empathic history, in the words of Dominick LaCapra, allows us to "recapture unrealized, desirable possibilities that have arisen in the past."[9] History written from the perspective of the historical subject enables us to see not only the world that came to be but also the worlds that might have been. It allows us to appreciate contingency. Indeed, in opposition to Walter Benjamin, who criticized empathic history for always adopting the victor's point of view, empathic history allows us to appreciate not simply past success but also failure and disappointment, the tragedy that characterizes much of human life and much of human history, and the reality that human beings live out their lives in an always uncertain, ever changing, and unpredictable world.[10]

The Wannsee Conference

Few events in the history of Nazi Germany have received as much attention from historians as the Wannsee Conference, which was held at a villa on a lake in the Berlin suburb of Wannsee on 20 January 1942. The conference had originally been scheduled for 9 December 1941 but was delayed as a result of the Japanese attack on Pearl Harbor. Convened and chaired by the head of the SS Reichssicherheitshaupt Amt (RSHA), Reinhard Heydrich, the conference was attended by fifteen officials representing the three institutions that constituted the Nazi regime: the State, the Party, and the SS (the regime's security services).[11] Despite their different institutional affiliations, all fifteen attendees were centrally involved in one way or another in dealing with the so-called Jewish question.[12] What we know about the conference derives primarily from the minutes of the proceedings, which were prepared by one of the attendees, Adolf Eichmann, Heydrich's close associate in the SS. The conference in general, and the transcript in particular, has been the focus of intense attention from historians because it is seen as coming far closer than any other documented event to constituting the "smoking gun" in the history of the Nazi decision to exterminate the Jews of Europe, even though the mass murder of Jews in Eastern Europe was already underway by the time of the conference and some deportations of Jews from the Reich had already begun in the fall of 1941.

Although there was a time when historians tended to minimize the significance of the Wannsee Conference, today most historians regard it to be an event of decisive significance in the history of the Holocaust.[13] Although they reject the notion that the actual decision to exterminate the Jews in Europe was taken at the conference, they nonetheless see the conference as the key moment when the Nazi authorities irrevocably committed themselves to the extermination of the Jews of Europe. Thus, the historian Christian Gerlach, author of a carefully researched article about the conference, makes a compelling case that Hitler had decided to kill the Jews of Europe in early December 1941, following the Japanese bombing of Pearl Harbor and Germany's declaration of war against the United States, thereby fulfilling Hitler's "prophecy" made in his Reichstag speech of 30 January 1939 that a world war would mean the annihilation of the Jewish race in Europe. What occurred at the conference was the bureaucratic validation of Hitler's decision to exterminate the Jews of Europe, not simply the Jews of Eastern Europe but also all Jews living in Germany and in the rest of Central and Western Europe, and the conference established the bureaucratic basis for the practical implementation of the genocide.[14] Specifically, the SS, conveners of the conference, on the one hand, secured Party and State approval of and participation in the extermination of European Jewry and, on the other hand, established the SS's ultimate authority to carry out the genocide over its State and Party rivals.[15] The significance of the Wannsee Conference is reflected in the fact that although some German Jews had been deported to the east before 20 January 1942, after that date they were killed there.[16] Before March 1942, less than 10 percent of the Jews who would die in the Holocaust had been killed. From mid-March 1942 until mid-February 1943, half of the Jews who would eventually die in the Holocaust had been killed. Thus, if not "the moment of decision," the Wannsee Conference was a pivotal moment in the history of the Holocaust that, in the words of historian Mark Roseman, "cleared the way for genocide."[17]

Based on Eichmann's transcript, Reinhard Heydrich opened the conference with the assertion that Reich Marshal Hermann Goering had designated him to be "the person responsible for the preparation of the final solution of the European Jewish question" and that the purpose of the conference was to clarify "basic questions" relating to this project and to coordinate the activities of "all central authorities directly concerned with these questions."[18] Regardless of geographic boundaries, the "supervision of the final solution was ... centralized in the hands of the Reichsführer SS and Chief of the German Police," that is, in the hands of Heydrich's immediate superior, Heinrich Himmler. Having asserted the SS's claim to authority over the final solution of the Jewish question, Heydrich then reviewed "the struggle which had been waged hitherto against these opponents," the measures to exclude Jews from German society, from the life of the German people, and from German living space. Initially the effort to achieve these goals had taken the form of encouraging Jewish emigration. Now, however, given the danger to emigration posed by the war and thanks to "the opportunities provided by the east," Himmler had banned emigration in favor of the forcible deportation of Jews to Eastern Europe. By alluding to the activities of killing squads in the east (the so-called *Einsatzgruppen*), Heydrich made clear to his listeners that the deported Jews were to be killed there. He next turned to the more than 11 million European Jews "who come into consideration for this final solution of the Jewish question," broken down by country, including those not under German control, and to how occupied and allied countries might be persuaded to turn their Jewish populations over to the Germans, thereby conveying the SS's intention to kill every single European Jew no matter where they might live.[19] Heydrich then discussed using Jews as forced labor in the east, how they would be conscripted and supervised. Most of these would die "through natural causes," effectively worked to death. Any who managed to survive would have to be killed, since these would be especially racially fit and therefore especially dangerous, potentially forming "the germ cell from which the Jewish race could regenerate itself." He suggested that, after combing Europe for Jews, Jews thus collected would be sent first to transit ghettos and then further east.

Thereupon, Heydrich raised the question that formed "an important precondition for the evacuation," namely, "the precise definition of the group of persons involved." He suggested that elderly Jews, Jewish war veterans, and

Jews with war decorations not be "evacuated" (i.e., exterminated) but transferred to an old people's ghetto. This apparently prompted a lengthy and intense general discussion—a full third of the transcript and surely the longest part of the conference—devoted to the question about what was to be done with people who were one-half or one-quarter Jewish, so-called *Mischlinge* of the first and of the second degree, and with Jews who were married to non-Jewish Germans along with their children, a discussion based on the "problem of defining a Jew,"[20] which, in the words of Mark Roseman, had "vexed the Nazis ever since they came to power."[21]

In contrast to the rest of the conference, where the participants apparently sat quietly listening to Heydrich hold forth, according to both the transcript and especially Eichmann's postwar testimony during his trial in Jerusalem, everyone became animated on this issue, openly disagreeing with one another, speaking out of turn and at cross purposes.[22] The animation of the participants reflected the fact that resolving "the mixed marriages and the Mischling questions" was, in Heydrich's words, "a precondition for the comprehensive resolution of this problem," a precondition, that is, for determining who would and who would not be deported and killed. Generally following the letter and/or the implications of the Nuremberg Laws and the Law for the Protection of German Blood and German Honor, both from 1935, Heydrich wanted half Jews (Mischlinge of the first degree), not married to a non-Jew with children or having special exemptions, to count as full Jews eligible for deportation. He advocated that half Jews not eligible for deportation should be subject to compulsory sterilization. Quarter Jews (Mischlinge of the second degree) were to count as Germans exempt from deportation except in certain unusual cases of unfavorable appearance or having an unfavorable criminal or political record, even if that person was "married to a person of German blood."[23] Full Jews married to persons "of German blood" would be sent to an old people's ghetto, but each case would need to be evaluated individually, "depending on the effect of such a measure on the German relatives of this mixed marriage." The same standard would apply to half Jews married to persons "of German blood." Half Jews and quarter Jews married to full Jews, and half Jews married to other half Jews or to quarter Jews, along with their children, would all be treated as full Jews and sent to a ghetto.

As noted above, Heydrich's proposals regarding the eligibility for deportation of the various categories of Mischlinge and Jews in mixed marriages produced, apparently for the first time in the conference, animated general discussion, although that spirit is only faintly captured in Eichmann's protocol. According to the minutes, SS-Gruppenführer Otto Hofmann of the Race and Resettlement Office expressed his support for the sterilization option, as Mischlinge would certainly choose it over deportation. Wilhelm Stuckart of the Ministry of the Interior also pressed for compulsory sterilization of half Jews as an alternative to deportation, and for the compulsory divorce of mixed-race couples. The representative of Goering's Four-Year Plan (responsible for the wartime economy) raised concerns about deporting Jews working in industries vital to the war effort. Finally, the representative of the General Government of Poland asked that the final solution begin there since there were already too many Jews in the territory. The representatives of the General Government in Poland and of the Ministry for the Occupied Eastern Territories urged that preparatory work be undertaken for the final solution in the occupied territories in the east, "though without upsetting the population," whether Germans in the Reich or the local population is unclear from the protocol. Finally, Heydrich asked the participants to support him going forward in "carrying out the solution." Thereupon the meeting adjourned.

Although the SS managed to establish its authority over the final solution at Wannsee, the issue of defining who was a Jew eligible for deportation and death, which so animated the participants at the conference, remained unresolved at the meeting's end.[24] Indeed, that issue was the subject of two further, equally inconclusive, meetings that focused on the forced sterilization of Mischlinge and on the forced dissolution of mixed marriages, on 6 March and 27 October 1942.[25] The inability of the participants in these three meetings, which stretched out over a ten-month period, to resolve the question of what to do with Mischlinge and with Jews in mixed marriages reflected the fact that the participants sought to square the circle. On the one hand, the Nazis (the SS in particular) wanted to include as many Mischlinge and Jews in mixed marriages in the final solution as possible. On the other hand, the Nazi leadership, particularly Hitler, Goebbels, and Goering, was deeply concerned about upsetting the non-Jewish German relatives and friends of any Jews deemed eligible for deportation and extermination. They feared popular unrest, even protest, if Jews connected to non-Jewish Germans were to be deported.[26] In the words of Mark Roseman, what helped "half and quarter Jews was Hitler's sensitivity to public morale. There were so many full-German relatives to consider. Ideologically, Hitler favored the hard line of the party radicals, but tactically he was hesitant."[27] Even Heydrich was not insensible to the reaction of the non-Jewish German public to the deportation of friends and relatives, at one point suggesting during the Wannsee Conference that Jews in mixed marriages be deported to a ghetto rather than "evacuated," the SS euphemism for extermination.[28] In the words of historian John Grenville,

> in assessing National-Socialist policies, one must take into account the fact that most "Mischlinge" and those living in mixed marriages had close family ties to non-Jewish Germans and that this fact had without a doubt lasting influence on the decisions taken by the Nazi leadership.

"The significance of this relationship," according to Grenville, "can hardly be overestimated." Had it not been for their fear of the reaction of the German public, the Nazis, given their "fanatical racism," would have included all Jews in mixed marriages and all half Jews in the final solution.[29]

Indeed, the efforts of Himmler and the SS to exterminate the Mischlinge of Central and Western Europe were largely unsuccessful.[30] According to Grenville, "the vast majority of German 'Mischlinge' survived the period of the National-Socialist terror in their homeland."[31] Mischlinge of the first degree "were treated with restraint until the end of the war, even though ... they were regarded biologically to be more Jews than Germans," and many managed to survive the Third Reich.[32] Attempts to challenge the privileged status of Mischlinge of the second degree also proved futile. Mass sterilization of Mischlinge never occurred.[33] And the same "restraint" characterized Nazi treatment of Jews in mixed marriages, particularly if they had produced children. The plan forcibly to terminate mixed marriages was only implemented in any sustained way during the last months of the war, and efforts to deport Jewish partners were generally not successful.[34]

Despite its central place in Eichmann's minutes of the conference, the fact that it was apparently the only subject openly discussed and debated by the participants, and indeed that, as Mark Roseman and John Grenville point out, it represented "the real policy *content* at Wannsee," historians have been uncertain what to make of the animated discussion about how to deal with Mischlinge and Jews in mixed marriages at the conference.[35] Some see it as essentially tangential, a pedantic, legalistic, and bureaucratic debate bizarrely set within the participants' lethal endorsement of the genocide of European Jewry. Thus, despite the investment of the historical participants in this issue, some historians focus little attention on that section of the conference.[36] Other historians recognize the importance of the discussion of Mischlinge and Jews in mixed marriages but tend to read it in light of the historically significant *results* of the conference: namely, that Wannsee established the bureaucratic basis for the extermination of the Jews of Europe with the SS in charge and State and Party complicit in the genocide. That is to say, the heated discussion about which Jews to deport is seen as more or less derivative of the meeting's ultimate outcome.[37] Thus, for the outside observer—who knows that after the Wannsee Conference the Jews of Germany and of those lands conquered by or allied with Germany were sent to extermination camps—the heated discussion about Mischlinge and Jews in mixed marriages seems either irrelevant or subsidiary. For the outside observer—who knows that the question about what to do with Mischlinge and Jews in mixed marriages would never ultimately be resolved, who knows that most Central European Mischlinge and Jews in mixed marriages would in fact survive the Holocaust, and who knows that (with one notable exception) popular protests against the deportation of German Jews never occurred (in part of course because of the reluctance of the Nazi leadership to deport Mischlinge and Jews in mixed marriages)—the heated debate at Wannsee did not much relate to what happened after the conference; at best, it related to what did not happen. What is important for us today, based on our knowledge of what happened after the conference, is different from what was important for the historical participants.

If we adopt the empathic position, if we think our way back into the space of experience and the horizon of expectation of the participants at the Wannsee Conference, the compelling importance of the question of Mischlinge and Jews in mixed marriages in light of its potential impact on non-Jewish Germans becomes completely understandable and, indeed from the Nazi perspective, appropriate. And what was the space of experience of the participants in the Wannsee Conference? It was the fate of the Nazi euthanasia program, which, following growing public unrest and the opposition of church leaders, had officially been suspended a mere three months before the decision to convene the original Wannsee Conference and five months before the conference was actually held.[38]

The euthanasia program was at the heart of the Nazis' biomedical vision. It was designed to protect and to strengthen the health of the *Volkskörper*, the body of the *Volk*, through racial hygiene. To that end, the regime sought to eliminate what it called "life unworthy of life" (*lebensunwertes Leben*) and "ballast existences" (*Ballastexistenzen*) from the racially pure and vital Volksgemeinschaft they were determined to create. By preventing those with hereditary illnesses or disabilities from reproducing, the genetic health of the Volk would be secured for generations to come. By eradicating the disabled, the chronically or terminally ill, the mentally ill, and other "ballast existences," valuable resources devoted to preserving this "life unworthy of life" would be freed to support healthy members of the Volk and, with the outbreak of the war, the German war effort. Thanks to the "progress of civilization" and Christian morality, natural selection had been compromised and people had been kept alive who, in a state of nature, would ordinarily have perished. The Nazi euthanasia program would therefore intervene on nature's behalf, restoring the natural order of things by preventing the unfit from reproducing and life unworthy of life from draining precious resources from the Volk.

Already in July 1933, compulsory sterilization was legalized in the Law for the Prevention of Hereditarily Ill Offspring. Based on the Law for the Protection of the Hereditary Health of the German Volk of October 1935, and following the outbreak of the war in September 1939, Hitler authorized the killing of the disabled and the chronically and hereditarily ill, with disabled children the first victims. People to be euthanized were sent to various specialized institutions where some 70,000 killings were carried out, through lethal injection and starvation and in gas chambers. Despite efforts to keep the killings secret by pretending that the victims of the euthanasia had died of natural causes, news of the program quickly leaked out and spread across the Reich, producing a crescendo of protests that began in February 1940. These protests generally took the form of letters of complaint from families of the victims of the euthanasia and of those targeted for euthanasia, from the general public, from church officials, both Protestant and Catholic, and even from party leaders. On one occasion, however, Hitler himself was apparently subjected to a demonstration by angry relatives when his train stopped at a station in Bavaria where handicapped children were being deported.[39]

Building on public anger over the euthanasia program, the event that brought the program to an official end was Bishop Clemens von Galen's sermon of 3 August 1941, in which he denounced the killing of the physically disabled and the congenitally and mentally ill. Thousands of copies of the sermon were quickly printed and circulated throughout the Reich, prompting public protests by other religious leaders.[40] In the words of historians Jeremy Noakes and Geoffrey Pridham, Galen's sermon had the effect of "a bomb-shell": "The Nazi leadership were [sic] furious but helpless."[41] According to historian Ernst Klee, "internal situation reports reveal the complete cluelessness [Ratlosigkeit] of the Nazis" following Galen's sermon.[42] Testifying to their desperation were demands by Party officials that Galen be arrested and even by one that he be hanged, a step prevented by Goebbels and Hitler as far too dangerous to the regime during wartime. In the words of John Grenville,

> Galen's public protest against the euthanasia was soon known all across Germany and did not fail to have an impact on Hitler. It was the "Führer's" constant worry that public protest could lead to the unrest in the population that he so feared.[43]

Thus, on 24 August 1941, Hitler ordered the suspension of the euthanasia program. Although officially terminated and the killing of disabled adults ceased, euthanasia continued in more or less unofficial forms and on a smaller scale after that date, with institutionalized children killed by lethal injection and starvation, and inmates unable to work in concentration camps gassed.[44] It is estimated that approximately 50,000 more people were "euthanized" after the program's official end.[45] Nevertheless, in the words of the historian Richard Evans, the public opposition to the euthanasia program "was the strongest, most explicit and most widespread protest movement against any Nazi policy since the beginning of the Third Reich."[46]

In order to understand Hitler's decision officially to suspend the euthanasia program in the face of public protest, it is important to appreciate the Nazis' sensitivity to popular opinion and their sense that their legitimacy and even power depended to a significant extent on their being in tune with the popular will. As the historian Frank Bajohr puts it, "the Nazi regime was no simple top-down dictatorship" that imposed its will on the German people through force and the threat of force "and condemned the society to play a strictly passive role. Instead, the 'Third Reich' was more a plebiscitary dictatorship that took full account of 'popular opinion'."[47] Hence, John Grenville traces Hitler's general cautiousness regarding Mischlinge and Jews in mixed marriages to the Führer's "pronounced instinct for the public opinion of the Germans, upon whose support the conduct of the war and his plans for the future depended."[48] In sum, it was the Nazis' acute sensitivity to and dependence on German public opinion that caused them officially to suspend a program designed to preserve the health of the German Volkskörper by eliminating the unfit that, along with their desire to eradicate the Jewish menace, stood at the very top of their racial agenda.

Hitler's termination of the euthanasia program on 24 August 1941 in the wake of protests by the churches and the families and friends of victims and potential victims of the program seems to have exacerbated concerns on the part of the Nazi leadership that popular protests could interfere with their other essential racial project—the elimination of the Jews from the German Volkskörper as part of the final solution of the Jewish question in Europe. Indeed, the reaction of the German public to the deportation of German Jews generally and Mischlinge and Jews in mixed marriages in particular pre-occupied the Nazi leadership in the months following the official suspension of the euthanasia program. Thus, a mere three weeks after suspending the program, Hitler decreed on 1 September 1941 that quarter Jews (Mischlinge of the second degree) did not need to wear the Yellow Star made compulsory for Jews on that date. Approximately two months later, the SS officer who had ordered the unauthorized execution of Berlin Jews deported to Riga in November 1941 was ordered to Berlin to receive an official reprimand, "the urgency" of that summons testifying to the fact, according to Mark Roseman,

> that Hitler and Himmler were intensely sensitive to issues of morale and public opinion. Or, as Goebbels put it just eight days earlier, the Führer "wants an energetic policy against the Jews that, however, does not cause us unnecessary difficulties."[49]

Himmler and Hitler were both concerned about the potential impact of public knowledge in Germany about the extermination project, which was well underway in conquered Eastern Europe and already becoming too much of an "open secret." On 14 December 1941, Himmler expressed the need to do the work of killing as quickly as possible in the interests of secrecy to Viktor Brack, one of those who had been in charge of the euthanasia pro-gram.[50] Concern about potential public reaction to the elimination of "more German Jews" helped put the issue of defining who was and who was not a Jew generally and of what to do with Mischlinge and Jews in mixed marriages specifically "high on the agenda" of the original Wannsee Conference that was to have been held on 9 December 1941.[51] Not only before Wannsee but, as reflected in the two subsequent conferences in March and October 1942, also after, the Nazi leadership remained concerned about the impact on German public opinion of deporting Mischlinge and Jews in mixed marriages. Indeed, Goebbels acknowledged in his diary in March 1942 that separating intermarried Jews and their Mischling children was an "extremely delicate" matter, and expressed his concern about separating Jews in mixed marriages from German society without upsetting the morale of the German people.[52]

Thus, the official termination of the euthanasia program in the face of public and church opposition was the space of experience of the participants in the Wannsee Conference. And their horizon of expectation was that the final solution to the Jewish question in Europe might suffer the same fate as the euthanasia program, were public protests to erupt in Germany. Thus if we adopt the empathic perspective, that is, if we adopt the perspective of most of the participants in the Wannsee Conference, the question of what was to be done with German Mischlinge and Jews in mixed marriages appears to have been, in its own right, perhaps *the* crucial issue to be considered and decided at the conference. On the one hand, the participants at the Wannsee Conference wanted to eliminate Jews and Mischlinge from the German Volkskörper. On the other hand, they feared that, if large numbers of half and quarter Jews with many non-Jewish German relatives and Jews in mixed marriages (particularly if these had produced children) were deported, public protest might seriously compromise the entire extermination project.

To the best of my knowledge, no historian, with the possible exception of John Grenville, has explicitly related the heated and lengthy discussion about what to do with Mischlinge and Jews in mixed marriages at the Wannsee Conference to the role that public protest had played in bringing the euthanasia program to an official end.[53] Even historians fully appreciating the importance of that discussion and its basis in anxiety about popular protest have failed to make that connection.[54] Nor, to the best of my knowledge, have historians of the euthanasia program connected its forced official suspension to the discussions at the villa in Wannsee.[55]

Why then have historians largely failed to see this connection? As was suggested above, given the advantages of hindsight afforded them by the outside observational position, historians have tended to understand the Wannsee Conference more on the basis of what came after the meeting than on what came before. By contrast, the historical participants understood the conference on the basis of what had come before (their space of experience) and based their actions on what, given their space of experience, they anticipated the future might bring (their horizon of expectation). Another reason why historians have failed to connect the heated discussion of Mischlinge and Jews in mixed marriages to the fate of the euthanasia program is that the termination of that program is nowhere mentioned in Eichmann's minutes of the conference. It seems possible that Hitler's suspension of the euthanasia program was in fact mentioned at the conference but those references were not included in the minutes or were subsequently edited out by Eichmann and Heydrich. Given that thirty copies of the conference protocol were made and distributed, including to each of the participants (with the potential for a wider distribution that apparently never occurred), Eichmann and Heydrich may have wanted to avoid acknowledging in writing and in an official protocol what was a major setback, indeed something of a defeat, in the Nazis' realization of their new racial order. It is also possible that the euthanasia program was in fact not mentioned at the conference. Perhaps, given its centrality to the Nazi racial project, the suspension of the euthanasia program was so distressing to the participants that they themselves were not conscious of the connection between it and their discussions in Wannsee. Or, rather more likely, the relevance of the suspension of the euthanasia program to the debate over Mischlinge and Jews in mixed marriages was so obvious to the participants that it simply went without saying.

Of course, the possibility must be acknowledged that the fate of the euthanasia program played no role at the Wannsee Conference at all. Although it brings us onto the thin ice of historical speculation, if one imagines one's way, thinks one's way, and feels one's way inside the participants' space of experience and horizon of expectation, it seems virtually inconceivable, given its central importance to the Nazi racial project, that the suspension of the euthanasia program in response to public protest did not exert a pervasive influence on the discussions about what to do with Mischlinge and Jews in mixed marriages at the Wannsee Conference.

Viewed from the empathic perspective, the history and significance of the Wannsee Conference become somewhat different than when viewed from the position of the external observer. Afforded the benefit of hindsight, the external observer reads the conference in light of the subsequent extermination of the Jews of Europe, seeing it as having "cleared the way for genocide" by establishing the bureaucratic foundation of the final solution, the SS's authority over the killing, and the complicity of State and Party in the genocide.[56] That is an authentic, valuable, and significant reading of the conference. Indeed, it explains Heydrich's evident satisfaction at the conference's outcome. Nevertheless, the reading yielded by the empathic observational position is also authentic, valuable, and significant. It focuses more sharply on the lengthy and heated debate at the conference about what to do with Mischlinge and Jews in mixed marriages, and provides a compelling explanation of that debate. It also brings contingency to light, illuminating not only what happened after the conference but also what might have happened. Seeing the conversation at the Wannsee conference as responding to the suspension of the euthanasia program reveals possibilities foreseen—and in this case feared—that might have prevented the full extent of the genocide. Indeed, viewing the conference from an empathic perspective brings home in an intellectually and emotionally compelling way how tenuous Nazi officials felt their plan to exterminate the Jews of Germany to be, how vulnerable, how much at risk, were popular protests against it to occur. The decision officially to suspend the euthanasia program had been a bitter blow to the Nazis. Therefore, the issue of how to handle Mischlinge and Jews in mixed marriages was of vital importance, for the fate of the "final solution to the Jewish question in Europe" appeared to them to hang in the balance.

Historians have frequently indicted the German people for having failed to protest against the final solution at any point along the way, thereby enabling the Nazis to carry out the genocide of the Jews.[57] And they have wondered how many lives might have been saved had non-Jewish Germans protested against the deportation of their Jewish neighbors. As John Grenville puts it,

> the policies of the National Socialists were emphatically influenced by concern about what the public reaction would be; that concern applied to their policies toward Jews. It is therefore appropriate to ask the at least hypothetical question, what could have been delayed and perhaps even prevented if more Germans, especially Germans in high positions, had more effectively expressed their concerns about their persecuted Jewish and Christian fellow citizens.[58]

An empathic history of the Wannsee conference conveys the Nazis' fear of public protest against the final solution in a particularly compelling way. That fear, reflected in the decision to suspend the euthanasia program and in the heated debate at the Wannsee conference about Mischlinge and Jews in mixed marriages, suggests that popular protest might indeed have significantly hampered the extermination of the Jews of Germany and Austria, and perhaps of Western Europe.[59] And an empathic history of the Wannsee conference testifies in a particularly compelling way to the tragic consequences of the fact, given the real possibility of their success, that, with one exception, there were no popular protests against the deportation of the Jews of Germany and Austria. Indeed, not only in the case of the euthanasia program, but also on two other occasions where significant public protest occurred, the Nazis backed down. Popular protests brought a halt to the Nazis' attempt to remove crucifixes from schools in Bavaria in 1941, although this attempt was far lower on the Nazi agenda than was the euthanasia program or the final solution to the Jewish question. And in February 1943, a year after the Wannsee conference, protests by hundreds of non-Jewish Germans, primarily women, led to the release of 2000 of their Jewish husbands and other Jewish relatives destined for deportation to the east from an SS internment center in the Rosenstrasse in Berlin. In the words of historian Nathan Stoltzfus, "the Rosenstrasse Protest was the singular incident of mass German protest against the deportation of German Jews."[60] Due to the cowardice, the anti-Semitism, and the general lack of empathy of non-Jewish Germans for their Jewish fellow citizens, and given the effective decision of the Nazis largely to spare Mischlinge and Jews in mixed marriages from deportation, no other significant popular protest against the final solution occurred in Germany.[61] And yet, the very success of the Rosenstrasse protest testifies to the Nazis' sensitivity to and fear of an aroused German public.[62] An empathic history of the Wannsee conference—one that focuses on the experience of the participants, their hopes, and above all their fears—affirms powerfully and tragically that popular protests might indeed have compromised the Nazis' plan to exterminate the Jews of central Europe.

Writing about the Holocaust

The crucial role played by our observational position in determining what we know about the past can be illustrated in relation to the language we use in writing about what we now call "the Holocaust." It was only in the 1960s that "the Holocaust" came to refer to the systematic killing of European Jews during the Second World War. It is a term that was unknown to killers or victims when the events it conveys took place. It is a term used by historians and others to define what they see looking back from an external observational position as a more or less coherent historical phenomenon. The millions of individual killings, the people being worked, starved, and marched to death, the people electrocuted on barbed wire, the people who committed suicide by taking poison, the extermination factories like Auschwitz, the killings by the *Einsatzgruppen*, the killings by Polish villagers of their Jewish neighbors, the killings that occurred in many different places and at many different times all across Europe, the killers from all across Europe, the victims who were religious Jews, secular Jews, people who did not consider themselves to be Jews at all, the vast and varied, isolated and incoherent, chaotic and willful killing of those designated "Jews" are in retrospect brought together under the term "the Holocaust."

There is absolutely nothing wrong with the term "the Holocaust" or with using it to characterize the mass killing of Jews during the Second World War. Indeed, as large-scale historical phenomena go, the Holocaust is perhaps among the more coherent. Nevertheless, we need to be aware that when we employ the term "the Holocaust" we are external observers looking back at a multiplicity of events, people, times, places, and experiences. The coherence lent by the term does not convey the experiences that would be captured from an empathic observational position that adopts the perspective of the victims. Indeed, the term distorts, even elides, those experiences: the incoherence, the confusion, the terrible uncertainty; the hopes, the dashed hopes, the intense individuality of the historical participants' experience. What seems more or less consistent and coherent when viewed from without was terrifyingly inconsistent and incoherent, atomizing and isolating, when viewed from within the experience of the Jews of Europe, who for the most part lacked an overview of the situation in which they found themselves. Our observational stance determines what we see and know about the past. The external perspective and the empathic perspective yield two radically different histories here. Although both histories are legitimate and valuable, it would seem that historians' tendency to observe the past from without, along with our preference for clarity and coherence, has meant that more history has been written of "the Holocaust" than of its ambiguous, incoherent, and traumatic experience by the Jews of Europe. In any event, given the fact that what we see is determined by the observational stance we adopt, it is important that historians recognize and appreciate the very different views of the past afforded by the external and the empathic observational positions, and that they attempt to be conscious of which observational position they are adopting when looking at the past.

Not only do we need to be conscious of whether we are viewing past people from our or from their perspective; it is also important when adopting the empathic position to be clear about whose particular perspective we are adopting, to be clear about which particular past people we are empathizing with.[63] Returning to the Holocaust and the language we use to describe it, how do we characterize the killing of the Jews? If we use the word "murder" to characterize the killing that took place at Auschwitz, for example, we are using a word that those doing the killing would not have used to describe their actions. Calling the killing at Auschwitz "murder" is a characterization made from outside the experience of the historical perpetrators at the time of their perpetration. It is also a characterization implying that the killing and the killers were fundamentally self-interested. One "murders" for personal gain—financial, sexual, or other forms of advancement—or out of personal passion, rage, jealousy, to take revenge. To be sure, members of the SS enriched themselves from their victims and/or took sadistic pleasure in their victims' suffering and death. But those were byproducts of the killing, not its primary motivation. What gave extermination camps like Auschwitz and the entire Nazi killing project life was less individually self-interested or the product of personal passion and more collectively impersonal and ideological. In addition, "murder" is, by definition, unlawful homicide. In English common law, it is the killing of those "under the King's peace" at the time of the murder, and who therefore enjoyed the protection of the State.[64] Under no circumstances could one claim that Jews were under anything like "the king's peace" in Nazi Germany or in the lands occupied by the Third Reich. The use of the term "murder" to characterize the killing of Jews during the Second World War, then, does not capture the experience of the perpetrators and obscures the impersonal, ideological nature of the genocide.

By contrast, calling the killing "extermination" means adopting the perspective of those who carried it out, for that was the word that the killers— whether from behind a desk in an office or with a machine gun in front of a ditch filled with dead and dying people—used themselves. It conveys the experience of the killers, or at least the experience they wished to have. The Jews they "exterminated" were not human beings but something like vermin or bacilli, dangerous threats to the Aryan race to be eradicated ruthlessly. Unlike murder, which one human being does to another, the word "extermination" captures the dehumanizing aspect of the killing, a dehumanization produced by the Nazi killers and experienced by their victims. Indeed, according to the psychoanalyst Heinz Kohut, it was the dehumanization that moved the killing "a step beyond an empathy-informed hatred that wants to destroy you," to murder you, to "an empathyless environment that just brushes you off the face of the earth." The Nazis "totally disregarded the humanness of their victims ... That was the worst."[65]

We need to be aware of the fact that when we use the terms "extermination" or the "final solution" to characterize the mass killing of the Jews of Europe during the Second World War we are not occupying the position of the external observer and we are not occupying the position of the many victims of the Nazis. We need to be aware of the fact that we are adopting the perspective of the perpetrators. Again, there is nothing wrong with doing that, particularly since empathy is *not* identification or sympathy. The killers' ideology and experience are captured by the words they used and conveyed when we as historians use their words as well. Indeed, employing the words used by the killers makes their inhumanity, their ghastly zealotry, their deformity, more apparent than when we use words to characterize their behavior imported as it were from outside their experience. Can the writing of any historian convey the horror of the Nazi extermination project more effectively than Himmler's speech to SS generals in Posen of 4 October 1943?[66]

Finally, it seems important for us to know the words and phrases used by Jews to describe what was being done to them, and by using their language to convey their experiences of what we now call the Holocaust. I am not a Holocaust historian; but it seems that in contrast to those of us looking back at this history, who can find terms that pull all the variety, individuality, and inconsistency of experience together to see a single more or less coherent historical phenomenon, and in contrast even to the Nazis, who used terms that reflected the fact that they saw themselves engaged in a more or less coherent process of achieving a "final solution" to the "Jewish question" in Europe, the experience of European Jews lacked the sense of closure and coherence that could be captured in a word or a phrase. I suspect that there was no one term or set of terms Jews used to describe what was happening to them, their friends, family, and fellow Jews. It seems important for the historian seeking to empathize with Jews during the genocide to discover and to employ the words they used themselves. This point is emphasized by the historian Amos Goldberg. In his view, "a major emphasis of historical analysis of the Holocaust and the Jews should be placed on language, which is ... much more forceful in revealing the human condition than any other factual evidence or description"—language expanded here to include symbolic practices "by which Jews produced, or at times failed to produce meaning."[67]

In finding the words that Jews used to try to capture and convey their experience, it is important to acknowledge that those words do not reflect a single Jewish experience but a multiplicity of experiences, a multiplicity of experiences of the millions of different Jews, and a multiplicity of experiences of even the same Jew. And it is important, in discovering and using those words, to recognize that Jewish lives during what we call the Holocaust were not deterministically focused exclusively on their ultimate deaths, but on experiences of hunger, humiliation, mourning, fear, helplessness, and, yes, dignity, agency, hope, and happiness. In the language we use to describe the experiences of Jews during what we now call the Holocaust, we should be careful not to reduce those lives to dying and to death, deterministically ignoring all experiences of Jews not necessarily connected with Auschwitz. We should be careful, in considering the experiences of Jews during the Second World War, not to see "the Holocaust" as a foregone conclusion, for to them it was not.

Thus, it is important for historians to know whose perspective they are adopting when they think and write about the people of the past, to know whose language they are using.[68] Are historians viewing and writing about the past from without, from outside the experience of their historical subjects, or are they viewing and writing about the people of the past from within the experience of their historical subjects? And if historians adopt the empathic perspective, exactly whose perspective are they adopting? I fully appreciate that this awareness is extraordinarily difficult to develop and to maintain. Indeed, even in the above paragraphs I have shifted points of view without noting that I have done so. I have used words like "killing," "killers," "perpetrators," "victims," and "genocide" that probably come from an external vantage point—"genocide" certainly does at any rate. We go back and forth in the perspective we adopt as historians, and it is extremely difficult—if important—to be conscious of the perspectival shifts that we make.

Adding to the challenge of being rigorously self-conscious when adopting the empathic perspective is the fact that people think about and experience themselves in different ways at different times. Take the word "Jew." On the one hand, there is the problem of labeling a person a Jew who, when viewed from without—or from the point of view of the Nazi racial laws—can be defined as Jewish based on racial, ethnic, or cultural criteria but who did not experience himself or herself to be a Jew. When we label such persons "Jews," we are imposing an identity on them. On the other hand, even people who identified themselves as Jews did not experience themselves to be Jews at all times and in all circumstances. Thus a person who at times experienced himself as a Jew might at other times have experienced himself first as a father, a son, a teacher, a resident of Munich, a German, a Socialist, etc. In empathizing with that person, it would be important to try to know and to communicate precisely how that person experienced him- or herself at the moment we are attempting to understand. The same can be said of course about people we label as "Nazis" or "Germans."[69] Thus, although consistently adopting the precise perspective of the historical subject based on that subject's momentary experience is extraordinarily difficult and probably ultimately impossible, it remains an ideal that we should strive to achieve, not least because it prevents us from imposing identities on past people, from reducing them to a single aspect of themselves, from rendering them something other than what they experienced themselves to be; and because it pushes us toward a truly human history, complex, nuanced, diverse, never fixed, always shifting, always on the move.

Notes

1 See, for example, Peter Fritzsche, *Germans into Nazis* (Cambridge, MA: Harvard University Press, 1998); Eric D. Weitz, *Weimar Germany: Promise and Tragedy—New and Expanded Edition* (Princeton: Princeton University Press, 2013). See, also, the article by Peter Fritzsche, "Review: Did Weimar Fail?" *Journal of Modern History* 68, no. 3(1996).

2 See, for example, Jeffrey Herf, *Reactionary Modernism: Technology, Culture, and Politics in Weimar and the Third Reich* (Cambridge: Cambridge University Press, 1986), 19–21; Charles S. Maier, *Recasting Bourgeois Europe: Stabilization in France, Germany and Italy in the Decade after World War I* (Princeton: Princeton University Press, 1975), 385–386; Peter Pulzer, *Germany, 1870–1945: Politics, State Formation, and War* (Oxford and New York: Oxford University Press, 1997), see 103–117 specifically and 97–129 generally.

3 Gordon Craig, *Germany: 1866–1945* (Oxford: Oxford University Press, 1978), 396–433.

4 Indeed, in a recent article in the German weekly *Die Zeit*, Matthias Geis and Bernd Ulrich, in arguing that the SPD has a long history of adapting itself to prevailing circumstances, accused the governing Social Democrats in 1918–20 of abandoning the SPD's revolutionary heritage by suppressing the Left and accommodating the Old Order in 1918–20. Indeed, the authors characterize the conduct of the majority Social Democrats after the war "as the historic guilt of the SPD." Geis and Ulrich see the behavior of the governing Social Democrats in 1918–20 as establishing a fateful and feckless pattern of "adaptation, self-sacrifice, and system stabilization," which continues to characterize the conduct of the SPD down to the present day. Matthias Geis and Bernd Ulrich, "Wacht auf, verdammt!" *Die Zeit*, 14 February 2019. In the following issue, the distinguished historian of Weimar Germany, Heinrich August Winkler, wrote a highly critical response to Geis and Ulrich's article defending the conduct of the SPD after the war, and indeed throughout its history. Nevertheless, even Winkler concedes "that the claim that the Social Democrats, into whose hands governmental power unexpectedly fell in November 1918, did too little to establish a firmer foundation in society for the desired parliamentary democracy is hardly disputed by historians today." Heinrich August Winkler, "Mehr Revolution wagen?," *Die Zeit*, 21 February 2019.

5 For a detailed account of how the space of experience and horizon of expectation of the majority Social Democrats and of the German military high command affected their understanding of and their conduct during the German Revolution, see Ute Daniel, "Erfahrene Geschichte: Intervention über ein Thema Reinhart Kosellecks," in *Zwischen Sprache und Geschichte: Zum Werk Reinhart Kosellecks*, ed. Carsten Dutt and Reinhard Laube, Marbacher Schriften (Göttingen: Wallstein, 2013), 23–28.

6 Crane Brinton, *The Anatomy of Revolution* (New York: Vintage, 1965; originally published 1938).

7 Ute Daniel emphasizes the challenges of writing the history of experience, that is, empathic history written from the subjective perspective of the people of the past—and its essential importance. Daniel, "Erfahrene Geschichte," 20–28.

8 Ibid., 16–17.

9 LaCapra, "Tropisms of Intellectual History," 503.

10 Walter Benjamin, *On the Concept of History*, trans. Dennis Redmond, vol. I:2, Gesammelte Schriften (Frankfurt: Suhrkamp, 1974).

11 All of the important state ministries were represented in Wannsee apart from the Propaganda Ministry, which had been scheduled to participate in the originally scheduled conference in December 1941. The Propaganda Ministry was represented at the two conferences that followed up on the Wannsee Conference in March and October 1942.

12 Richard J. Evans, *The Third Reich at War* (New York: Penguin, 2009), 260.
13 Michael Burleigh, *The Third Reich: A New History* (New York: Hill and Wang, 2000), 647.
14 Christian Gerlach, "Die Wannsee-Konferenz, das Schicksal der deutschen Juden und Hitlers politische Grundsatzentscheidung alle Juden zu ermorden," in *Krieg, Ernährung, Völkermord: Forschungen zur deutschen Vernichtungspolitik im Zweiten Weltkrieg* (Hamburg: Hamburger Edition, 1998), 87, 123–124, 126, 142. This article has also appeared in English translation: "The Wannsee Conference, the Fate of German Jews, and Hitler's Decision in Principle to Exterminate All European Jews," *Journal of Modern History* 70, no. 4(1998). I cite the German article here throughout.
15 Doris L. Bergen, *War and Genocide: A Concise History of the Holocaust* (Lanham, MD: Rowman and Littlefield, 2003), 159; Burleigh, *The Third Reich*, 646–649; Evans, *The Third Reich at War*, 264, 267; Saul Friedländer, *The Years of Extermination: Nazi Germany and the Jews, 1939–1945* (New York: HarperCollins, 2007), 339, 342; Gerlach, "Die Wannsee-Konferenz," 140–141; Mark Roseman, *The Wannsee Conference and the Final Solution* (New York: Metropolitan, 2002), 97, 119–121, 124, 145; Leni Yahil, *The Holocaust: The Fate of European Jewry, 1932–1945*, trans. Ina Friedman and Haya Galai (New York and Oxford: Oxford University Press, 1990), 312–313.
16 Gerlach, "Die Wannsee-Konferenz," 93.
17 Roseman, *The Wannsee Conference and the Final Solution*, 155, 156.
18 All quotations from the Wannsee Conference transcript come from Jeremy Noakes and Geoffrey Pridham, eds., *Nazism 1919–1945: Volume 3. Foreign Policy, War and Racial Extermination: A Documentary Reader* (Exeter: University of Exeter Press, 1995), 1127–1134.
19 Friedländer, *The Years of Extermination*, 341.
20 Roseman, *The Wannsee Conference and the Final Solution*, 114.
21 Ibid.
22 Christopher R. Browning and contributions by Jürgen Matthäus, *The Origins of the Final Solution: The Evolution of Nazi Jewish Policy, September 1939–March 1942* (Lincoln and Jerusalem: University of Nebraska Press and Yad Vashem, 2004), 412; Gerlach, "Die Wannsee-Konferenz," 105.
23 The Nuremberg Laws and the Law for the Protection of German Blood and German Honor had defined half Jews as Mischlinge of the first degree and quarter Jews as Mischlinge of the second degree. Mischlinge of the first degree were forbidden to marry non-Jewish Germans and could only marry Mischlinge of the second degree (quarter Jews) with special permission. Mischlinge of the second degree were allowed to marry non-Jewish Germans but not other Mischlinge of the second degree or other people with more than a quarter "Jewish blood." The implication of the Nuremberg Laws and the Law for the Protection of German Blood and Honor was that Mischlinge of the first degree were to be regarded as Jews, whereas Mischlinge of the second degree were to be regarded as having sufficient "German blood" to count as citizens of the Reich. For a reasonably clear account of these confusing distinctions and of the policies based on them in the context of the Wannsee Conference, see John A. S. Grenville, "Die 'Endlösung' und die 'Judenmischlinge' im Dritten Reich," in *Das Unrechtsregime: Internationale Forschung über den Nationalsozialismus*, ed. Werner Jochmann, Werner Johe, and Ursula Büttner (Hamburg: Christians, 1986), 105; Beate Meyer, *"Jüdische Mischlinge": Rassenpolitik und Verfolgungserfahrung, 1933–1945*, ed. Monika Richarz and Ina Lorenz, Studien zur jüdischen Geschichte, vol. 6 (Hamburg: Dölling und Galitz, 1999), 98–99. For a sensitive study that examines the

perspectives of the various officials trying to determine who counted as "Jews" in the interstices of Nazi racial thought and policy and how the individuals affected by these policies petitioned to have their status or the status of their relatives changed, see Thomas Pegelow Kaplan, *The Language of Nazi Genocide: Linguistic Violence and the Struggle of Germans of Jewish Ancestry* (Cambridge: Cambridge University Press, 2011).

24 Roseman, *The Wannsee Conference and the Final Solution*, 147–148.

25 Nuremberg Trial Documents: "NG-2586 (H), Record, Conference on the Final Solution of the Jewish Problem, Berlin, March 6, 1942" (ca. 1945) and "NG-2586 (M): Minutes of Conference, the Jewish Problem, October 27, 1942" (23 January 1948). See here Roseman, *The Wannsee Conference and the Final Solution*, 146; also Grenville, "Die 'Endlösung' und die 'Judenmischlinge' im Dritten Reich," 111–112.

26 Gerlach, "Die Wannsee-Konferenz," 115; Roseman, *The Wannsee Conference and the Final Solution*, 117–118.

27 Roseman, *The Wannsee Conference and the Final Solution*, 116.

28 Ibid., 105. See also the summary of the conference protocol presented above.

29 Grenville, "Die 'Endlösung' und die 'Judenmischlinge' im Dritten Reich," 92, 94.

30 Gerlach, "Die Wannsee-Konferenz," 88.

31 Grenville, "Die 'Endlösung' und die 'Judenmischlinge' im Dritten Reich," 91; see also Friedländer, *The Years of Extermination*, 334.

32 Grenville, "Die 'Endlösung' und die 'Judenmischlinge' im Dritten Reich," 111–112.

33 Meyer, *Jüdische Mischlinge*, 6, 51–52, 99.

34 Grenville, "Die 'Endlösung' und die 'Judenmischlinge' im Dritten Reich," 111–112.

35 Roseman, *The Wannsee Conference and the Final Solution*, 194.

36 For example, both the Holocaust historian, Leni Yahil, and the historian of Nazi Germany, Richard Evans, despite extensive treatment of the Wannsee Conference in their respective books, devote a single sentence to this lengthy and animated portion of the conference. Yahil, *The Holocaust*, 313; Evans, *The Third Reich at War*, 265.

37 Even Mark Roseman, who fully appreciates the central importance of the debate over Mischlinge and Jews in mixed marriages at the Wannsee Conference and beyond, sets the debate within the "concerted, coordinated campaign by Himmler and Heydrich to assert their supremacy" over the final solution. Thus Heydrich's radicalism in regard to the Mischlinge and Jews in mixed marriages at the conference was part of his attempt to assert "the RSHA's preeminence in all aspects of the Jewish question." Roseman, *The Wannsee Conference and the Final Solution*, 105, 119–121.

38 Invitations to the original Wannsee Conference were sent out on 29 November 1941.

39 Noakes and Pridham, *Nazism 1919–1945*, 1039–1040.

40 Henry Friedlander, *The Origins of Nazi Genocide: From Euthanasia to the Final Solution* (Chapel Hill: University of North Carolina Press, 1995), 116.

41 Noakes and Pridham, *Nazism 1919–1945*, 1039.

42 Ernst Klee, "'Euthanasie' im NS-Staat: Die 'Vernichtung lebensunwerten Lebens'," in *Die Zeit des Nationalsozialismus*, ed. Walter H. Pehle (Frankfurt: Fischer, 2009), 335. See also Nathan Stoltzfus, *Resistance of the Heart: Intermarriage and the Rosenstrasse Protest in Nazi Germany* (New York: Norton, 1996), 15, 110–111, 144–145, 147–148.

43 Grenville, "Die 'Endlösung' und die 'Judenmischlinge' im Dritten Reich," 115.

44 See here various articles by Lutz Kaelber as well as the volume he co-edited with Raimond Reiter, *Kindermord und "Kinderfachabteilungen" im Nationalsozialismus: Gedenken und Forschung* (Hamburg: Peter Lang, 2011).

45 Noakes and Pridham, *Nazism 1919–1945*, 1048.

46 Evans, *The Third Reich at War*, 98.

47 Frank Bajohr, "Vom anti-jüdischen Konsens zum schlechten Gewissen: Die deutsche Gesellschaft und die Judenverfolgung, 1933–1945," in *Der Holocaust als offenes Geheimnis: Die Deutschen, die NS-Führung, und die Allierten*, ed. Frank Bajohr and Dieter Pohl (Munich: Beck, 2006), 17.

48 Grenville, "Die 'Endlösung' und die 'Judenmischlinge' im Dritten Reich," 114.

49 Gerlach, "Die Wannsee-Konferenz," 95; Roseman, *The Wannsee Conference and the Final Solution*, 75–76.

50 Browning and Matthäus, *The Origins of the Final Solution*, 409–410; Gerlach, "Die Wannsee-Konferenz," 119.

51 Indeed, it was hoped by some planning to attend that the conference would "achieve a 'breakthrough' on the treatment of mixed race Jews." Roseman, *The Wannsee Conference and the Final Solution*, 77, 83–85; Gerlach, "Die Wannsee-Konferenz," 88, 102–103.

52 Stoltzfus, *Resistance of the Heart*, xxx.

53 Grenville connects Hitler's concern about German public opinion in relation to Mischlinge and Jews in mixed marriages to the fate of the euthanasia program, although he does not mention the Wannsee Conference in this regard. Grenville, "Die 'Endlösung' und die 'Judenmischlinge' im Dritten Reich," 115.

54 Thus, Doris Bergen recognizes that the Nazi leadership worried about the reaction of non-Jewish German relatives if Jews married to "Aryan Germans" or half Jews were included in the extermination. Nevertheless, she fails to make the connection between the discussion of this issue at the Wannsee Conference and the fate of the euthanasia program. Bergen, *War and Genocide*, 168–169. Similarly, Michael Burleigh recognizes the central importance of defining which Jews or partial Jews were to be included in or exempted from the final solution at the Wannsee Conference, and appreciates the role played by protests on behalf of individual Jews or half Jews in prompting discussion of the issue. Nevertheless, even though Burleigh had previously written a book that focused centrally on the euthanasia program, he does not consider the impact of its suspension on the discussion of what to do with Mischlinge and Jews in mixed marriages at the villa in Wannsee. Burleigh, *The Third Reich*, 647. See also Gerlach, "Die Wannsee-Konferenz."

55 It is particularly striking that Henry Friedlander, in a book that established the link between the euthanasia program and the genocide of the Jews and showed how the latter emerged out of the former, failed to connect the discussion of Mischlinge and Jews in mixed marriages at the Wannsee Conference to the fate of the euthanasia program. Friedlander, *The Origins of Nazi Genocide*, 290.

56 Roseman, *The Wannsee Conference and the Final Solution*, 156.

57 See, for example, Ian Kershaw, "Alltägliches und Ausseralltägliches: Ihre Bedeutung für die Volksmeinung, 1933–1939," in *Die Reihen fast geschlossen: Beiträge zur Geschichte des Alltags unterm Nationalsozialismus*, ed. Detlev Peukert and Jürgen Reulecke (Wuppertal: Peter Hammer, 1981), 286.

58 Grenville, "Die 'Endlösung' und die 'Judenmischlinge' im Dritten Reich," 116.

59 To understand the absence of popular protests against the persecution, deportation, and, to the extent they knew about it, extermination of the Jews of Germany, one needs to think, feel, and imagine one's way inside the spaces of experience and the horizons of expectation of non-Jewish Germans. I am indebted to the psychoanalyst Armin Vodopiutz for bringing the importance of empathic focus in this context to my attention.

60 Stoltzfus, *Resistance of the Heart*, xxv.

61 It is one of the central arguments of my book that it was the closing off of empathy that made it possible for the Nazis to carry out what they called the "final solution" to the Jewish question in Europe. Kohut, *A German Generation*, 132–141, 167–172, 240–241. See, also, LaCapra, *Understanding Others*, 47.

62 According to Stoltzfus, "Goebbels reported that Hitler understood his response to the 'psychological' conditions of unrest that caused him to release the inter-married Jews." Stoltzfus, *Resistance of the Heart*, 16. Gerlach claims that the plan forcibly to dissolve mixed marriages was dropped as a result of the Rosenstrasse protests. Gerlach, "Die Wannsee-Konferenz," 149–150.

63 See, here, note 59 above.

64 David Mitchell Aird, *Blackstone Economized: Being a Compendium of the Laws of England to the Present Time* (London: Longmans, Green, and Co., 1873), 311. I am indebted to Eric Knibbs for this definition of murder in English common law.

65 Kohut, "On Empathy," 530.

66 Heinrich Himmler, "Speech of the Reichsführer SS at the Meeting of SS Major-Generals at Posen, October 4th, 1943, Document 1919-Ps," in *Nazi Conspiracy and Aggression*, ed. Office of United States Chief Counsel for Prosecution of Axis Criminality (Washington, DC: United States Government Printing Office, 1946). For penetrating and empathic analyses of Himmler's speech, see Saul Friedländer, *Reflections on Nazism: An Essay on Kitsch and Death*, trans. Thomas Weyr (Bloomington: Indiana University Press, 1993), 102–106; Dominick LaCapra, *Representing the Holocaust: History, Theory, Trauma* (Ithaca: Cornell University Press, 1994), 106–110; LaCapra, *Understanding Others*, 87–88.

67 Amos Goldberg, "The Victim's Voice and Melodramatic Aesthetics in History," *History and Theory* 48(2009): 236–237.

68 Dominick LaCapra, whose views on empathy generally align with those presented here, fully appreciates the empathic stakes involved in the language that we use and the names we employ. LaCapra, *History and Memory after Auschwitz*, 53–54, 206–207; *Understanding Others*, 166–167. Indeed, LaCapra implicitly suggests that historians adopting the external perspective on what we now call the Holocaust adopt the problematic role of "the bystander, which deceptively seems closest to objectivity." Ibid., 167.

69 I regret not having spelled out these distinctions in my first book, *Wilhelm II and the Germans*. I would have avoided misunderstanding and criticism had I defined "the Germans" in the way considered here. "The Germans," as I ought to have defined them then, were "those people who experienced themselves to be Germans at the moments when they did so." Thomas A. Kohut, *Wilhelm II and the Germans: A Study in Leadership* (New York and Oxford: Oxford University Press, 1991).

Chapter 5

How We Know in Empathy

In the foregoing, I have sought to demonstrate the importance of historians being aware of their observational position vis-à-vis the past, not least because the external and the empathic observational positions yield different, if both valuable, histories. Having hopefully established that historians need to be self-conscious in their use of empathy, I shall in what follows focus primarily on other issues relating to the role of empathy in historical knowledge. This chapter addresses the important question of how we know in empathy. Specifically, it considers three factors that are frequently seen as making empathic knowledge and understanding in history possible: knowledge of the historical subject's context; the existence of specific experiences shared by historian and historical subject; and, closely related to the last, the existence of universal experiences or of a universal human nature.

The Role of Context in Empathy

Philosophers going back as far as Adam Smith have contended that knowing another empathically involves reconstructing the other person's context and then imagining oneself in the other person's place within that reconstructed context.[1] Indeed, neuroscientific research has found that understanding another's actions requires knowledge of the context in which the other's actions were performed.[2] Our mirror neurons do not fire in response to decontextualized action. The fuller the knowledge of the context of an action, in fact, the more robust the mirroring neurological response will be.[3]

So in using empathy in history do we simply recreate in our minds, as comprehensively and as deeply and as subtly as we can, the context of the person or persons of the past we wish to know and understand and then imagine ourselves in that context? Do we in effect simply fill an imaginary past room with imaginary past furniture and then imagine ourselves living in that room when we empathize?[4] Is there not a danger here of privileging the historical context over the people who lived in it? Past actions and experiences are then attributed not to the people who performed or had them but to the context in which they found themselves. In this account of empathy, the people of the past lose agency and become solely a product of their circumstances, effectively interchangeable with anyone, including with the historian. In effect, this was the view of empathy proposed by Collingwood and those advocating for empathy in the debate over the role of covering laws in history some fifty years ago. Collingwood and those following him generally assumed that past actors were rational actors whose actions were more or less dictated by the circumstances in which they found themselves. Indeed, given the rationality of the historical actor and the pressure of circumstances, the empathizing historian merely needed to rethink or re-enact the rationale that *must* have guided the actor given the circumstances in which he found himself. In this account, empathy with past people is possible because both historian and historical actor possess what Jane Heal calls a "shared rationality." The rational historian puts herself in the place of the rational historical actor and reconstructs the rationale for that actor's actions. Given their shared rationality, it is assumed that historian and historical actor would behave in the same way under the same historical circumstances.[5]

Not only irrational action but individual difference along with free will and contingency would seem to be lost in accounts of empathy that depend solely or largely on recreating historical context and then imagining oneself within it. Moreover, if empathy depends solely on the reconstruction of historical context, the humanity of the historical subject is reduced as well. For the historian Mark Roseman, empathy in history requires more than knowledge of past context, of filling an imaginary room with furniture and imagining what one can see from one of the armchairs in the room. Empathy "should involve more than the mechanical reconstruction" of what could be seen from "a particular vantage point."

> [E]mpathy feels as if it is not just about what could be seen, but also what could be felt, or what was actually perceived, and that means not just arranging the room and the lighting, but somehow entering the mind of the person.[6]

Dominick LaCapra, while seeing contextualization as "altogether necessary but not sufficient for historical understanding," expresses concern that an overreliance on context to do the work of historical empathy "objectifies" history.[7] Indeed, for LaCapra, "objectification" and "contextualization" can prevent empathizing historians from recognizing that they are in a cognitive and affective relationship with their historical subjects.[8] LaCapra argues that we need to free historical subjects from bondage to context in order to allow historians to experience more fully and more self-consciously their interaction with the people of the past.[9]

The definition of empathy as vicarious introspection proposed by Heinz Kohut seems relevant to the consideration of the role of context in empathy.[10] What exactly does "vicarious introspection" mean? Does the phrase mean that, as the philosopher Louis Agosta claims, "I feel what you feel and when I look at myself having this feeling, this is what I see and understand"?[11] Or does it mean that, "if I were you, and I looked at myself, this is what I would see and understand"? The distinction between these two accounts may be difficult to grasp or seem insignificant, but the latter definition of vicarious introspection demands a second imaginative step. One does not simply imagine oneself in the place of the other, in the context of the other; one imagines oneself being the other in the other's place, being the other in the other's context. The second account allows for the possibility that the empathizer might experience a particular mental state differently from the way the empathized would. As an example, the philosopher Amy Coplan cites the case of the introvert, who loves being alone, imagining himself in the place of an extrovert, who hates being alone. When the extrovert describes being alone, the introvert would wrongly assume, given his proclivities, that the extrovert was feeling comfortable since he, the introvert, would feel happy in those circumstances.[12]

The distinction between these two accounts of vicarious introspection is echoed in the debates between various philosophers and psychologists adhering to simulation theory. Most simulation theorists follow Alvin Goldman in seeing empathy as simply putting oneself in the shoes of the other.[13] Others like Amy Coplan argue for the view that in empathy one imagines being not oneself but the other in the other's shoes. The standard account Coplan calls "self-oriented" perspective-taking, resulting generally in a "quasi empathy" where the self is simply projected into the other's situation, into the other's context. "Other-oriented" perspective-taking represents true empathy in her view, and is able to go beyond projection of oneself into the circumstances, the context, of the other to better recognize and account for differences between empathizer and empathized.[14] The psychoanalyst Evelyne Schwaber puts this distinction nicely:

> That we must rely on some echo of experiential alikeness does not mean, however, that we are to share the patient's experience as our own. To place ourselves in the other's shoes, into what he or she is feeling, is not the same process as considering what *we* would feel if *we*—who *we* are— were in those shoes. It requires a considerable degree of self-awareness to make this crucial distinction.[15]

It seems likely that people use both "self-oriented" and "other-oriented" perspective-taking depending on how deeply they know the person they wish to understand. When we know very little about how a particular individual or group of individuals might respond to a particular set of circumstances, we have no choice but to put *ourselves* in their place; when we know more about them we are better able to imagine ourselves being *them* in their place. Defining empathy as thinking and/or imagining one's way inside the "space of experience" and "horizon of expectation" of the people of the past would seem to give context a role in historical knowledge that is attuned to the individuality of the historical subjects. As was noted above, empathy in historical knowledge is not about imagining that the people of the past are like us, but simply occupying a different historical context; rather, empathy in historical knowledge is about recognizing that the people of the past are different from us, not merely by virtue of their historical context, and then trying to imagine that we are like them.

And yet, perhaps the distinction between imagining oneself in the place of the other and imagining being the other in the other's place is a false distinction, or at least a distinction that makes little sense. Although the difficulty of imagining being the other in the other's place is obvious, perhaps imagining being *ourselves* in the place of the other is ultimately impossible. Indeed, the criticism that empathy reduces historical understanding of past people to their historical context, that empathy is akin to filling a room with imaginary furniture and imagining oneself in that room, underestimates not only the power of historical imagination but also the role played by context or the environment in shaping the self. In one of his 1982 William James lectures, the philosopher Richard Wollheim discussed at length imagining Sultan Mahomet II's ceremonial entrance into Constantinople in 1453, having read Edward Gibbon's account of this event.[16] Wollheim considered various vantage points from which he could imagine the sultan's entrance. He could imagine it from the outside, as an external observer. He could imagine it from within the scene as a spectator along the parade route. Or he could imagine it from within the scene as Sultan Mahomet II himself. In reference to this last perspective, Wollheim appears to discuss the distinction under consideration here, the distinction between imagining himself in the sultan's situation and imagining himself being the sultan in the sultan's situation.

As best I understand him, Wollheim contends that we in fact do have the capacity to imagine ourselves being other people and not merely being ourselves in their shoes, a view that more fully acknowledges the power of the human imagination. Nevertheless, what Wollheim and others do not seem to consider is that our self is not wholly psychologically or cognitively autonomous, not wholly impervious to its environment. When we imagine ourselves in a different context, that context changes us, changes who we are at that moment. When we imagine ourselves in Mahomet II's shoes as he entered Constantinople, our self is altered. We become a different person for the duration of our imaginary journey, and perhaps even beyond. To some degree at least, context, including an imagined context, determines not just what we experience but who we are. Or, as Edmund Hussserl put it,

> I cannot literally transpose myself into the other, but only into the other's situation. All I can do is to "conceive how I would feel if I were in the

other's shoes. But then I am really no longer myself and can no longer properly maintain my identity."[17]

Not only did the context in which the people of the past found themselves affect what they felt and thought and did, affect who they were; when we imagine ourselves in their context (their past, present, and anticipated future), we too are changed. And we are in a cognitive and emotional relationship with the people of the past, a relationship that affects and also changes us. We do not simply impose ourselves on the past. The past imposes itself on us as well.[18]

In his wonderful book, *The Problem of Unbelief in the Sixteenth Century: The Religion of Rabelais*, Lucien Febvre used his deep knowledge of Rabelais' historical context to demonstrate that Abel Lefranc's portrayal of Rabelais as a forerunner of the coming skeptical, rationalistic, scientific, and atheistic era was an anachronistic projection of the present onto the past. In his book, Febvre presented Rabelais' historical context, a deeply religious life world, and then read Rabelais and the writings of others about him in light of that life world to make clear that Rabelais could not have been anything like the proto-Enlightenment figure drawn by Lefranc. In recreating the atmosphere of sixteenth-century France, Febvre enables the reader to imagine at least to an attenuated degree what it would have been like to live in that environment, saturated as it was with religious belief.[19]

Imaginary experiences are real experiences, powerful experiences, experiences that bring us into new worlds, experiences that change us. People who do not have imaginary experiences are the poorer for it. Historical accounts based upon a deep and sophisticated knowledge of a past context that enable us to experience that context, to put ourselves imaginatively into that context, bring the past to life in us, help us to understand the past better, and change us—not least by expanding the horizon of our experience. Empathy, then, represents not a loss of self but its enrichment and its expansion.[20]

The Role of Subjective Experience in Empathy

Central to most accounts of empathy, apart from that of the phenomenological position, is the notion that we know others by analogy with ourselves. Empathic understanding by "imaginatively placing myself" in the situation of the other "is a form of reasoning by analogy," according to the philosopher Robert Nozick, "in that I am the thing to which he is analogous. It is inferred that he is behaving as I would in that situation."[21] Indeed, the notion that we know others' minds and mental states by analogy with ourselves and that we use our own personal experiences to understand the experiences of others goes back to David Hume and Adam Smith.[22] As Hume put it,

> now 'tis obvious, that nature has preserv'd a great resemblance among all human creatures, and that we never remark any passion or principle in

others, of which, in some degree or other, we may not find a parallel in ourselves ... and this resemblance must very much contribute to make us enter into the sentiments of others, and embrace them with facility and pleasure.[23]

Wilhelm Dilthey, too, thought that we know the external world through "inferences by analogy."[24] In the early Dilthey account of empathy, we understand another by observing the other's expression, then connecting that expression with the thoughts and feelings associated with that expression for us; and finally, based upon the relationship of expression and thought for us, we infer the thought and feeling of the other.[25] Following Dilthey, the psychoanalyst Heinz Kohut cited the example of using inference by analogy to understand the experience of an extraordinarily tall person upon entering a room full of people of average height by reviving "inner experiences in which we had been unusual or conspicuous, only then do we begin to appreciate the meaning that the unusual size may have had for this person."[26]

Although our subjectivity can inhibit or distort historical knowledge and understanding, it would seem that our subjectivity also makes knowledge and understanding of the past possible. The historian's own experiences and personality, in the words of Georg Simmel, "provide indispensable raw material for the understanding of another person."[27] Leopold von Ranke's wish that he could efface himself in order to know the past completely on its own terms, uncontaminated by his subjectivity, is therefore neither possible nor desirable.[28] As if in response to Ranke, Simmel argued that, "if my personal identity is eliminated, then there is nothing left for me to use in order to comprehend what lies beyond it."[29] Just as our observational position determines what we are able to see, so our subjectivity enables us to see and understand historical phenomena that would otherwise remain invisible to us.[30] Thus, historians with different life experiences are able to see and understand different aspects of the same historical phenomenon.[31] Our own experiences enable us to empathize with the experiences of others, experiences different from our own but sufficiently related or comparable to enable us to imagine our way, to think our way inside them.[32]

One of the implications of the notion that we know others by analogy with ourselves, that we use our own experiences to know and to understand the experiences of others, is that empathizing is easier with people who are similar to us, with experiences similar to our own, than with people very different from ourselves.[33] However, as the sociologist Charles Cooley neatly put it, we must strike a balance between similarity and difference:

The likeness in the communicating persons is necessary for comprehension, the difference for interest. We cannot feel strongly toward the totally unlike because it is unimaginable, unrealizable; nor yet toward the wholly like because it is stale—identity must always be dull company.[34]

In striking contrast to Cooley, the Swiss historian Jacob Burckhardt argued that not our disinterest in the more familiar recent past but our investment in it creates problems for historical knowledge. The "worst enemy of knowledge," in Burckhardt's view, was that

> we can never free ourselves entirely from the intentions of our own time and from our own personality ... The clearest test of this is [that] as soon as history approaches our own century and our own worthy selves, we find everything more "interesting", when in fact we are only more [self] "interested".[35]

Hence, for history to contribute even slightly to solving "the great and profound mystery of life,"

> we must again quit the regions of individual and temporal foreboding and return to a region where our view is not immediately dimmed by [our own] egotism. It is perhaps only through calmer observation from a greater distance that we can take a first step toward understanding the true nature of our activities here on earth.[36]

Thus, to comprehend and critique his own times, Burckhardt looked back to the Italian Renaissance, which he saw as the origin of his own modern, individualistic, secular age.

Moreover, excessive closeness can pose a problem for empathy beyond self-interestedness. People very like us can actually be harder to understand than people who are very different, in no small measure because we may overlook or fail sufficiently to appreciate what distinguishes them from us.[37] In the account of empathy as knowledge through inference by analogy, then, there would seem to be a sweet spot where one is neither too close nor too distant from those one wishes to know and understand. Finally, given the role that knowledge of context plays in facilitating empathy, an extensive and sophisticated knowledge of another's circumstances or, perhaps better, of another's space of experience and horizon of expectation would work to reduce the difference separating empathizer from empathized.

And yet the question arises: Do we only know others, including others in history, by analogy with ourselves? Can we only know those experiences of others, whether in the present or the past, that we have had ourselves? This account of empathy implies, to quote Dilthey, that "a feeling that we have not experienced ourselves we cannot find again in someone else."[38] At worst, empathy as knowing the other by analogy with ourselves would suggest that we can only know that which we already know.[39] At best, it would suggest that we can only know that which is related to what we already know. According to Max Scheler, all accounts of empathy as inference by analogy beg the question. We must actually already know what it is that we seek to know: If we do not already know what the other is feeling, we cannot select the proper analogy to use in knowing that feeling.[40] Thus, returning to the example of empathizing with the unusually tall person, one must already know that the tall person experienced discomfort in standing out in a room full of people of average height in order to mobilize relevant experiences of one's own where one felt conspicuous, self-conscious, and uncomfortable.

At the heart of the account of empathy as knowing others by analogy with oneself lies the problematic assumption that we know our own minds better than we know the minds of others. It assumes a fundamentally Cartesian view of the world, where knowledge of others is ultimately based upon knowledge of the self. As Edith Stein put it, however, we cannot simply "take the self as the standard" of knowledge, for if we do, "we lock ourselves into the prison of our individuality. Others become riddles for us, or worse still, we remodel them into our own image and so falsify historical truth."[41] Others can only be known indirectly, by analogy, and by putting *ourselves* in their context as recreated in our imagination. This account of empathy then appears to privilege self-knowledge and to presume psychological and epistemological autonomy. As was discussed in Chapter 2 in considering the phenomenological position, it overlooks the fact that our knowledge of ourselves can be problematic, partial, and flawed and how difficult it is to empathize with oneself. And it overlooks the extent to which our inner life is shaped by our experience of the outer world, a world populated by other human beings. "The self," in the words of George Herbert Mead, "is essentially a social structure, and it arises in social experience."[42] In fact, "there could not be an experience of a self simply by itself"; we need others to be able to experience our self in the first place.[43]

Viewed psychologically, the self is never wholly autonomous. Its boundaries are shifting, ambiguous, and permeable. Indeed, the self is formed through the internalization and transmutation of the responses of the familial and broader social environment.[44] In early childhood, the boundaries between self and environment are not yet firmly established. The infant lives to a degree in a world of merger, experiencing the world as part of itself and itself as part of the world. As we mature, our ability to distinguish between self and other develops, and we come to experience ourselves as cohesive in space and continuous in time. Nevertheless, even in mature psychologically healthy adults, the self is never wholly autonomous.[45] Not only in infancy but throughout our lives we remain psychologically connected to our environment, experiencing ourselves in subtle and differentiated ways as part of others and others as part of ourselves, as what Heinz Kohut called "selfobjects."[46] We inhabit other people's psychological and mental worlds and other people inhabit ours. Or, as the philosopher Kathleen Haney put it, we are not distinct, autonomous selves: we touch each other; "we may even dwell in each other."[47] Empathy, in fact, can be conceptualized psychologically as a "selfobject relationship." The developmental origin of empathy lies in the experience of merger during infancy, which, as we mature psychologically, develops into the capacity to adopt the position of another.[48] Indeed, simultaneously having a secure sense of self and the capacity to share feelings with and to know others in empathy is a feature of psychological maturity and strength.

We are not psychologically autonomous. We are not epistemologically autonomous either. As we have seen, the phenomenological position is based upon a critique of empathy as knowing others by analogy with the self, for presuming that we begin with and never really leave our own minds, and for failing to appreciate the degree to which our minds are social and cultural constructs. The experiences we call our own ultimately come from a vast world of shared experiences. How we articulate, comprehend, and assess our thoughts, emotions, and sensations comes from without, not least through our use of language. In interacting with another, we are part of another's experience and the other is part of ours. The phenomenological account of empathy focuses on the interactive, intersubjective dimension of knowledge. We share an intersubjective space with those around us, and much of what we know about ourselves and about others occurs in that space. We know the mind of another not simply because we assume that the other's mind is like our own but because we are in a communicative and cognitive relationship with the other mind, because on some level our minds are interrelated and interconnected, "inhabiting" one another.

This blurring of epistemological boundaries would apply not only to the relationship between individuals in the here and now but, in contradistinction to the phenomenological position, also to the relationship we develop to the people of the past through our engagement with their expressions, their creations, the sources they have left behind. Perhaps we know them not simply because we are like them, because we mirror or mimic them, because we have had analogous experiences to theirs. Perhaps we know past people because we are in a relationship with them in which, analogous to everyday relationships, we in some more limited sense become them and they become us. The fact that the boundary between human beings, both psychologically and cognitively, is never fixed or impermeable, that we are changed through human interaction, means that the people of the past impress themselves on us as we impress ourselves on them. We do not merely put ourselves in their place; they put themselves in our place as well. Knowing in history is a process not simply going from the historian to the people of the past, but also from the people of the past to the historian. Collingwood described the reciprocal relationship between the thought of the historian and that of the historical subject beautifully:

> historical knowledge is that special case of memory where the object of present thought is past thought, the gap between present and past being bridged not only by the power of present thought to think of the past, but also by the power of past thought to reawaken itself in the present.[49]

Although we exercise authority over the people of the past as historians, they exercise authority over us as well.[50] In fact, the past has more power over us in historical knowledge than we might care to admit. By immersing ourselves in the worlds and experiences of the people of the past, we ourselves are changed such that we can know and understand them.

Following the phenomenologists, it would certainly seem that we have the capacity to know that which we have not experienced ourselves. In Max Weber's memorable phrase, "one need not have been Caesar in order to understand Caesar."[51] Or, as Weber's contemporary Georg Simmel put it,

> we are able to recreate mental contents that have never appeared in our own subjective experience. Given the satisfaction of certain conditions—which are, nevertheless, purely external—we are able to share the mental life of persons who have nothing at all in common with us.[52]

Perhaps restricting our empathic capacities too much, Weber thought us unable to empathize with people whose experiences are beyond our emotional grasp (a mass murderer, a psychotic person, a person suffering extreme trauma). Nevertheless, he continued:

> The more we ourselves are susceptible to such emotional reactions as anxiety, anger, ambition, envy, jealousy, love, enthusiasm, pride, vengeful-ness, loyalty, devotion, and appetites of all sorts, and to the "irrational" conduct which grows out of them, the more readily can we empathize with them. Even when such emotions are found in a degree of intensity of which the observer himself is completely incapable, he can still have a sig-nificant degree of emotional understanding of their meaning and can interpret intellectually their influence on the course of action and the selection of means.[53]

For Weber, then, we can empathize with experiences of another that we share qualitatively if not quantitatively with that person. Wilhelm Dilthey too thought we could know past people very unlike ourselves through "the substratum of a general human nature." Thus, an atheist can understand Luther, for example:

> Now inasmuch as the interpreter [of Luther] tentatively projects his own sense of life into another historical milieu, he is able within that perspec-tive to momentarily strengthen and emphasize certain psychic processes and to minimize others, thus making possible within himself a re-creation of an alien form of life.[54]

And yet Weber's and Dilthey's views of our empathic capacities, although expanding their range beyond that of immediate personal experience, were still based on the assumption that we ultimately know others in empathy by analogy with ourselves. Therefore, Edith Stein's conceptualization of our ability to empathize with people very different from ourselves seems preferable. We do not need to have had an experience to understand that experience in another, according to Stein. We need merely to have the *capacity* to have that experience.[55] Put another way, we can empathize with experiences that we can imagine having. Only that which we cannot imagine, can we not know. It is imagination that enables us to transcend the limits of personal experience. In the words of Karsten Stueber, nature "has endowed us with a mind that has the power of imagination ... to think about actual or possible worlds."[56] We should not underestimate that power—nor should we underestimate our ability to learn (through works of art, literature, academic writing, etc.). Learning increases not only our knowledge of the world but also our capacity to empathize. Through learning, we gain access to countless experiences that we have never directly had ourselves. These learned, vicarious experiences are real experiences, experiences that expand the storehouse we can draw on to know and understand others, in the present and in the past.

The Role of Universal Experience in Empathy

Closely related to the notion that we can know and understand the experiences of the people of the past by using analogous experiences of our own is the notion that we rely on certain basic human similarities or certain basic human experiences to empathize with past people. As the Roman playwright Terence put it, "I am a human and hold nothing human alien to me."[57] Similarly, in lectures from the late 1860s, Jacob Burckhardt wrote: "we regard the *recurrent, constant*, and *typical* as echoing in us and understandable through us."[58] As we have seen, the early Dilthey conception of Verstehen was based upon this notion: "I myself, who experience and know myself from within, am a constituent of this social body and that the other constituents are similar to me and are thus for me likewise comprehensible in their inner being."[59] We can accept that aspects of human nature are unchanging without having to go as far as David Hume, who famously claimed:

> It is universally acknowledged that there is a great uniformity among the actions of men, in all nations and ages, and that human nature remains still the same, in its principles and operations ... Mankind are so much the same, in all times and places, that history informs us of nothing new or strange in this particular.[60]

Contemporary historians taking an empathic approach to the past acknowledge the role played by the universal in historical understanding. Thus, the historian Lyndal Roper writes that "it does not endanger the status of the historical to concede that there are aspects of human nature which are enduring, just as there are aspects of human physiology which are constitutional."[61] Not just our knowledge of people in the past but of people in general is made possible "because nature has provided all human beings with a mind that is structured and that functions psychologically in a similar manner."[62] Indeed, according to historian Barbara Taylor, "historical understanding involves empathic connection between historian and her human subjects, a connection made possible by the species similarity between individual subjectivities across place and time."[63]

As we have seen, there is considerable physiological evidence that the capacity for empathy itself is an essential aspect of human nature. The fact that human beings and monkeys are endowed with mirror neurons, perhaps as part of a sophisticated and complex system of sensorimotor learning that functions in comparable ways for both species, suggests that people throughout all of human history have had the capacity for empathy. It seems undeniable that the universal plays a role in history and that, despite all that separates people of different times and in different places, they share some fundamental experiences and even an unchanging core human nature that historians rely on in knowing the past.[64] Hence, in my own work, I relied on two aspects of universal human nature to help me understand the behavior of young middle-class Germans during the Third Reich. Although its intensity may vary from person to person and from culture to culture, human beings have a need to belong to the group and, hence, to exclude others from it—a need that accounts in part for the attraction of what I regard to be Nazism's fundamental ideological tenet, the racially exclusive collective of the Nazi *Volksgemeinschaft* or "community of the people." And human beings have the capacity to close off empathy for others, a capacity that enabled German perpetrators and bystanders to dehumanize their Jewish fellow citizens, enabling their persecution, deportation, and extermination. On some level, the human need to belong helped motivate the genocide of European Jewry; on some level, the human capacity to close off empathy enabled the genocide to be carried out.[65] Indeed every historical interpretation can be said to presuppose certain regularities, certain generalizations about human beings and their make-up and behavior.[66] These assumptions are so basic, so obvious, that we are generally unaware of our reliance on them,[67] for, in the words of the political theorist John Connelly and the psychologist Alan Costall, "without the presupposition of the constancy of at least some aspects of human nature ... historical knowledge as such ... would be rendered impossible."[68]

Not only do human beings share a fundamental physiology and human nature; there may also be certain universal human customs and institutions. That at least was Giambattista Vico's conviction when he wrote in 1725 that:

> all nations, barbarous as well as civilized, though separately founded because remote from each other in time and space, keep these three human customs: all have some religion, all contract solemn marriages, all bury their dead. And in no nation, however savage and crude, are any

human actions performed with more elaborate ceremonies and more sacred solemnity than the rites of religion, marriage and burial.

Indeed, "these three eternal and universal customs" provided Vico with the "universal and eternal principles" of his new "Science" of history.[69] A number of philosophers, especially those coming from the hermeneutic tradition like Hans-Georg Gadamer, reject the existence of a universal human nature or of universal human experiences, which we use to gain access to people and life worlds different from our own. And yet the assertion that change is the only universal and that nothing remains constant in the human world seems a conclusion more deduced from a philosophical position than based upon empirical observation and historical evidence. Perhaps each society or life world has its own unique language game played by its own unique rules, but every society has a language game governed by rules. Each society or life world may make sense of itself in its own unique way, but all societies and life worlds seek to make sense of themselves and those who inhabit them. That effort, for the philosopher Peter Winch, is universal in human society and in human history. Returning to Vico's notion that all cultures have customs relating to birth, sexual relations, and death, Winch concluded that these universal human experiences enable us to know other societies:

> In any attempt to understand the life of another society, therefore, an investigation of the forms taken by such concepts—their role in the life of the society—must always take a central place and provide a basis on which understanding may be built.[70]

Notes

1 Smith, *Theory of Moral Sentiments*, 13–15. For a recent account of the role played by context in empathic understanding, see Retz, *Empathy and History*, 8, 216, 218.
2 Watson and Greenberg, "Empathic Resonance," 126; Zahavi, "Empathy and Mirroring," 219–220; De Vignemont and Singer, "The Empathic Brain," 437–438.
3 Watson and Greenberg, "Empathic Resonance," 129–130.
4 Personal communication from Mark Roseman.
5 Heal, *Mind, Reason, and Imagination*, 29 and 44.
6 Personal communication from Mark Roseman.
7 LaCapra, "Tropisms of Intellectual History," 502.
8 LaCapra, *Understanding Others*, 3, 165–166.
9 LaCapra, *History in Transit*, 18.
10 Kohut, "Introspection, Empathy, and Psychoanalysis," 206–209. See, also, Köhler, "Von der Freud'schen Psychoanalyse zur Selbstpsychologie Heinz Kohuts," 38–39.
11 Agosta, *Empathy in the Context of Philosophy*, 134.
12 Coplan, "Understanding Empathy," 9–11.
13 Kögler and Steuber, "Introduction," 9.
14 Coplan, "Understanding Empathy," 9–11. The first philosopher to articulate "other-oriented empathy" was Robert Gordon. Kögler and Steuber, "Introduction," 9–10.

By contrast, Peter Goldie explicitly rejects "empathetic perspective-shifting" that takes the form of imagining being the other person in the other's situation, which he appears to see as coming close to merger and false identification. Peter Goldie, "Anti-Empathy," in *Empathy: Philosophical and Psychological Perspectives*, ed. Amy Coplan and Peter Goldie (Oxford: Oxford University Press, 2011), 302, 317. Curiously, in an earlier article, Goldie appears to take the opposite position. Putting oneself in the other's shoes, "unlike empathy, involves the narrator having a mixture of my own characterization and some of his; empathy, if successful, does not involve any aspect of me in this sense, for empathetic understanding is a way of gaining a deeper understanding of what it is like *for him*, not of what it would be like for a person with some mixture of his and my characterization." Peter Goldie, "How We Think of Others' Emotions," *Mind and Language* 14, no. 4(1999): 398.

15 Evelyne A. Schwaber, "Empathy: A Mode of Analytic Listening," *Psychoanalytic Inquiry* 1, no. 3(1981): 385.

16 Richard Wollheim, *The Thread of Life* (New Haven: Yale University Press, 1984), 73–78.

17 Husserl quoted in Makkreel, "How Is Empathy Related to Understanding?," 210.

18 The fact that we are in a cognitive and affective relationship with past people that influences what we know and write about them and that affects and even changes us as well does not mean that we lose our sense of self or become one with them. While we are in a relationship with our historical subject, we need to reflect consciously and critically on that relationship as it impacts our knowledge and understanding of the historical subject and, indeed, as it impacts us as well.

19 Lucien Febvre, *The Problem of Unbelief in the Sixteenth Century: The Religion of Rabelais* (Cambridge, MA: Harvard University Press, 1985).

20 Fritz Breithaupt presumes, wrongly in my view, that empathy represents a loss of self rather than its expansion. Breithaupt, *Kulturen der Empathie*, 9, 109; "A Three-Person Model of Empathy," *Emotion Review* 4(2012): 85; "Empathy for Empathy's Sake," 154; *Die dunklen Seiten der Empathie*, 44–78.

21 Robert Nozick, *Philosophical Explanations* (Cambridge, MA: Harvard University Press, 1981), 637–638.

22 Smith, *Theory of Moral Sentiments*, 11–13; Janet Strayer, "Affective and Cognitive Perspectives on Empathy," in *Empathy and Its Development*, ed. Nancy Eisenberg and Janet Strayer (Cambridge: Cambridge University Press, 1987), 229.

23 Hume, *Treatise of Human Nature*, 318, also 359.

24 Dilthey, *Understanding the Human World*, 29.

25 Dilthey, *Hermeneutics and the Study of History*, 230; *Understanding the Human World*, 29–30, also 244–245. The psychologist Silvan Tompkins follows Dilthey here: Silvan Tompkins, "Affects: Primary Motives of Man," *Humanitas* 3, no. 3 (1968): 328–329.

26 Kohut, "Introspection, Empathy, and Psychoanalysis," 207–208.

27 Simmel, *Problems of the Philosophy of History*, 88.

28 Leopold von Ranke, *Englische Geschichte*, Sämtliche Werke, vol. 2 (Leipzig: Duncker and Humblot, 1880), 103.

29 Simmel, *Problems of the Philosophy of History*, 88–89. See, also, Walsh, *Introduction to the Philosophy of History*, 106. See also Dominick LaCapra, "History and Psychoanalysis," *Critical Inquiry* 13, no. 2(1987): 229.

30 Peter Gay, *Freud for Historians* (New York: Oxford University Press, 1985), viii–ix; Loewenberg, "Cultural History and Psychoanalysis," 19.

31 Simmel, *Problems of the Philosophy of History*, 91.

32 Kohut, *A German Generation*, 242. One of the implications of this view is that the more life experiences the investigator has, the more experiences of the investigated he or she will be able to know and understand. Breithaupt, *Die dunklen Seiten der Empathie*, 20.

33 Hume, *Treatise of Human Nature*, 318; Simmel, *Problems of the Philosophy of History*, 65; Weber, *Economy and Society*, 1, 5–6; Aschheim, "The (Ambiguous) Political Economy of Empathy," 27–28; Assmann and Detmers, "Introduction," 8; Breithaupt, *Kulturen der Empathie*, 18, 22; Coplan, "Understanding Empathy," 13; Schwaber, "Empathy," 382.

34 Cooley, *Human Nature and the Social Order*, 153.

35 Jacob Burckhardt, *Weltgeschichtliche Betrachtungen*, 2nd edition, ed. Jakob Oeri (Berlin and Stuttgart: Spemann, 1910), 10.

36 Ibid. Also Jacob Burckhardt, *Reflections on History*, ed. Gottfried Dietze, trans. M. D. Hottinger (Indianapolis: Liberty Classics, 1979), 40–41; *The Civilization of the Renaissance in Italy*, trans. S. G. C. Middlemore (London and New York: Penguin, 1990).

37 Georg Simmel, "Vom Wesen des historischen Verstehens," in *Gesamtausgabe*, ed. Gregor Fitzi and Otthein Rammstedt (Frankfurt: Suhrkamp, 1999), 156.

38 Dilthey, *Formation of the Historical World*, 3, 218.

39 Zahavi, "Empathy and Other-Directed Intentionality," 131.

40 Scheler, *The Nature of Sympathy*, 12, 241–242.

41 Edith Stein, *On the Problem of Empathy*, trans. Waltraut Stein (The Hague: Martinus Nijhoff, 1970), 105.

42 Mead, *Mind, Self, and Society*, 140.

43 Ibid., 195.

44 Leonard S. Cottrell, "Some Neglected Problems in Social Psychology," *American Sociological Review* 15(1950): 707.

45 Scheler, *The Nature of Sympathy*, 247–248; Hoffman, "Interaction of Affect and Cognition in Empathy," 103–131; Doris Bischof-Köhler, "Empathy and Self-Recognition in Phylogenetic and Ontogenetic Perspective," *Emotion Review* 4, no. 1(2012): 43.

46 Our psychological attachment to the environment in self psychology is conveyed by the concept of the "selfobject," that is, an object, an "other," that is experienced as part of the self. The sociologist Leonard Cottrell, in 1942, articulated a similar concept that he connected with empathy. Leonard S. Cottrell, "The Analysis of Situational Fields in Social Psychology," *American Sociological Review* 7(1942): 370 and 378.

47 Kathleen Haney, "Empathy and Otherness," *Journal of Philosophy: A Cross-Disciplinary Inquiry* 4, no. 8(2009): 11.

48 The psychoanalyst Lotte Köhler presents a cogent account of the development of the capacity for empathy in human beings, a capacity that generally is consolidated at between 48 and 60 months. At that age, the child—recognizing that other minds are different from its own and grasping cognitively the difference between its own feelings and those of others—is able "to adopt the perspective of the other," which is "the last step in the development of empathy." Köhler, "Von der Freud'schen Psychoanalyse zur Selbstpsychologie Heinz Kohuts," 40–49, quotation on 47.

49 Collingwood, *The Idea of History*, 294.

50 LaCapra, "Tropisms of Intellectual History," 502; Retz, *Empathy and History*, 12, 65, 69.

51 Weber, *Economy and Society*, 1, 5.

52 Simmel, *Problems of the Philosophy of History*, 93–94.

53 Weber, *Economy and Society*, 1, 6.

54 Dilthey, *Hermeneutics and the Study of History*, 249.

55 Stein, *On the Problem of Empathy*, 103–105.

56 Stueber, *Rediscovering Empathy*, 111.

57 Translation in Bolognini, "Empathy and 'Empathism'," 287.

58 Burckhardt, *Weltgeschichtliche Betrachtungen*, 4; *Reflections on History*, 34 (emphasis in translation).
59 Dilthey, *Introduction to the Human Sciences*, 1, 89.
60 Hume, *Enquiries Concerning Human Understanding*, 83–84. Indeed, the particular value of history was that it expanded "our experience" to "all past ages, and to the most distant nations; making them contribute as much to our improvement in wisdom, as if they had actually lain under our observation. A man acquainted with history may, in some respect, be said to have lived from the beginning of the world, and to have been making continual additions to his stock of knowledge in every century." Hume, "On the Study of History," 566–567.
61 Lyndal Roper, *Oedipus and the Devil: Witchcraft, Sexuality and Religion in Early Modern Europe* (London and New York: Routledge, 1994), 13.
62 Stueber, *Rediscovering Empathy*, 111.
63 Taylor, "Historical Subjectivity," 195.
64 Walsh, *Philosophy of History*, 107; White, *Foundations of Historical Knowledge*, 216.
65 Kohut, *A German Generation*, 240.
66 See, here, Chapter 1, note 68 explicating Carl Hempel's position that all explanations are based upon general laws, or at the very least general hypotheses.
67 Walsh, *Philosophy of History*, 58; Gardiner, *Historical Explanation*, 82, 93, 99, 125; Michael Scriven, "Truisms as the Grounds for Historical Explanations," in *Theories of History*, ed. Patrick Gardiner (Glencoe, NY: Free Press of Glencoe, 1964), particularly 444, 458; Kohut, "Psychohistory as History," 339.
68 John Connelly and Alan Costall, "R. G. Collingwood and the Idea of an Historical Psychology," *Theory and Psychology* 10(2000): 165.
69 Vico, *The New Science*, 53.
70 Peter Winch, "Understanding a Primitive Society," *American Philosophical Quarterly* 1, no. 4(1964): 324.

Chapter 6

Is Historical Empathy Unique?

As was noted at the outset, the fields in which empathy has been the subject of recent attention have focused on empathy's role in knowing others in the here and now. Hence, the question naturally arises: Is empathy as it is used to know people in the past different from empathy as it is used to know people in the present? This chapter explores that question. Before tackling it more or less head on in the second section, I shall first consider the relationship between feeling and knowing in empathy, since empathy's affective dimension appears to play an important role in our everyday interactions, including in knowing other minds and mental states. Most historians would probably deny that shared feeling plays much of a role in historical knowledge and understanding, however. Certainly, if affective sharing does occur in historical work, historians are frequently unaware that feelings from the past are coming to life in them.

Feeling and Knowing in Empathy

Although historians may not always fully appreciate the fact, there is an affective dimension to their engagement with the past. Not only do our own emotional investments and commitments influence what we study and how we study it;[1] the past also exerts an emotional influence on us, frequently a powerful influence.[2] The impact of history on the historian is particularly evident in relation to trauma. Not only does past trauma powerfully affect those who experienced it firsthand; trauma also powerfully affects those experiencing it secondarily, not simply their children and grandchildren but also the historian of trauma. Traumatic events like the Holocaust are only extreme and obvious examples of the power that history exerts on people generally and on historians in particular.

We not only inhabit the past in our imagination; the past inhabits us as well. This can be a difficult and upsetting experience. The powerful feelings that history evokes in us account more often than we may realize for some of the difficulty we experience in doing historical work. It is not simply that we become personally invested in our work. From the outset, we choose to work on topics that are important to us, intellectually and personally as well. When we study the past, we in some ways also study ourselves. And our immersion in past historical worlds can arouse feelings and raise personal issues that may be difficult to deal with. To take one example, my book *A German Generation* dealt significantly with the Third Reich and with the persecution, deportation, and extermination of Jews. I found thinking and writing about the topic distressing. It made me uncomfortable—although I was long unaware that the source of my distress and discomfort was the past. Progress was painfully slow, and I blamed myself for not working more effectively, more quickly, in a more sustained fashion, failing to recognize that there were good reasons why I was having difficulties. Gradually I became aware that my immersion in the Third Reich generally and my study of the reactions of non-Jewish Germans toward their Jewish fellow citizens in particular were arousing feelings of helplessness, passivity, and potential victimhood in me.

With that awareness, I was able to write more quickly and with less discomfort and anxiety. I was also able to reflect critically on how those feelings evoked by the past may have influenced my work. I articulated first to myself and ultimately to the reader my concern that my interpretations and the way I had chosen to structure the book may have helped me counteract the feelings of helplessness, passivity, and potential victimhood aroused in me by the past. I became aware of what in classical psychoanalysis would be called my "countertransference" to the Germans I was studying in my book, aware of feelings they had evoked in me that had the potential to interfere with my understanding and representation of them—indeed, to interfere with my empathy for them.[3] And that awareness led me to understand myself better, to more fully appreciate the powerful psychological role that the Holocaust played in my family and plays in my life.[4] Indeed, understanding the past can help us gain a certain mastery over the personal issues that have brought us to our particular historical topic in the first place and over the issues that our engagement with that topic have aroused in us over the course of our work. Put another way, as historians we are on some level working on ourselves and for ourselves and with ourselves in doing history. We are emotionally engaged participants in history.[5]

Thus, our emotional engagement with the past can interfere with our ability to research and write, can make it harder for us to imagine ourselves in the place of the people of the past, and can distort our vision and understanding of them. But our emotional engagement with the past can also facilitate our historical knowledge and understanding, beyond the fact that our emotional investments and commitments give direction and energy to our historical work. Indeed, we can learn from our emotional responses to the past. To cite one example, in several courses that I teach at Williams College I show the 1935 Nazi propaganda film *Triumph of the Will* to the students, the full-length version. In class, students frequently report that despite the beauty of many of the images in the film, they soon became bored with the endless marching, the constant blaring martial music, the film's relentless repetition. I ask the students to reflect upon their experience of boredom, to think not only about whether Germans in 1935 would have found the film boring but also to think about and analyze their own reactions. Doing that work enables the students to appreciate the important role played by repetition in the film, its effort to drum experiences of individuality out of the viewer, to eradicate individualizing thought, and to create a common, passive, emotional experience. Indeed, our boredom in watching the film not only reflects its efforts to pacify us; it also may reflect our affective effort to protect our individuality from the film's collectivist assault.

Empathy, particularly in relation to history, has been understood here as a form of cognition, as a way of knowing; and yet empathy is considered by most psychologists and many philosophers, particularly those subscribing to simulation theory, to include shared feeling, even by those who emphasize empathy's ultimate cognitive status. The question then arises: Do historians not only have their own subjective emotional responses to the past, which may interfere with but also facilitate historical understanding, but do historians also experience the emotions of past people, and does that shared feeling facilitate historical knowledge and understanding?

Empathy as affective-sharing plays an important role in many psychological and philosophical accounts of empathy as a way of knowing the minds and mental states of others. As discussed in Chapter 3, given the fact that empathy requires a clear awareness of the distinction between self and other, merger and affective contagion do not qualify as empathy. However, shared affect that comes with an awareness that what one is feeling has been taken over from another represents the standard account of empathy as "affective mindreading" in simulation theory. Called by some the "sharing first" account, the empathizer experiences the emotion of the other person, subjects that emotion to introspective scrutiny, and then attributes that emotion, now identified, to the other person, putting the empathizer in a position to understand why the other person, given his or her situation, is experiencing that particular emotion.[6] This affective form of cognition in a controlled and structured setting is what frequently occurs in psychoanalysis when the analyst, who is maintaining evenly hovering attention, experiences an emotion and recognizes that the emotion he or she is experiencing is in fact the analysand's feeling and ultimately not the analyst's. Subjecting that feeling to "vicarious introspection," the analyst seeks to identify and understand the meaning of that feeling for the analysand based on what the analyst knows about the patient.

The philosopher of history Dominick LaCapra has consistently emphasized not simply the cognitive but also "the affective dimension of historical understanding," including especially in relation to empathy.[7] He uses the psychoanalytic concept of "transference" to characterize the cognitive and affective relationship that is established between the historian and the historical subject.[8] Indeed, he sees transference, defined as "the mutual but differential implication of the self in others," as forming "a basis for empathy."[9] Transference in history is not simply the implication of the historian in the historical subject, where the historian unconsciously projects or "transfers" his or her own issues onto the people of the past, comparable to "countertransference" in classical psychoanalysis. Transference, for LaCapra, is also the implication of the historical subject in the historian. It is a "co-implication" that "includes affective involvement and the tendency to repeat what is found in or projected into the other."[10] That is to say, the past also projects or "transfers" itself onto the historian, such that "the problems at issue in the object of [historical] study reappear (or are repeated with variations), in the work of the historian," generally without the historian being conscious that such a transfer has taken place.[11]

This book, then, follows LaCapra in emphasizing the reciprocal cognitive and affective relationship that exists between the historian and the past, particularly past people. We do not simply project ourselves onto them; they project themselves into us. Most historians seem more aware of the former than of the latter, in part perhaps because to recognize the influence of the past on the historian means to recognize the limits imposed by the past on the historian's autonomy and authority over history, both lived and written.

An illustration of transference in LaCapra's sense of the term is provided by the historian of early America John Demos. Demos' own work demonstrates the productive affective relationship that exists between historian and historical subject in a way that is analogous to the relationship between psychoanalyst and patient. Curious and knowledgeable about psychoanalysis, Demos was well aware of the problem of countertransference, when the historian's personal issues blind his vision or distort his understanding of the past. And yet, Demos realized, that "psychoanalysis cuts another way as well. Viewed from the opposite end of the analytic couch, the self [of the analyst] could actually be a source of insight—and thus of treatment benefit." Indeed, the analyst's "reactions [to the patient] may be a tip-off not only to aspects of his own inner life but also to those of his patient."[12] Demos applied this insight derived from psychoanalytic treatment to his historical work. In his essay "Using Self, Using History," Demos describes how his own life experiences enhanced his knowledge and understanding of the early modern American past. Thus, in researching and writing the book *A Little Commonwealth*, his relationship with his own small children facilitated and deepened his understanding of Puritan families and childrearing practices.[13] The experience of social interactions and of "the power and play of human emotions" in Demos' personal and professional life informed his study of witchcraft in early America, *Entertaining Satan*. And a powerful experience of altered sense perception freed him to write about what he calls the "spooky parts of the witchcraft record."[14]

But Demos' personal experiences not only influenced his historical work; his historical work also influenced Demos. This mutual influence was particularly striking in his study of the famous "Indian captive," Eunice Williams.[15] As Demos puts it, "not only was I using myself and my experience for the sake of my project; the project, for its part, was using me."[16] Specifically, Eunice Williams' decision not to return to the Puritan family into which she had been born but to remain with the Mohawk family to which she had been brought as a kidnapped child affected Demos powerfully, in no small measure because it resonated with the departure of his own daughters from the family home to establish independent lives. Ultimately, the story of Eunice Williams helped him gain insight into and mastery over his emotional response to the loss of his own daughters to adulthood.[17] Demos' choice of that particular historical topic can hardly have been accidental. Indeed, he recognizes that all historians choose to work on subjects that are "inextricably rooted in the self. Far from being a matter of serendipity … such a choice is powerfully, and personally, determined." Every topic, "no matter how public and impersonal its most visible aspects, carries internal resonances" to which historians "are inclined (or compelled) to respond." What we study as historians is deeply influenced by who we are. And who we are is deeply influenced by what we study.[18]

Therefore, affective sharing in historical work may generate knowledge and insight in ways that are analogous to affective sharing in psychoanalytic treatment. Nevertheless, not all interpretations in psychoanalysis—not to speak of psychoanalytic psychotherapy—involve the simulation theorists' "sharing first" model. Indeed, I suspect that most psychoanalytic under-standing does not begin with the analyst experiencing the patient's feeling but remains purely or mostly cognitive as the analyst thinks rather than feels his or her way inside the patient's experience. Philosophers who subscribe to the phenomenological position believe that in empathy we can know and under-stand the emotional and mental state of another without our having to experience the other's emotional or mental state ourselves in any way. Indeed, Max Scheler cited the novelist, the playwright, and the "historian of motives" as all possessing "in high degree the gift of visualizing the feelings of others, but there is not the slightest need for them to share the feelings of their sub-jects and personages."[19] Contemporary phenomenologists like Dan Zahavi and Søren Overgaard follow Scheler in contending that we can empathize with the thoughts and feelings of another without having the other's experi-ence literally transmitted to us. In empathy, the focus is on the experience of the other, not on our own experience. "Thus empathy does not entail that we ourselves undergo the emotion we observe in the other. We might, but this is not a requisite."[20]

Nevertheless, there is a strong case to be made for the connection between knowing and affective sharing in empathy. According to the anthropologist Douglas Hollan, empathy is a cross-cultural phenomenon. And yet what distinguishes empathy in Western cultures from empathy in other parts of the world is the tendency in the West sharply to distinguish between thought and feeling.[21] Recent research in neuroscience and psychology confirms the non-Western view, suggesting that empathy cannot be conceived as either cognitive or affective but always, according to Karsten Stueber, "as encompassing both." Specifically, Stueber sees the discovery of mirror neurons as bolstering "such a unified conception of empathy."

If mirror neurons are indeed the primary underlying causal mechanisms for *cognitively* recognizing certain emotional states in others by looking at their facial expressions, then it is quite understandable how such an observation could also lead to the feeling of an emotion that is more congruent with the situation of the other; that is, to empathy in the affective sense. Such affective responses are due to the fact that the perception of another person activates similar neurons in the subject and the target.[22]

Indeed, the interrelationship of thought and feeling is captured by the concept of "experience," which generally conveys a state that is neither exclusively intellectual nor exclusively emotional, but an amalgam of both. As a noun (experience as a phenomenon) and as a verb (experience as a way of apprehending), as what we seek to know and how we seek to know it, "experience" brings thought and feeling together.[23]

So, if feeling and knowing are connected in everyday life and in the concept of experience, and if historical knowledge has an important affective dimension, does that mean that when historians empathize with the people of the past they experience the feelings of their historical subjects as part of the process of knowing them? Collingwood contended that to know past thought, the historian needs to rethink it. Does knowing the feelings and experiences of past people mean that the historian feels the feelings, relives the emotional life, and re-experiences the experiences of those people? It seems unlikely that empathy in the "sharing first" account occurs with any frequency in historical knowledge, at least in anything like the self-conscious and disciplined way it occurs in psychoanalysis. Unlike psychoanalysts, historians are not trained to be aware of affective-sharing or to subject shared emotional responses to introspective scrutiny so that they can serve as a vehicle for understanding the experience of another. Nevertheless, it seems likely that historians frequently do experience emotional resonance with past people, although they are probably mostly unaware that what they are feeling comes from and ultimately belongs to their historical subjects. That seems to be the view of the historian Michael Roper. Like LaCapra, Roper emphasizes that knowing in history is "an affective process" and draws attention to the "unconscious communication" that goes on between the people of the past and the historian. That communication may well include our re-experience, if to an attenuated degree, of the feelings of our historical subjects.[24] Given its largely unconscious nature for historians, affective sharing in history then would have much the same status as affective sharing in everyday life, where, according to simulation theory, we unconsciously mimic the emotional states of others in the process of knowing them.

I do not know if empathy as affective sharing always or only occasionally plays a role in historical knowledge. I suspect, however, that deep empathic knowledge of past experience involves emotional resonance. Could one empathically understand, say, Hitler's anti-Semitism without experiencing at least a trace of his fear and his hatred of Jews? One does not need to become an anti-Semite in order to understand one; but perhaps one does need to dip one's toe into the pool of the anti-Semite's fear and hatred of Jews. Would a purely intellectual understanding of Hitler's anti-Semitism be a deeply empathic understanding? Can one deeply understand someone else's experience without feeling anything at all of what the other feels or, in the case of history, felt? It does seem likely, then, that historians at times share—if to an attenuated degree—the experience of the people of the past in knowing them, although that shared experience may be as much a byproduct of the empathizing process as essential to it. Given its largely unconscious nature, affective sharing or emotional resonance between historian and historical subject is different from the deliberate and self-conscious application of empathy, however.

Whatever role shared feeling may play in knowing the minds and mental states of others, empathy as it is understood here ultimately serves cognition. Apart from the basic empathy we employ mostly intuitively in everyday life, re-enactive empathy is a highly developed, psychologically and cognitively mature, human capacity. It is employed deliberately and self-consciously and centrally involves adopting the perspective of the person or persons one wishes to know and understand. We may at times *feel* our way into the experience of the people of the past, but, even more, we *think* our way inside their experience. The emphasis on shared feeling in empathy threatens to obscure its cognitive aim and its largely rational character. Max Weber's contention that understanding is either rational or arrived at through emotional "sympathetic participation" and that therefore empathy, while of heuristic value, must be supplemented by logic, abstraction, and comparison fails to appreciate that empathy, while it can involve shared feeling, is a rational cognitive process.[25] Indeed, in the words of the psychoanalyst Lotte Köhler, "the systematic use of empathy ... does not presume the rejection of rational knowing but leads instead to its expansion, deepening, and differentiation."[26]

Empathy in Everyday Life and in History with a Detour through Hans-Georg Gadamer

Although the current intense interest in empathy relates almost exclusively to empathy in everyday human interaction, R. G. Collingwood has been the focus of considerable attention in recent years, particularly on the part of those who see his philosophy of history as consistent with simulation theory. Nevertheless, Collingwood's work too is generally considered in relation to empathy in everyday life.[27] Curiously, the philosophers and psychologists who discuss Collingwood generally do so without addressing the difference or the potential difference between empathy as a way to know people in the present and empathy as a way to know people in the past. Indeed, they frequently seem implicitly to equate knowledge of others in everyday life with knowledge of others in history. For the two other contemporary philosophical accounts of how we know the minds and mental states of others, the relationship between empathy in everyday life and in history would appear to be a non-issue. According to "theory theory," there is only one world of knowledge, and hence no difference between how we know people in the present and in the past. In both instances we simply apply hypotheses informed by theory to the people we want to know, and there is no place or need for empathy at all. According to "the phenomenological position," we know other minds directly, without resorting to analogy or imitation, and empathic knowledge is restricted to unmediated, face-to-face encounters. Therefore, since we cannot empathize with people whom we only encounter through their expressions, empathy implicitly would appear to play no role in historical knowledge according to the phenomenological account.

But can we really only empathize with other people in direct, unmediated, personal interaction? Would a letter or an e-mail from a friend expressing his or her thoughts and feelings not enable us to empathize with that friend? Would our knowledge of that friend's mind or mental state really be so different from knowledge gained through face-to-face interaction? Can empathy not bridge that gap?[28] And if a letter or an e-mail gives us empathic access to another, then surely we have similar empathic access to the inner lives of past people who have left various forms of self-expression that we can re-experience. Conversely, is a face-to-face encounter really an unmediated interaction? After all, we know the minds and mental states of others in face-to-face encounters in part through their clothing, posture, gestures, facial expressions, and, above all, spoken words. These too are "texts" that we "read." In everyday life and in history we gain access to the inner life of people through their expressions, by reading the texts, broadly defined, they have produced. And when we read a friend's letter, we do not so much experience ourselves being in dialogue with the letter. We experience ourselves being in dialogue with our friend. Perhaps as we read we can hear her voice or visualize his face. Similarly, historians who are interested in past people, when reading a document generally experience themselves as engaging not merely with a text but also with the person who produced it. To be sure, some historians are more interested in texts than in their authors. Still many historians *are* interested in past people and study their texts in order to know and understand them, their minds and mental states, their experience—the philosopher Hans-Georg Gadamer notwithstanding.

Despite following Vico, Droysen, Dilthey, et al. in seeing a fundamental epistemological distinction between the natural and the human sciences, Gadamer rejected empathy as a way of knowing in the human sciences generally and in history in particular. Like those who preceded him, Gadamer saw the natural sciences as concerned with "the concrete phenomenon as an instance of a universal rule" and the human sciences as concerned with "the phenomenon itself in its unique and historical concreteness."[29] Yet what characterized knowledge in the human sciences for Gadamer is the understanding of the *meaning* of the particular through the interpretation of texts. Indeed, the interpreter engages in dialogue with texts. It is through that dialogue—not empathy—that understanding is achieved in the human sciences. Regarding history specifically, Gadamer saw the historian not as standing outside of history but as a historical being. We neither can escape our historical moment nor should try to leave that moment to transpose ourselves into the past in order to understand the past on its own terms:[30]

> To think historically always involves mediating between those [past] ideas and one's own thinking. To try to escape from one's own concepts in interpretation is not only impossible but manifestly absurd. To interpret means precisely to bring one's own conceptions into play so that the text's meaning can really be made to speak for us.[31]

Historicity for Gadamer meant that the historian belongs to a particular historical tradition and occupies a time and place bounded by a particular historical horizon. Why and how historians read historical texts is determined by the tradition to which they belong and by the horizon that circumscribes their field of view. Historians bring their own horizon and interests and beliefs to bear on the text and the horizon to which it belongs and on the interests and beliefs it expresses, an interaction that produces something new through "a real fusing of horizons."[32] As a result, "understanding is not merely a reproductive but always a productive activity as well."[33] We approach past texts with a question prompted by our own contemporary situation. Those past texts were themselves responses to questions prompted by the contemporary situation in which they were produced. The present question comes together with the past answer to produce new answers connected with the past but transcending it to become relevant in the present day.[34] For Gadamer, then, we are not interested in the past for its sake but for ours.[35]

Thus interpretation for Gadamer is a dialectical interaction between the interpreter and the interpreted, with the latter understood as a text whose meaning expresses not so much the author's intentions as the tradition and horizon to which the text belongs.[36] Gadamer saw understanding in history as closely related to understanding in everyday life. In history, understanding is achieved in dialogue *with* a text; in everyday life, understanding is arrived at in dialogue *over* a text or a topic, over what he called a *Gegenstand*. For Gadamer, two people do not so much understand one another directly as they arrive at an understanding with one another over "a subject matter that is placed before them."[37] "Understanding each other ... is always understanding each other with respect to something." Hence, there is no place for "sympathetic understanding of the other person" since we only proceed "via the subject matter" over which we are in dialogue.[38]

In history, for Gadamer, the role of the historical Gegenstand or of the historical text is, if anything, even more important than in everyday life. Like his contemporaries Collingwood and those like Hempel, Gardiner, and Dray engaged in the debate over covering laws in historical explanation, Gadamer presumed that historians are primarily concerned with ideas or events, that is, with historical *Gegenstände*, not with those who produced them. In seeking to understand those ideas or events, the historian, according to Gadamer, would be wrong to assume that their meaning reflected the original intention of the author or actor.[39] "The hermeneutical reduction to the author's meaning is just as inappropriate as the reduction of the historical events to the intentions of their protagonists."[40] Knowing the experience of past people is at best a flawed and partial way to get at the ideas and events they produced. It never seems to have occurred to Gadamer, however, that one might be interested in past people not as the producers of ideas and events, of Gegenstände, but in their own right. For historians of experience, past people do not so much help us understand the texts or actions they produced; those texts or actions help us understand the people who produced them. And, despite the fact that our own historical position influences what we choose to look at in the past and what we see there, historians are interested in trying to understand the people of the past more on their terms than on ours.

So if we are willing to reject theory theory and its unlikely bedfellow Gadamer in dispensing with empathy altogether and the phenomenological position for its restriction of empathy to face-to-face encounters, and if we are willing to accept that we use empathy to know and understand people in the present *and* in the past, then the question naturally arises as to the relationship between empathy in everyday life and empathy in history. Already Wilhelm Dilthey distinguished between "elementary understanding," which we use more or less unconsciously when there is an immediate unity between mental content and its expression, and higher and more complex forms of understanding, which are self-conscious and relate to context and general patterns of meaning. This higher and deliberate form of understanding is necessary when the relationship between mental content and expression is unclear. In this higher form of understanding, we know the mental content of the other's mind through *Nacherleben* or re-experience. According to Dilthey, we use "elementary understanding" in everyday life, whereas "higher understanding is the province of the human sciences."[41]

As was discussed at the end of Chapter 2, contemporary philosophers, neuroscientists, and psychologists echo Dilthey in distinguishing between a lower-order, more affective and unconscious form of empathy, which the philosopher Karsten Stueber calls "basic empathy," and a higher-order, more cognitive, deliberate, and self-conscious form of empathy, which Stueber calls "reenactive empathy." According to those making this distinction (albeit using various terms), we use both forms of empathy in everyday life. Most simulation theorists implicitly or occasionally explicitly contend that we use what Stueber calls basic empathy more or less automatically, unconsciously, and ubiquitously; but we employ re-enactive empathy more or less deliberately when we are faced with a response of another that basic empathy fails to comprehend. In effect, we employ re-enactive empathy when we are faced with an explanatory puzzle, when someone else's feelings, thoughts, or actions do not seem to be self-evident responses to their situation. It is then, in the language used here, that we consciously adopt the position of the internal, empathic observer, and try to think our way inside that person's situation and experience in order to understand why his or her feelings, thoughts, and actions made sense.

The philosopher Jane Heal makes a different if related and relevant distinction between basic and re-enactive empathy. According to Heal, although we are generally able to know another's emotional or mental state directly (perhaps through something like basic empathy or simply in an unmediated fashion as the phenomenological position contends), we employ re-enactive empathy if we wish to *understand* that state rather than simply identify it.[42] The need to understand the emotional or mental state of the other is what prompts us to imagine our way inside the other's situation and experience. In re-enactive, *understanding* empathy, then, we are "not looking at the subject to be understood but at the world around that subject."[43] In everyday life, we use empathy to identity what others are thinking and feeling, often in order to be able to anticipate how they will respond in a given situation. By contrast, in history, we generally know what the people of the past did; we know how they responded, and we may even know something of what they experienced. We imagine ourselves in their place, in their context, generally not to know their mental state or to anticipate their actions but to *understand* why they felt, thought, or acted as they did, to *understand* why their actions and/or experience made sense from their perspective. In that regard, one can say then that the historian has an empathic advantage over the person using empathy to know the other in the moment in everyday life.[44]

Karsten Stueber is one of the few contemporary philosophers to consider the relationship between knowing and understanding people in everyday life and knowing and understanding people in history. He sees narrative playing a heightened role in historical explanation.[45] Unlike those who conceptualize empathy as a form of narrative, discussed briefly in "Imagination and Per- spective-Taking in Empathy" in Chapter 3, Stueber sees narrative as *facilitating* empathic understanding of historical actors. Historical narratives support "the empathetic act of grasping another person's beliefs and desires as his or her reasons for acting" by enabling the historian to set those beliefs and desires within a biographical and cultural context.[46] By embedding individual action "in a larger story," historical narratives "support our empathetic grasp of" historical actors' "reasons for acting."[47] Narratives also help the historian determine which explanation of an actor's behavior makes most sense "in the larger context that the narrative identifies. In this manner, a narrative allows us to develop greater confidence in our judgment that those are indeed the reasons that caused a person to act."[48] Specifically, Stueber considers the role played by what philosophers of mind and cognitive scientists call "folk psychology," that is, the commonsense psychology we use to explain and predict the behavior and mental state of other people, in historical knowledge.[49] Despite the reluctance of philosophers of history to acknowledge the fact, historians, according to Stueber, use "folk psychological understanding" in knowing past people; indeed, folk psychological understanding and historical understanding are frequently the same.[50] Empathy for Stueber is central to knowing others in folk psychology and, to the extent that folk psychology plays a role in historical knowledge, in historical understanding as well, particularly in knowing the intentions of historical actors.[51]

In knowing others in everyday life and in knowing others in history, then, it would seem we make use of both lower-order, unconscious basic empathy and higher-order, deliberate, and self-conscious re-enactive or perspective-taking empathy. Whether in knowing people in the here and now or in history, it would seem that we are using basic empathy when the behaviors, ideas, and experiences of people seem self-evident or intuitively intelligible. But when the behaviors and experiences of past people seem puzzling and do not intuitively make sense, and when, following Heal, the historian wishes to *understand* those behaviors and experiences, then, according to Stueber, the historian employs re-enactive empathy deliberately and self-consciously—a view shared by the anthropologist Douglas Hollan.[52] Like Heal, Hollan sees basic, intuitive, more affective empathy able to identify the emotional and mental states of others but not to understand them. To understand the emotional and mental states of others, particularly those belonging to other cultures, we must employ the more sophisticated, self-conscious, and deliberate cognitive form of what he calls "complex empathy," which, according to Hollan, requires cultural knowledge, imagination, and perhaps even theory.[53]

The focus of these reflections on the role played by empathy in historical knowledge is on re-enactive, perspective-taking, or complex empathy, rather than on basic empathy. Given its automatic, intuitive character, in basic empathy we are not always aware of our observational position, whereas in re-enactive or complex empathy we need to be aware of the fact that we are at least partially leaving our own observational position to adopt in our imagination the position of the other. Furthermore, affective sharing and cognition would seem to be entirely bound up with one another in basic empathy, whereas affective sharing would seem to take a back seat to cognition in re-enactive empathy. In everyday human interaction, affective sharing or emotional resonance plays a crucial, life-sustaining, and life-enhancing role in how we relate to and support one another.[54] By contrast, empathy in history is primarily a way of knowing, a mode of observation. Whereas shared feeling plays a central role in human relationships, emotional resonance is secondary to cognition in history, occasionally facilitating cognition, more often its byproduct.

Nevertheless, historians of experience, specifically, and historians who study human beings more generally, when all is said and done, are people attempting to understand other people. It seems reasonable to assume that the skills in understanding others that we have developed over a lifetime of human interactions (our "folk psychology") help us to empathize with and understand the past people we encounter as historians. Whether in the present or the past, we employ basic empathy unconsciously and instinctively when we know and understand past behavior and experience that seems self-evident, so self-evident in fact that it may not require explanation; and we employ re-enactive or perspective-taking empathy consciously and deliberately when we seek to make sense of and understand feelings, thoughts, or actions that do not make immediate intuitive sense.

Notes

1 Michael S. Brady, *Emotional Insight: The Epistemic Role of Emotional Experience* (Oxford: Oxford University Press, 2013).
2 One philosopher of history who fully appreciates the power—including the affective power—that history exerts upon the historian is Dominick LaCapra: *Writing History, Writing Trauma*, 502; "Tropisms of Intellectual History." Another is the historian Saul Friedländer: "Trauma, Transference and 'Working through' in Writing the History of the 'Shoah'," *History and Memory* 4, no. 1(1992); "Introduction," in *Probing the Limits of Representation: Nazism and the "Final Solution"*, ed. Saul Friedländer (Cambridge, MA: Harvard University Press, 1992).
3 Kohut, *A German Generation*, in particular 17 and 241–242.
4 Roger Frie, "Psychoanalysis and History at the Crossroads: A Dialogue with Thomas Kohut," in *History Flows through Us: Germany, the Holocaust, and the Importance of Empathy*, ed. Roger Frie (London and New York: Routledge, 2018), 167–168, 176–179.
5 LaCapra, *History in Transit*, 5; "History and Psychoanalysis," 228.
6 De Vignemont and Jacob consider this account, which they associate with Alvin Goldman, critically in Frederique De Vignemont and Pierre Jacob, "What Is It Like to Feel Another's Pain?," *Philosophy of Science* 79, no. 2(2012): 310–311.
7 LaCapra, *Writing History, Writing Trauma*, 218; "Tropisms of Intellectual History," 503; "History and Psychoanalysis," 228; *History in Transit*, 43–44.
8 For LaCapra, the basis of empathy in history is the social relationship that is established between the historian and historical subject. *Understanding Others*, 36, also 165–166.
9 Ibid., 2.
10 Ibid., 57, also 122.
11 LaCapra, "History and Psychoanalysis," 228; "Representing the Holocaust: Reflections on the Historians' Debate," in *Probing the Limits of Representation: Nazism and the Final Solution*, ed. Saul Friedländer (Cambridge, MA: Harvard University Press, 1992), 110; *Representing the Holocaust*, 72. Saul Friedländer also argues that the historian should follow the model of the psychoanalyst in being aware of his or her own countertransference and also of the power of the past to evoke experiences in the historian that reflect the reality of past experience. Friedländer, *History and Psychoanalysis*, 18–19.
12 John Demos, "Using Self, Using History … ," *Journal of American History* 89, no. 1(2002): 38.
13 Ibid.; John Demos, *A Little Commonwealth: Family Life in Plymouth Colony* (New York and Oxford: Oxford University Press, 1970).

14 John Demos, *Entertaining Satan: Witchcraft and the Culture of Early Modern New England* (New York and Oxford: Oxford University Press, 1982); "Using Self, Using History," 39.

15 John Demos, *The Unredeemed Captive: A Family Story from Early America* (New York: Knopf, 1994).

16 Demos, "Using Self, Using History," 40.

17 Ibid., 40–41.

18 Ibid., 41.

19 Scheler, *The Nature of Sympathy*, 9.

20 Zahavi and Overgaard, "Empathy without Isomorphism," 7.

21 Douglas Hollan, "Emerging Issues in the Cross-Cultural Study of Empathy," *Emotion Review* 4(2012): 72.

22 Stueber, "Empathy" (2014, Conclusion). See, also, Gerdes, "Empathy, Sympathy, and Pity," 41; Bischof-Köhler, "Empathy and Self-Recognition"; Vaage, "Fiction Film and Empathic Engagement," 164.

23 For a philosophically, psychologically, and historically sophisticated and insightful consideration of the concept of experience, see Donna M. Orange, "Experiential History: Understanding Backwards," in *History Flows through Us: Germany, the Holocaust, and the Importance of Empathy*, ed. Roger Frie (London and New York: Routledge, 2018); also Ankersmit, *Sublime Historical Experience*; Martin Jay, *Songs of Experience: Modern American and European Variations on a Universal Theme* (Berkeley: University of California Press, 2005).

24 Michael Roper, "The Unconscious Work of History," *Cultural and Social History* 11, no. 2(2014): 186 and 171–172.

25 Weber, *Economy and Society*, 1, 5; *Roscher and Knies*, 169.

26 Köhler, "Von der Freud'schen Psychoanalyse zur Selbstpsychologie Heinz Kohuts," 51.

27 Philosophers who have written on Collingwood in recent years include: Giuseppina D'Oro, "Collingwood on Re-Enactment and the Identity of Thought," *Journal of the History of Philosophy* 38(2000); "Re-Enactment and Radical Interpretation"; "Collingwood, Psychologism and Internalism"; Karim Dharamsi, "Re-Enacting in the Second Person," *Journal of the Philosophy of History* 5, no. 2(2011); Jacquette, "Collingwood on Historical Authority and Historical Imagination"; and Sandis, "A Just Medium." Philosophers sympathetic to simulation theory who have written on Collingwood include: Heal, *Mind, Reason, and Imagination*; Stueber, *Rediscovering Empathy*; and Stephen Turner, "Collingwood and Weber vs. Mink: History after the Cognitive Turn," *Journal of the Philosophy of History* 5, no. 2(2011).

28 Certainly, David Hume thought it could: "Sympathy [empathy] is not always limited to the present moment, but that we often feel by communication the pains and pleasures of others, which are not in being, and which we only anticipate by the force of imagination." Hume, *Treatise of Human Nature*, 385.

29 Gadamer, *Truth and Method*, 4.

30 For a succinct account of Gadamer's rejection of historicism, see Retz, *Empathy and History*, 153.

31 Gadamer, *Truth and Method*, 414–415. Indeed, Gadamer was interested primarily in understanding his own cultural tradition and interpreting past texts to which his thought was related and in some form heir.

32 Ibid., 317.

33 Ibid., 307.

34 Ibid., 383.

35 Gadamer's *Truth and Method* exemplifies his hermeneutic philosophy. He enters into dialogue with the texts of the past, with the writings of Plato, Schleiermacher,

Dilthey, and Heidegger. To a certain extent, he seeks to set these writings within the context of the tradition to which they belonged, but mainly he engages in dialogue with these writings to help him develop and articulate his own hermeneutical philosophy. For Gadamer, one engages in dialogue with past texts not simply out of historical interest in those texts. For Gadamer, historical study must have an application, a use in the present. He is not a historian, and he does not study historical texts as historians do—that is, to understand those historical texts and the people who produced and read them as much as possible on their own terms. He is a philosopher, and he studies historical texts in relation to their relevance to today, to our tradition, within the context of our horizon that, in his view, we cannot escape and should not attempt to escape.

36 Gadamer, *Truth and Method*, 345.

37 Ibid., 386.

38 Ibid., 187.

39 Kögler and Stueber agreeing with Gadamer here in "Introduction," 30. This is Gadamer's critique of Schleiermacher for studying a text in order to know the intended meaning of its author, whereby the interpreter thinks his or her way back from the text to the author rethinking the thoughts and re-experiencing the experience of the author through empathy. Gadamer, *Truth and Method*, 191–201.

40 Gadamer, *Truth and Method*, 382.

41 Ermarth, *Wilhelm Dilthey*, 247; Makkreel, *Dilthey*, 325–329.

42 Heal's distinction is affirmed by neuroscience research conducted by Alvin Goldman showing that "mirroring empathy" is more accurate in determining *what* emotional state the other is experiencing, whereas "reconstructive empathy" is more accurate in determining *why* the other is experiencing that emotional state. Goldman, "Two Routes to Empathy," 42–43.

43 Heal, *Mind, Reason, and Imagination*, 15.

44 Ibid., 31. Obviously, in everyday life we use empathy analogously to the way a historian uses empathy when we seek to understand why a person did or felt something in hindsight. Indeed, it is the historian's maintenance of the external observational position before, during, and after empathizing that gives him or her what Fritz Breithaupt calls an "advantage in clarity" over the historical subject. Breithaupt, *Die dunklen Seiten der Empathie*, 17.

45 Stueber seems to imply that we have to be more attentive to difference in empathizing with historical figures than in empathizing in daily life. He argues that, more than in daily life, historians use narrative as a way to overcome cultural and social difference by making interpretations that fit into the narrative of the historical figure's life. Karsten Stueber, "Reasons, Generalizations, Empathy, and Narratives: The Epistemic Structure of Action Explanation," *History and Theory* 47, no. 1(2008): 34–36, 41–43; "Intentionalism, Intentional Realism, and Empathy," *Journal of the Philosophy of History* 3, no. 3(2009): 299–300.

46 Stueber, "Reasons, Generalizations, Empathy, and Narratives," 34–35.

47 Ibid., 41.

48 Ibid., 42–43.

49 Although associated with theory theory, "folk psychology," in Stueber's use of the term, seems less an implicit theory about human psychology that we apply to those we encounter and more our understanding of others using basic empathy.

50 Stueber, "Intentionalism, Intentional Realism, and Empathy," 291, 296–297.

51 Ibid., 292.

52 Ibid., 301; Stueber, "Understanding Versus Explanation," 26.

53 Hollan, "Emerging Issues in the Cross-Cultural Study of Empathy," 71.

54 I am indebted to the philosopher Bojana Mladenovic for emphasizing the importance of affective-sharing in our everyday human interactions and, indeed, the role played by shared feelings in historical knowledge and understanding. The importance of affective sharing in everyday life may account for the fact that, according to Tyson Retz, empathy is ordinarily conceived of as shared feeling and not as a form of cognition. Retz, *Empathy and History*, 218.

Chapter 7

The Authority of the Empathizing Historian

This chapter explores the empathizing historian's "authority" understood in several slightly different but closely related, even overlapping, ways. The chapter considers the authority that the empathizing historian exercises over and relinquishes to the people of the past, particularly in comparison with historians who occupy more or less exclusively the external observational position; put another way, it considers the empathizing historian's autonomy, or, perhaps better, sovereignty in relation to the past. The chapter also considers the authority of empathically derived historical reconstructions and interpretations, their validity, the evidentiary- or truth-value of empathic claims about the past. And the chapter considers the authority of the empathizing historian as author, as re-presenter and interpreter of the past, as writer of history, including his or her empathic responsibility to the reader. In considering the authority of the empathizing historian in these various forms, I take the position, as I have throughout, that the past has considerably more autonomy and exerts considerably more authority over historians than they have traditionally been wont to acknowledge. Indeed, to maintain their sense of autonomy and the illusion that their authority over the past is more or less complete, some historians apparently would rather face the charge that historical knowledge is self-projection than recognize how powerfully the past affects what they know and understand, what they write, and even who they are.

Empathy and the Historian's Authority over the Past

It would seem that the historian who adopts the empathic position relinquishes considerable authority over the past by restricting what can be known to the perspective of the historical subject. Indeed, the empathizing historian would actually always seem to know less than the historical subject, to be lagging behind and scrambling to keep up. Frustratingly, empathic knowledge appears at best a pale reflection of the original experience of the people of the past. By contrast, the historian who adopts the external observational vantage point can view the past directly and clearly; can see and know more than the people of the past did, including, with the benefit of hindsight, the consequences of their actions; and can pass judgment on them and on their deeds.

Traditionally, social scientific historians saw the position of the external observer as making more or less objective knowledge of the past possible. They rejected empathic history for narrowing what can be known about history to the always limited and frequently distorted perspective of the historical actors. Thus, according to the analytic philosopher Arthur Danto, participants in historical events "have no privileged status when it comes to historical explanations," and the historian who adopts their perspective generally understands those events less well than the externally observing historian.[1] For Marxist historians, empathic history with its focus on motivation and experience overlooks what really matters in history, human productive activity, its material context, and its consequences. That activity, which ultimately determines motivation and experience, can best be known from the external observational position—not from the subjective perspective of the historical actors. Indeed, in understanding historical activity, what the people of the past thought they were doing might well be irrelevant, limited, or in error. The empathizing historian would fail to critique, appreciate, or perhaps even perceive the "false consciousness" of historical actors.

Similarly, historians influenced by Michel Foucault, like Joan Scott, see the empathic historian, who accepts the experience of the people of the past, as failing to question and even as unwittingly affirming the power structures and dominant discourses that helped create and shape past people's experience in the first place. Acceptance of the evidence of experience, according to Scott, "precludes analysis of the working of this system [of the construction of experience] and of its historicity; instead, it reproduces its terms."[2] Even, or perhaps especially, for marginalized groups, the empathic historian effectively reinforces their marginal status by failing to interrogate how their experience of marginalization was socially and culturally constituted.[3] In criticizing empathic historians for accepting rather than critically examining the subjective experience of past people from a detached observational position, Scott echoes Bertolt Brecht's critique of theater that encouraged the audience to identify "itself with the characters in the play." Rather than develop empathy for those characters, Brecht sought deliberately to "alienate" the audience from them, thereby putting the audience in a position of emotional detachment that would enable it to view the characters, their actions, and their situation critically.[4] Critical detachment would in turn put the audience in a position to change the status quo rather than simply accept it.

Following the shift away from high political history, historians have tended to privilege accounts that see history created not *by* people but *for* people, that see human beings as more shaped by than shaping history, perhaps in part because these accounts empower the historian at the expense of the people of the past. In such accounts the historian is able to see and analyze what the people of the past frequently could not: namely the economic forces, the structures and processes, or the discourses that shaped their feelings, thoughts, and actions; their experience and understanding of themselves and of their world; the way they lived their lives.

As we have seen, however, historians never occupy the empathic position continuously or completely; and, when occupying the external observational position, they preserve the authority over the past that the external observational position affords—albeit an authority limited and mediated by what they see and know and understand from the empathic perspective, from the perspective of the historical subject. It is from our own observational position that we decide which aspects of historical experience we wish to know, aspects that may be more important to us than they were to the people of the past. In particular, hindsight can influence which experiences of past people we seek to understand empathically. When weaving empathically reconstructed experiences into a narrative and when forging empathically derived insights about those experiences into an analysis, we write from a perspective that transcends the perspective of the people of the past and we incorporate factors of which those people were unaware, including again the consequences of their actions.[5] Following our empathic immersion in the experience of past people, we return to the position of the outside observer should we wish to assess or judge them. Even while empathizing, we maintain our own sense of self, remain with at least part of ourselves in the external observational position. From that position, we are able to empathize critically, to reflect on what we are re-experiencing.

Nineteenth-century theorizers of empathy like Droysen and Dilthey already recognized that the re-experience of past experience in one's imagination was not by itself sufficient for historical understanding. By bringing contexts and coherences of which the person of the past was unaware to bear on his experience, historians were in a position to understand that person better than he understood himself.[6] Likewise, Collingwood dismissed historians who simply took the historical subject's account at face value and presented that account to tell a story as "scissors-and-paste" historians.[7] The empathizing historian, according to Collingwood, not only rethought past thought; he also thought *about* past thought in a "labour of active and therefore critical thinking." Transcending the experience of the historical actor, the historian brought his knowledge, particularly of the actor's context, to bear on the thought of the actor and judged that thought. Indeed, active criticism of past thought while rethinking it was for Collingwood "an indispensable condition of historical knowledge itself."[8] Thus, although the historical subject's experiences and motives remain, in the words of Karsten Stueber, the "proper objects of interpretation," the empathizing historian cannot be bound by the historical subject's perspective. The historian must understand the historical subject's experiences and motives within the context of "a complex environment" that transcended the subject and to which the subject consciously and unconsciously responded.[9]

Thus we occupy the external observational position before, after, and even while empathizing, a position that enables us to transcend the perspective of the historical subject. It would also appear that knowledge of the historical subject's personality, commitments, values, desires, fears, and so forth—and especially of the historical subject's whole "life curve"—is actually integral to the empathizing process itself.[10] That knowledge enables us to focus and fine-tune empathy; to see, appreciate, and understand aspects of the subject's experience of which the subject may have been more or less unconscious at the particular moment in his or her life we are seeking to understand. Our knowledge of the historical subject's personality and life does not enable us to transcend the subject's experience by viewing it from without but deepens our empathic knowledge of that experience while viewing it from within.

Despite the fact then that understanding the people of the past empathically always means on some level scrambling to keep up with them, despite the fact that we must concede our ultimate empathic inadequacy, that we can only know another empathically to an attenuated degree, we nevertheless can *on some level* understand the people of the past more deeply and comprehensively than they understood themselves. It is the notion of the "unconscious" that allows for that deeper, more comprehensive understanding. On the one hand, following Koselleck, the historian can know experiences and expectations of which the historical subject may have been unconscious in a cultural and social sense. Our experiences are not all fully conscious because they include cultural and social experiences and practices so imbedded in us that we are unaware of them. And expectations need not be wholly conscious either because they represent at once our own personal hopes and fears and those of the culture and society to which we belong.[11] On the other hand, the historian can know experiences and expectations of which the historical subject may be unconscious in a more traditionally psychoanalytic sense. According to Gadamer, Friedrich Schleiermacher, one of the nineteenth century's principal advocates of empathy, believed that the interpreter can "claim superiority over his object" since the aim of understanding "is not the author's reflective self-interpretation but the unconscious meaning of the author that is to be understood." The interpreter, "through thought, through elaborating the implications of an author's ideas," is able "to achieve insights into the real intention of the author—insights he would have shared if his thinking had been clear enough."[12] Similarly, according to Karim Dharamsi, Collingwood's view of historical knowledge "involves understanding others as they *might* understand themselves."[13] In William Dray's account, Collingwood "doesn't hesitate to ascribe to historians what is often ascribed to psychoanalysts: the capacity to discover in the record of what a person did various thoughts of which that person was quite unaware."[14]

Indeed, historians should be reassured about their ability to empathize with aspects of past experience that were not altogether conscious for the people who had them, about their ability to understand the people of the past better than they understood themselves, by the example of psychoanalysts who are able to think and feel their way inside experiences of patients of which the patients are largely or even completely unaware. In psychoanalysis or psychoanalytic psychotherapy, the analyst is able to offer empathic interpretations that are in tune with and make sense of the patient's experience but which the patient is unable to arrive at on his own. If expressed in the appropriate language and at the appropriate time (when the patient is in some sense ready to hear it), the analyst's understanding is then validated by the patient himself, by his sense that he has been understood. Obviously, such validation is not possible in history. But if our empathic interpretations capture and make sense of our historical subjects' experience, we can at least *imagine* that they might have been accepted, might have been validated, by those subjects. The philosopher Karl-Otto Apel, in arguing for a view of understanding in the human sciences that makes the people of the past not "objects" of investigation but "virtual co-subjects of interaction and communication," suggests that the historian engage in an imaginary empathic conversation with the people of the past, in which the historian brings the voices of those people to life in the present.[15] Such an imaginary conversation suggests the possibility that the historian, like the psychoanalyst, might bring the people of the past to a knowledge and understanding of themselves that they could not have arrived at on their own. In my own work, first on Kaiser Wilhelm II and then on Germans who had been active in the youth movement during the Weimar Republic, I made interpretations that neither the Kaiser nor this group of Germans had made about themselves, interpretations that transcended their conscious knowledge of themselves. Nevertheless I fantasize and on some level actually believe that if my interpretations were empathic interpretations, if they captured and made sense of the experience of Kaiser Wilhelm II and of those former youth movement members, then both might ultimately have come to accept my interpretations, have come in fact to feel understood.

In writing history, the historian—including the empathic historian—imposes meaning and coherence on the people of the past in ways that go beyond their experience. But the people of the past also impose meaning on historical writing. As has been emphasized here again and again, we should not overlook the power that the past exerts over us. The writing of history is a dialectical process involving present and past, historian and historical material. In effect, history writing is a collaboration between historian and historical subject.[16] The externally observing historian cedes less authority to the people of the past in that collaboration; the empathically observing historian grants them considerably more.[17]

Empathy's Heuristic and Evidentiary Value

As was discussed in the historical excursus, a number of those who insisted that we know the human and the natural worlds in essentially the same way, such as the positivist philosopher Carl Hempel, did not reject empathy outright.

Imagining one's way inside the experience of historical actors could conceivably have heuristic value if it allowed the historian to arrive at hypotheses about the motivation for their actions. Those hypotheses possessed no evidentiary value, however. The explanations they inspired still needed to be verified using the methods of the natural sciences, data, logic, and empirically proven universal laws.[18] Max Weber also thought that empathy could be used to gain access to the subjective meaning that was the focus of knowledge in the human sciences; but empathy needed to be supplemented by logic, abstraction, and comparison if empathically derived explanations were to have social-scientific validity.[19] He expressly derided the notion that the historian should attempt to evoke empathized feelings in the reader, where emotional contagion takes the place of rigorous causal analysis: "Subjective, emotional 'interpretation' in this form does not constitute empirical, historical knowledge."[20] Empathy meant shared feeling for Weber, and, as noted above, he failed to connect logic, reason, and evidence with empathic understanding. Empathizing historians, in his account, merely felt but did not think or reason their way inside the subjective experience of the historical subject. He failed to see that empathy, although it may involve shared feeling, is a rational mode of cognition based on historical evidence.[21]

In seeking to refute Weber's claim that empathy, while able to generate hypotheses, has no evidentiary value, the philosopher Peter Winch argued that, to be accepted, an empathic interpretation does not require logical and empirical verification from without. Instead, an empathic interpretation needs to be verified from within, within the context of the life world or within the rules of the language game to which that being interpreted belongs and is given meaning.[22] In essence, the empathic nature of the interpretation itself is what ultimately lends it validity.[23]

And yet the question remains: Who in history determines that an interpretation has empathic validity; that it makes sense from within the subjective experience of the people of the past; and that it is verified from within the context of the world it seeks to comprehend? In history, it is the reader who, at least initially, plays an important role here. In the case of empathically derived interpretations, these are accepted when readers are able to follow the historian's empathy along, when they come to empathize with the people of the past as a result of the empathic work that the historian has done. Empathy then has, in Hempel's phrase, "scientific value" in and of itself. Keeping in mind that empathy in history is largely a rational form of cognition, based on logic and evidence, the historian's ability to engender empathy for the historical subject in the reader "verifies" the interpretation of the historical subject for that reader. Indeed, it is one of the empathizing historian's principal tasks to engender empathic understanding on the part of the reader.

In the literature on empathy, the historian's task of engendering empathy for the historical subject on the part of the reader appears to have been almost entirely overlooked. One notable exception is Karsten Stueber.[24]

Another is Peter Winch, who considered empathy more in an anthropological than in a historical context. According to Winch, who was much influenced by Wittgenstein's concept of language games, the investigator must translate the language game and life form of the people being studied into a language game and a life form that readers can understand.[25] What Winch effectively calls translation, I would characterize as fostering empathy in the reader, helping readers to step out of their space of experience and horizon of expectation in order to adopt in their imagination the space of experience and the horizon of expectation of the people of the past.

Perhaps a parallel can be drawn between empathic validation in history and in psychoanalysis or psychoanalytic psychotherapy. As noted above, the psychotherapist is able to arrive at an understanding of her patient, can make sense of her patient's experience, in a way that the patient himself cannot. And yet in psychotherapy, the validity of the therapist's understanding is ultimately determined not by the analyst but by the patient, who feels understood by the interpretation that has been made of him and his experience. Although I suggested above that as a historian one can imagine the people of the past ultimately coming to accept one's interpretation of them, in history the validation provided by the patient in psychotherapy would seem to be provided by each individual reader, at least until a professional consensus about the validity of the interpretation emerges. In both psychoanalysis and history, then, interpretations are designed to make the subject empathically understandable. The validity of explanation in psychoanalysis and in history depends to some degree on the psychoanalyst or the historian being able to communicate empathic understanding in such a way that the person being addressed, be he patient or reader, empathically understands the subject as well.[26] The reader needs to be able to join the historian in his or her empathic work, not simply to accept its results but to think along the way those results were arrived at.

The Criticism that Empathy Cannot Bridge the Gulf of Place and Time

Whereas those who see history as a rational social science criticize empathy for being emotional, overly reliant on the imagination, and lacking empirical rigor, those at the opposite end of the philosophical spectrum criticize empathy for failing to appreciate the gulf separating the historian from the people of the past.[27] For the former critics, empathic history fails to attend sufficiently to human similarities, generalities, and regularities, even to the universal laws governing human nature and human conduct; for the latter critics, empathic history fails to attend sufficiently to historical and cultural difference, difference that makes empathic understanding ultimately impossible. For these critics, often influenced by postmodernism and/or belonging to the hermeneutic tradition, empathizing historians do not so much imagine their way or think their way inside the experience of past people; instead, they impose themselves, their life world, and/or their historical horizon on past people. Empathy in this account is simply projection masquerading as knowledge of the other.[28] The fundamental problem, according to critics like Hans-Georg Gadamer, is that empathic historians fail to appreciate their own historicity.[29] We are so much suffused by the values, norms, language, by the ways of being, feeling, and thinking of our own time that we simply cannot put them to one side. They define us; they shape us; they constitute us. They create an "insuperable distance" separating the interpreter from what is being interpreted.[30] As the historian William V. Harris puts it, "what really makes life difficult for historical empathizers, and indeed seems to put them out of business, is the sheer *otherness* of the people we are normally trying to investigate."[31]

As has been emphasized here, the view of empathy as projection is based upon the false assumptions that we are more or less impervious to the influence of the past and that our authority over the past is more or less complete. It fails to recognize and to appreciate the considerable authority that the past exercises over us. And it fails to recognize and to appreciate that we are in a reciprocal emotional and cognitive relationship with the past. The past is not some lifeless object awaiting our dissection, and we do not simply determine what we know and write about it. Instead, the past calls out to us. It collaborates with us, codetermining what we think and what we write. And our interaction with the past influences us, changes us, makes us different than we were before.

The assertion of insuperable distance in the postmodern and hermeneutical critique of empathy seems not to have been arrived at empirically or introspectively, but to be the logical product of a particular abstract philosophical position. What evidence do those asserting absolute historicity present or can they present to invalidate the claim that certain universal human experiences connect historian and historical subject, shared experiences that enable the historian empathically to understand the historical subject? What evidence do these critics of empathy present or can they present to demonstrate that we lack the imaginative capacity to transcend our historical moment, to know historical difference, to understand things we have never experienced, to step outside of our life world into another, to learn the language games played by other cultures in other times?[32] After all, in living our lives, we are able to step outside of our own skin and into the skin of others, and do so all the time.

Not only does this critique of empathy seem derived less from life than from a philosophical position; the philosophical position, on which this critique is based, seems problematic. Many adopting this philosophical position would reject the Cartesian assumption that all we can ultimately know is ourselves, and would emphasize the fact that the self and knowledge are culturally constituted. Nevertheless, in critiquing the possibility of empathy in history, they appear to introduce what might be called "cultural Cartesianism"—that human beings lack the capacity to transcend their own historical and cultural moment, that we can only really know the time and culture to which we belong and whose product we ultimately are. This "cultural Cartesianism" seems uncomfortably close to the claim that all we can really know is ourselves. Individual epistemological autonomy is rejected in favor of cultural epistemological autonomy. Now we are not imprisoned within ourselves; now we are imprisoned within our own culture and historical moment. But we are neither personally nor culturally autonomous. We are trapped neither within ourselves nor within our own culture or historical moment. As individuals, we are influenced and even changed by the people with whom we interact. As historians, we are influenced and even changed by the past people and past cultures with whom we interact as well. And we possess the imaginative capacity to transcend ourselves and our personal experiences and to transcend our cultural and historical moment, to empathize with and know other people, including those of other times and other places.

On the one hand, the criticism that those using empathy in the human sciences fail to appreciate differences of place and time seems an apt response to traditional histories that either ignored non-Western cultures or projected Western European cultures and Western European psychologies on the non-Western world. On the other hand, that criticism seems curious since in recent decades it has been empathizing cultural historians who have generally most appreciated cultural and historical difference and the role played by culture and history in shaping the self and the ways people experience themselves and their world. Despite the tendency of some historians in the nineteenth and twentieth centuries to ignore or overlook historical and cultural difference, the appreciation of difference on the part of scholars who use empathy in knowing other times and places goes back as least as far as Herder, whose central message, according to Isaiah Berlin, was:

> that one must not judge one culture by the criteria of another; that differing civilizations are different growths, pursue different goals, embody different ways of living, are dominated by different attitudes to life; so that to understand them one must perform an imaginative act of "empathy" into their essence, understand them 'from within' as far as possible, and see the world through their eyes.[33]

According to John Connelly and Alan Costall, Collingwood was highly critical of Sigmund Freud for drawing conclusions about "savages" in *Totem and Taboo*, based on his work with neurotic patients in his practice in early twentieth-century Vienna. In Collingwood's view, Freud was unable to enter the "savage mind" because he approached it as an outward phenomenon, "completely separate from the 'civilized mind' that is studying it." Likewise William James in his study of religion failed to empathize, according to Collingwood, and only gave "an 'external' account of the object of study," thereby "cutting himself off from any kind of real sympathy or participation in the very thing he is studying—this man's mental life and experiences."[34] By contrast, Collingwood, very like Peter Winch as quoted above, "advocated a historical psychology that captured and mapped the mental life of people at a particular moment in their history, as a form of history"; and he rejected "transnational and transhistorical" psychological "generalizations, concepts, and categories" that were not subject to historical change.[35]

On the one hand, empathic history, like psychoanalysis, seeks to reveal the underlying rationality of the apparently irrational. On the other hand, empathic history seeks to historicize irrationality. In considering the behavior of the various historical actors in Germany at the end of the First World War, I emphasized that it is important from the empathic perspective to identify the "laws" of historical development as defined not by an "objective" outside observer but by the historical participants themselves. In the same way, it is important from the empathic perspective to know not what seems irrational to us about past people and their conduct but to know what seemed irrational to the people of the past and to work out how they based their thoughts and actions on their particular definitions of the "irrational" and the "rational," the "abnormal" and the "normal."[36]

It is precisely the awareness of cultural and historical difference that prompts the historian to seek to empathize, and it is precisely the attenuated nature of empathy that enables the historian to grasp that the other is in fact different.[37] As Magdalena Nowak puts it, "the feeling of empathy" helps us not only to understand the historical actor "but also to see the difference, the incompatibility between his feelings" and our own, to experience what Dominick LaCapra calls "empathic unsettlement."[38] Empathy, then, allows us to connect emotionally and intellectually with people who initially seem very different from us, perhaps even alien. And yet empathy also allows us to appreciate and to respect their difference from us. Stepping into another's space of experience and horizon of expectation, into another's skin, conveys on a deep emotional and intellectual level the gulf separating us from others even as we seek to bridge that gulf through the exercise of our imagination. Indeed, it is precisely the awareness of difference that distinguishes empathy from contagion, merger, and identification. In sum, empathy allows us to experience simultaneously how we can be like the people of the past and how very different we are from them all at the same time.[39]

Notes

1. Danto, *Analytical Philosophy of History*, 232.
2. Scott, "Evidence of Experience," 779.
3. Ibid., 771.
4. Sandis, "A Just Medium." Sandis contrasts Brecht's conscious efforts to hinder the development of empathy on the part of the theater audience with Constantin Stanislavski's "overly empathetic" method, whereby the actor was to "enter the character of the person whose actions are in question." Ibid., 187. See, also, Nowak, "The Complicated History of Einfühlung," 314; Oliver, "The Aesth-*Ethics* of Empathy," 167, 176.
5. This is Karsten Stueber's account of the criticism of the "intentionalist" or empathic position for restricting historians to the perspective on the past taken by

the historical actors, a criticism which Stueber himself rejects. Stueber, "Intentionalism, Intentional Realism, and Empathy," 296–297. See also his "Reasons, Generalizations, Empathy, and Narratives"; also Carr, "Narrative Explanation and Its Malcontents," 21; LaCapra, *Understanding Others*, 113.

6 Maclean, "Droysen and the Development of Historical Hermeneutics," 358–359; Ermarth, *Wilhelm Dilthey*, 276, 278.

7 Collingwood, *The Idea of History*, 275.

8 Ibid., 215, 246, 292; Dray, *History as Re-Enactment*, 40–42, 199; Retz, *Empathy and History*, 118, 127–128, 131, 133.

9 Stueber, *Rediscovering Empathy*, 197, 201.

10 This is a phrase coined by the psychoanalyst Heinz Kohut.

11 Koselleck, "'Erfahrungsraum' und 'Erwartungshorizont'," 354–355; "'Space of Experience' and 'Horizon of Expectation'," 272.

12 Gadamer, *Truth and Method*, 199–201.

13 Dharamsi, "Re-Enacting in the Second Person," 165.

14 Dray, *History as Re-Enactment*, 40, also 111.

15 Apel, "The Erklären-Verstehen Controversy," 33.

16 Kohut, *A German Generation*, 13; also LaCapra, *History in Transit*, 105; Retz, *Empathy and History*, 12, 65, 69, 118, 166.

17 LaCapra, *History in Transit*, 78–79.

18 Hempel, "The Function of General Laws in History," 44–45. See, also, Abel, "The Operation Called Verstehen," 217; Gruner, "Understanding in the Social Sciences and History," 160–162; Nagel, *The Structure of Science*, 483–485.

19 Weber, *Roscher and Knies*, 185–186.

20 Ibid., 180–181.

21 Collingwood, *The Idea of History*, 246; Dray, *History as Re-Enactment*, 199.

22 Peter Winch, *The Idea of a Social Science and Its Relation to Philosophy* (London: Routledge and Kegan Paul, 1970; originally published 1958), 113–115.

23 In what seems a related argument, the philosopher Robert Nozick sees empathy as having more than simply heuristic value. Empathic understanding is plausible understanding, according to Nozick, and plausibility is a respected criterion in science. Nozick sees "the inferential reliability" of empathic understanding "as empirical, just like any other inference by analogy." Nozick, *Philosophical Explanations*, 636 and 638.

24 While acknowledging that re-enactment (in the mind first of the historian and then in the mind of the reader) cannot allow the reader to judge between competing interpretations, Stueber asserts that re-enactment remains "essential in judging the intrinsic plausibility of each interpretive proposal as a reconstruction of rational agency." Stueber, *Rediscovering Empathy*, 204.

25 Winch, "Understanding a Primitive Society."

26 Kohut, "Psychohistory as History," 344. Although he makes no reference to empathy in this context, see, also, Mink, "Autonomy of Historical Understanding," 45.

27 Taylor, "Historical Subjectivity," 203–204.

28 Clifford Geertz, for example, is critical of the use of empathy in anthropology, yet his definition of empathy as some form of mystical merger or communion is not empathy as defined here. Indeed, what Geertz advocates in understanding other peoples—setting one's own Western conceptions aside in order to "view their experiences within the framework" of their own conceptions—is precisely how I define empathy. That said, Geertz's view remains perhaps more that of the external observer than of the empathic one. He seems reluctant, once the framework of the other people's conceptions has been reconstructed, to try to think his way inside that worldview in order to understand specific actions, thoughts, and experiences

from within it. Clifford Geertz, "'From the Native's Point of View': On the Nature of Anthropological Understanding," *Bulletin of the American Academy of Arts and Sciences* 28, no. 1(1974): 31.

29 Gadamer, it seems, has not escaped a serious and troubling philosophical and ethical problem connected with his own historicity. His fundamental critique of those belonging to the historical school is that they never acknowledged their own historicity, never appreciated that their own position in history affected how and what they saw in the past. According to Gadamer, the historian can never escape his own historical position. It is only within the context of his own cultural and historical horizon that he engages in dialogue with texts embedded in their own very different historical positions, the product of very different historical moments, bounded by their own very different cultural and historical horizons. He emphasizes the critical importance of recognizing and being conscious of one's own historical position, of one's own horizon, in seeking to engage in dialogue with past texts. Yet Gadamer's own book, *Truth and Method*, seems entirely divorced from its own historical moment, its own historical position, its own historical horizon. Gadamer is mostly in dialogue with Socrates and Plato, with Kant and Hegel, with Schleiermacher and Dilthey, and most recently with Heidegger. This is a book published in the 1950s, and much of it was probably written before then, during the Third Reich and the Second World War. Where are Hitler and the Third Reich in *Truth and Method?* Where is the defeat of Nazi Germany in the book? Where is the Holocaust? How does Gadamer's own position in history inform this work? By not bringing in his own historical position into explicit view, Gadamer's book can be read as an effort to reclaim German Romanticism and nineteenth-century hermeneutics from Western social science. Indeed, the historian Richard Wolin, in a compelling intellectual and political critique of Gadamer, makes clear that the philosopher's conservative embrace of Germany's unique intellectual historical path brought him uncomfortably close to National Socialism during the Third Reich. Richard Wolin, *The Seduction of Unreason: The Intellectual Romance with Fascism from Nietzsche to Postmodernism* (Princeton: Princeton University Press, 2004), 89–128.

30 Gadamer, *Truth and Method*, 307.

31 Harris, "History, Empathy and Emotions," 10; see also Jenkins, *Re-Thinking History*, particularly 47–49. For an account of Jenkin's critique of empathy, see Retz, *Empathy and History*, 67–68.

32 Winch, *Social Science and Its Relation to Philosophy*; "Understanding a Primitive Society."

33 Berlin, *Vico and Herder*, 210.

34 Connelly and Costall, "Collingwood and the Idea of an Historical Psychology," 155–156.

35 Ibid., 160.

36 In Peter Winch's example of the Freudian psychoanalyst trying to understand a patient from the Trobriand Islands, the psychoanalyst could not simply "apply without further reflection the concepts developed by Freud for situations arising in our society. He would have first to investigate such things as the idea of fatherhood amongst the islanders and take into account any relevant aspects in which their idea differed from that current in his own society. And it is almost inevitable that such an investigation would lead to some modification in the psychological theory appropriate for explaining neurotic behaviour in this new situation." Winch, *Social Science and Its Relation to Philosophy*, 90.

37 Zahavi and Overgaard, "Empathy without Isomorphism," 9.

38 Nowak, "The Complicated History of Einfühlung," 317; LaCapra, *Writing History, Writing Trauma*, xi, 78; *History in Transit*, 65, 125.

39 Kohut, *A German Generation*, 18–19.

Chapter 8

Concluding Remarks

Empathy in Psychoanalysis and in History

As I argued more than thirty years ago, both psychoanalysis and history rely on empathy to know and understand their human subjects.[1] In both disciplines, one seeks to transcend one's own subjective responses in order to try to experience, if to a necessarily attenuated degree, the experience of the other. In both disciplines, one thinks and feels and imagines one's way inside the experience of the other in order to understand why—given one's knowledge of the other, of the other's past and present circumstances, and of the other's expectations for the future—it makes sense that the other felt, thought, and acted as he or she did.[2] And both history and psychoanalysis assume that people in the present and in the past felt, thought, and acted for good reasons, although those reasons may not be obvious at first glance.

It is empathy that sets psychoanalysis and psychoanalytic therapy apart from other forms of psychology and other types of psychological treatment. Thus, psychiatry and the psychopharmacological treatment of mental illness are generally not based upon empathy. Here, the psychiatrist occupies the position of external observer who, on the basis of the manifestations of the patient's mental and emotional state, diagnoses that state, and, based on that diagnosis, prescribes the appropriate medication.[3] Cognitive behavioral therapy also is not based on empathy. Instead, it helps clients develop cognitive and behavioral strategies to manage their mental and emotional states. There is little attempt in cognitive behavioral therapy to understand *why* clients feel as they do. Empirical psychology, the dominant form of contemporary academic psychology, does not rely primarily on empathy either and focuses instead on phenomena that can be externally observed and very often measured.[4] By contrast, psychoanalysis as "depth psychology" investigates complex mental states that cannot be directly observed and are ultimately knowable through introspection and empathy. Of course, knowledge obtained via introspection and empathy can inform empirical psychological studies, and knowledge obtained via empirical psychological studies can facilitate and/or confirm the empathic understanding of underlying complex mental states. Nevertheless, it is the introspective-empathic stance of the observer that defines psychoanalysis as a discipline and that distinguishes it from empirical psychology, which observes psychological phenomena largely from an external, "extrospective" perspective.[5]

As in history, the psychoanalyst does not occupy the empathic observational position exclusively, however; and psychoanalytic listening involves, in the words of Martha Nussbaum, a "'two-fold attention,' in which one both imagines what it is like to be in the sufferer's place, and, at the same time, retains securely the awareness that one is not in that place."[6] As the psychoanalyst Evelyne Schwaber puts it, "analytic listening has employed the use of two realities—that of the observer from 'outside,' and that from within (albeit the expressed province of our analytic concern lies with the latter—the patient's subjective reality)."[7]

To illustrate perspective-shifting in psychoanalytically informed psychotherapy, let me present an example from my brief career as a therapist. I had a young man in his first year of law school in treatment. At one point in our work together, he came to a session and announced that he was thinking of dropping out of law school in order to become a professional magician. As an outside observer, I was struck by his announcement in much the same way historians have traditionally been struck by the decision of the majority Socialists to ally with the anti-republican forces of the authoritarian Right at the beginning of the Weimar Republic. In the case of the majority Socialists, their decision seemed worthy of explanation primarily because we know its ultimate consequences. In the case of my client, his intention to become a magician seemed worthy of explanation both because it represented a radical departure from his previous life trajectory and because I had concerns about its potential consequences for him. With my client, I left the external observational position, from which his intention seemed unrealistic and inappropriate, to adopt the empathic position, his subjective position. From that vantage point, from his vantage point, I sought to explore with the young man, from within his "space of experience" and "horizon of expectation," why it made sense for him to want to drop out of law school to become a magician. I tried to understand my client's wish on as deep a level as I could, to understand why from his perspective the idea of becoming a magician made psychological sense, and I communicated that understanding to him in the form of interpretations. Although I tried to empathize with his desire to become a magician, from the position of an external observer I certainly did not "sympathize" with that desire. Indeed, from my point of view I thought his becoming a magician would be a mistake.

The nature and challenge of psychoanalytic empathy is beautifully captured by the advice that the psychoanalyst and psychiatrist Elvin Semrad gave to a group of first-year psychiatric residents who were about to encounter seriously ill psychiatric patients for the first time at the Massachusetts Mental Health Center in Boston in the late 1960s. Semrad's remarks, as reported by one of those residents, deserve to be quoted in full.

There were twenty-two of us, scared to death. Semrad gathered us into his office and gave us the following lecture. "Very shortly, you will be going onto your assigned wards. Within those wards, you will see over fifty of the sickest, craziest, most bizarre people you will ever encounter. They will be hallucinating, gesticulating, and delusional in the most grotesque ways. Every cell in your body will rebel and want to block out the experience. But here is the thing you must remember. Every one of those symptoms, as strange as they may seem to you, makes perfect sense to those people. Every single one has been evolved and carefully crafted to try to deal with some impossible family situation. Every one represents an attempt by that person to adapt to the hand that fate has dealt him. You are to regard each one as an artistic, creative endeavor to survive. Your job, and your only job, is to appreciate, and admire that effort."[8]

Both psychoanalysis and history, then, can be described as rationalizing disciplines, and, in both, empathy can play a central role in the rationalizing process. Both history and psychoanalysis seek in part to understand how what seems "irrational," bizarre, or simply odd from an external observational perspective (e.g., the majority Socialists' decision to ally with the Old Order, the central focus of attention on defining who was a Jew during the Wannsee Conference, my client's desire to become a professional magician, the delusions of patients on a hospital psychiatric ward) makes sense from an empathic perspective. Both psychoanalysis and history seek in part to find the underlying rationale or at least the underlying meaning of what may seem irrational or meaningless when viewed from without.[9] To be sure, both psychoanalysts and historians never understand their human subjects completely, and psychoanalytic and historical empathy is always attenuated. Indeed, certain psychological experiences—like those of psychotic patients on a psychiatric ward—and certain historical experiences—like that of an SS man standing with a machine gun before a trench filled with helpless naked people—may lie at the very limit of our empathic-imaginative capacities.[10] Nevertheless, we have an obligation to attempt to understand those extreme experiences and the people who had them, not least to avoid dehumanizing those people by closing off our empathy for them, to appreciate the bond that connects us to them, and to recognize that we have within us the capacity to be as they were.[11]

Some Implications of Recognizing Empathy's Role in Historical Knowledge

When we seek to understand the people of the past empathically, to adopt their observational position, we take a different approach to the past than when we approach the past as social scientists who know the past more or less exclusively from the position of the outside observer. These different observational stances promote different research strategies. The historian as external observer would generally approach historical subjects with a hypothesis. Intensive research would then either validate or invalidate the hypothesis or, more likely, cause the historian to revise and rearticulate the hypothesis. The empathizing historian would generally approach historical subjects in a way closer to that taken by the psychoanalyst, who seeks to listen to the patient with an open mind, who seeks to immerse herself in the patient's experience, to suspend judgment, to push theory into the background, to listen to the patient's voice. This seems to me to be what the empathic historian should do in listening to the voices of past people.[12] To be sure, we may approach those people with a question or a problem in mind based on our personal commitments and concerns, or on the commitments and concerns of our cultural and historical moment. Our knowledge of the ultimate consequences of historical actions and ideas may influence what we wish to know and understand about the past. And, finally, as I have suggested, we employ empathy when we are confronted with something that does not make sense to us viewed from without. Nevertheless, the empathic historian should still be inclined to let his or her question emerge not from present-day concerns, perhaps even present-day historiographical concerns. The empathic historian's question generally should emerge from the past itself.

An appreciation of the central role that empathy can play in historical knowledge of the human past has implications for graduate education in history. Indeed, first in 1942 and then in 1950, the sociologist Leonard Cottrell argued that graduate students should be trained in the use of empathy. Such training would make social scientists more effective in using themselves as instruments of investigation, he thought, in part by heightening their self-consciousness while empathizing.[13] My graduate education in history at least did not seek to develop my historical imagination or my capacity to empathize. Empathizing with the people of the past was never mentioned, let alone taught. Instead, my graduate education focused on developing my critical skills, as week after week I learned to identify historical arguments and to critique them. Although speaking in the context of psychoanalytic training, Lotte Köhler's admonition applies equally to the training of historians: "Scientific empathy ... is a highly specific way of knowing that must be learned and practiced."[14] Although over the last decades in the United States, Canada, Australia, and the United Kingdom there has been discussion about teaching secondary-level students to empathize, as far as I know there has been no discussion about teaching college or graduate students how to use empathy to know the past.[15] If imagination is an essential aspect of the historian's craft, then we need to think explicitly about its role in historical understanding and we need to train graduate students in its use. Graduate education that focuses on critique fosters the development of critical thinking; graduate education that focuses on empathy fosters understanding. These are potentially related but ultimately distinct intellectual projects.

Résumé

Over the course of this book, I have presented my ideas about empathy in relation to the ideas of others, for in virtually every instance my ideas derive from
theirs. Perhaps as a result, my own views on empathy have been insufficiently
salient. Let me conclude, therefore, by summarizing the principal points I have
sought to make regarding the role of empathy in historical knowledge.

Historians have long used empathy to know and understand the human
past. Indeed, with the advent of cultural history, they are using empathy more
than ever before perhaps. Nevertheless, historians have tended to use empathy to
know the past unselfconsciously, oft even unawares. Moreover, in contrast to
scholars in other fields of inquiry where empathy is the focus of intense
interest and discussion, historians have generally neither theorized empathy
nor engaged in sustained discourse about its role in historical knowledge.
Therefore, this book is designed to convince historians less to use empathy to
know the past and more to be self-conscious in doing so. On the one hand, the
book seeks to raise the consciousness of historians about the concept by introducing them to its history and to the contemporary literature on empathy in a
number of fields, including but not restricted to history. Specifically, it seeks to
encourage and to contribute to an informed, sophisticated, and rigorous discussion by historians about empathy and its use in historical knowledge.
Indeed, this book can be regarded in part as a sort of primer on empathy for
historians. On the other hand, the book seeks to raise the self-consciousness of
historians about their actual use of empathy in doing historical work. Historians need to be explicit, self-aware, and unashamed about their use of empathy
to know and understand the human past.

History written from the perspective of the outside observer is different
from history written from the empathic perspective, that is, from the perspective of the historical subject. Whereas, the former has the advantage of
hindsight, distance, and scope and the latter faces the challenge of attempting
to quarantine what one knows from outside the experience of the historical
subject, history written from the empathic perspective enables the historian to
write history that is not deterministic—bringing ideas, actions, hopes and
fears, experiences into view that were important to the people of the past but
failed to contribute to history's eventual outcome. Given the fact that the
position of the observing historian determines what he or she is able to know
and write about the past, it is important that historians be conscious of which
observational position they are occupying at any given moment, of when they
are empathizing and when they are not. And, when empathizing, it is important that historians also be conscious of which historical subject's perspective
they are adopting at any given moment.

Consciousness of the distinction between the external and the empathic
observational positions makes clear the categorical difference between sympathy (a response coming from the position of the external observer) and

empathy (a response reflecting the position of the historical subject): sympathy is *my* feeling for someone else; empathy is my attempt to feel what *someone else* is feeling. Throughout the process of empathizing, the historian needs to remain self-conscious and self-reflective. Indeed, it is the awareness of empathizing historians of their own independent sense of self that distinguishes empathy from contagion, merger, and identification, where the distinction between self and other is lost, and that enables empathizing historians to recognize the attenuated nature of their empathy and to appreciate and respect difference even as they attempt to know and understand it.

Self-consciousness on the part of empathizing historians demands that they have a clearly articulated and consistently employed definition of the concept. Here, empathy has been conceived of in largely cognitive terms, as a way of knowing, as a mode of observation. In historical empathy, we seek to know and understand past people by imagining, by thinking, and at times feeling our way inside their experience. When historians write history from the perspective of the historical subject, that is, from the empathic perspective, they employ empathy self-consciously and deliberately when the feelings, thoughts, and actions of the historical subject do not make immediate or intuitive sense. In the language of simulation theory, we deliberately employ re-enactive empathy in history when basic empathy fails to comprehend the thoughts, feelings, and actions of the historical subject, and particularly when we seek to *understand* those thoughts, feelings, and actions. Since empathy is neither identification nor sympathy, we can and should empathize with perpetrators and other unsympathetic historical figures we have no wish to resemble, for their feelings, thoughts, and actions frequently do not make intuitive or immediate sense.

Thus, the distinction between basic empathy and deliberate re-enactive empathy made in simulation theory can usefully be applied to the use of empathy in historical knowledge. Similarly useful is the phenomenological position's rejection of epistemological Cartesianism (the assumption that all we can ultimately know is ourselves) and its emphasis on the intersubjective nature of knowledge.

In history, we do not know past people empathically simply by reconstructing the context in which they lived and then projecting ourselves into that context, although knowledge of their "space of experience" and "horizon of expectation" is surely an important condition of historical knowledge and understanding. Nor do we know past people simply through shared experiences or a universal human nature, although shared experiences or a shared humanity surely facilitates empathic understanding. We should not restrict historical knowledge only to what can be known by analogy with ourselves, however. The presumption that we can ultimately know only ourselves, or that which is like ourselves, overlooks the difficulty of self-knowledge and the fact that we know people, in the past as in the present, because we are in a reciprocal cognitive and affective relationship with them. In history, the people of the past are better thought of less as the passive subjects of our investigation and more as our active collaborators. Our autonomy and our authority over past people are more limited than we may wish to acknowledge. In knowing past people, we do not simply impose ourselves on them; they impose themselves on us as well. They call out to us, communicate with us, and profoundly influence what we know, understand, and write about them. Indeed, our relationship with past people changes us, affecting what we think and feel, even who we are.[16]

The assumption that we can only know others by analogy with ourselves overlooks the intersubjective nature of knowledge and the fact that we are neither cognitively nor affectively autonomous. It also underestimates the power of the human imagination. Through its exercise, we are able to transcend direct personal experience to know and understand experiences in others that we have not had ourselves. Our imagination enables us to step inside the skin of other people and the life worlds they inhabited.[17]

The Cartesian assumption that we can only ultimately know ourselves, individually and culturally, is not only false but also has problematic political and ethical implications. This assumption can result in the reduction of complex human beings with multiple, shifting identities to one single "essential" or defining aspect of themselves, on the basis of which we can allegedly know and understand them provided we share their essential or defining characteristic. The assumption that we can ultimately only know ourselves, or that which is like ourselves, fails to recognize that we can know and understand people who are different from us, in everyday life, in psychotherapy, and in history.[18] And we know and understand them not simply because we discover some underlying similarity beneath the apparent difference separating us from them, but also because we establish a relationship with them and because we possess an imagination that allows us to step inside their experience and the worlds they inhabited. Empathy, as revealing essential human alikeness, has been presented by a number of scholars as a source of the conception of universal human rights.[19] Empathy is essential to the liberal humanist project not only because it reveals our underlying similarity to others, but also because it reveals our capacity to know and understand others who are *different* from us, whether in the here and now or in the past, through the cognitive and affective relationship we establish with them (where their contributions to what we know about them are at least as great as our own) and through the exercise of our imagination. Empathy is not only about recognizing essential alikeness; empathy is also about simultaneously recognizing and respecting difference while attempting to know and understand it. What is universal in empathy is not only *what* we know. What is universal in empathy is also the process of empathic knowing itself.

Notes

1 Kohut, "Psychohistory as History." See also Loewenberg, "Cultural History and Psychoanalysis," in particular 26, 30, 34. Freud, in one of his rare uses of the term Einfühlung, saw empathy as *the* essential way to know the psychic life of another:

"Von der Identifizierung führt ein Weg über die Nachahmung zur Einfühlung, das heißt, zum Verständnis des Mechanismus durch den uns überhaupt eine Stellungnahme zu einem anderen Seelenleben ermöglicht wird." This passage has been poorly and confusingly translated in the *Standard Edition of the Complete Psychological Works of Sigmund Freud*. For an accurate rendering of the meaning of the German, see Michael Basch, "Empathic Understanding: A Review of the Concept and Some Theoretical Considerations," *Journal of the American Psychoanalytic Association* 31(1983): 103, n. 101. For an excellent overview of the history of the concept of empathy in psychoanalysis, see Pigman, "Freud and the History of Empathy." See also Gladstein, "Historical Roots of Contemporary Empathy Research."

2 Kohut, "Psychohistory as History," 344–345.

3 It should be noted, however, that in recent years there have been efforts by psychiatrists to bring an empathic, psychoanalytic perspective to bear on the use of medication to treat mental illness. Indeed, at the time of writing, the psychiatrist David Mintz of the Austen Riggs Center was finishing a book entitled *The Manual of Psychodynamic Psychopharmacology*.

4 R. G. Collingwood rejected the empirical psychology of his day on precisely these grounds, namely that it looked at the inner life of people from without and adopted the procedures of the natural sciences in part as a result. Connelly and Costall, "Collingwood and the Idea of an Historical Psychology," 158–159.

5 This is the argument made by Heinz Kohut in his classic 1959 article "Introspection, Empathy, and Psychoanalysis." See also the transcription of remarks made in Berkeley days before his death: Kohut, "On Empathy," 527. For a lucid, knowledgeable, and thoughtful account of Kohut's view of empathy, see Elizabeth Lunbeck, "Empathy as a Psychoanalytic Mode of Observation: Between Sentiment and Science," in *Histories of Scientific Observation*, ed. Lorraine Daston and Elizabeth Lunbeck (Chicago: University of Chicago Press, 2011), 255–275. For an appreciation of Kohut from an intellectual historian's perspective, see Lunbeck's *The Americanization of Narcissism* (Cambridge, MA: Harvard University Press, 2014). Kohut's claim that psychoanalysis is defined by its introspective, empathic approach is overstated perhaps in that, like the empathizing historian, the empathizing psychoanalyst does not adopt an exclusively introspective empathic viewpoint. Extrospection, i.e., external observation, helps determine which experience of the patient the analyst seeks to empathize with and, even while empathizing, the analyst maintains an extrospective perspective on his or her own empathy. Indeed, as has been pointed out in critiquing Kohut's position, analysts routinely use data collected extrospectively—observations of expression, dress, demeanor, and verbal expressions of the patient to understand the patient, indeed to facilitate empathy with the patient. The role played by introspection and empathy in combination with the external observation of the patient's appearance, demeanor, and behavior in psychoanalysis is articulated in James H. Spencer and Leon Balter, "Psychoanalytic Observation," *Journal of the American Psychoanalytic Association* 38, no. 2(1990). Nevertheless, Balter and Spencer have also demonstrated, following Kohut, that "radical differences among theories and psychoanalytic thought may derive in part from critical differences in methods of observation." Leon Balter and James H. Spencer, "Observation and Theory in Psychoanalysis: The Self Psychology of Heinz Kohut," *Psychoanalytic Quarterly* 60(1991): 361.

6 Nussbaum, *Upheavals of Thought*, 328. As Sophie Oliver puts it, "Similarly, in psychotherapeutic definitions of the term, empathy *does not* call for the empathiser to 'lose' him or herself in the other's pain, since to do so in the therapeutic context would inhibit the therapist's ability to offer assistance; 'pure' empathy here involves more than the ability to put oneself in another's shoes and to see the world from

his or her perspective, it also expressly demands the ability to *return to self*. The suggestion, then, that we should for ethical reasons seek to nurture feelings of empathy need not and *must* not for all that imply that we should abandon our own—relatively secure—subject position. Empathy and exotopy [viewing from the external observational position] can and should be thought of as two sides of the same coin." Oliver, "The Aesth-*Ethics* of Empathy," 178.

7 Schwaber, "Empathy," 364. See, also, Robert Knight, "Psychotherapy of an Adolescent Catatonic Schizophrenia with Mutism: A Study in Empathy and Establishing Contact," *Psychiatry* 9(1946): 324.

8 Personal communication from the psychoanalyst Edward Shapiro. Semrad's remarks are quoted in Edward R. Shapiro, *Finding a Place to Stand: Developing Self-Reflective Institutions, Leaders, and Citizens* (Bicester: Phoenix, 2020), Epigraph.

9 Dray, *Laws and Explanation in History*, 122–126.

10 I am indebted to Karsten Stueber for emphasizing the potential limits to empathic understanding and the importance of nonetheless seeking to overcome them.

11 Kohut, *A German Generation*, 172; Frie, "Psychoanalysis and History at the Crossroads," 184–185.

12 Indeed, Saul Friedländer argues that the historian, particularly the historian interested in the unconscious meaning of a historical phenomenon, adopt the psychoanalyst's "free-floating attention." Friedländer, *History and Psychoanalysis*, 18.

13 Cottrell, "Situational Fields in Social Psychology," 381; "Neglected Problems in Social Psychology," 708; Gladstein, "Roots of Contemporary Empathy Research," 46.

14 Köhler, "Von der Freud'schen Psychoanalyse zur Selbstpsychologie Heinz Kohuts," 50.

15 For a knowledgeable and thoughtful consideration of the discussions about the role of empathy in history on the part of "history educationalists," those responsible for developing graduate curricula for students in training to be secondary-school history teachers in Great Britain, Australia, and Canada since the early 1970s, see Retz, *Empathy and History*. In the process, Retz considers the influence of Collingwood and, through Collingwood, German historicism, on education curricula in those countries. See, also, O. L. Davis Jr., Elizabeth Anne Yeager, and Stuart J. Foster, *Historical Empathy and Perspective Taking in the Social Studies* (Lanham, MD: Rowman & Littlefield, 2001).

16 I am paraphrasing the comments of the art historian Keith Moxey here, written in response to a draft of this work. Moxey's own art historical writing focuses in part on the power that objects exert over the viewer.

17 As a thought experiment, imagine that a space alien lands on earth. At first contact, there would be no knowledge or understanding between us. However, through the relationship that would be established between us, our ability to understand one another would gradually increase. Our relationship would generate shared experiences that we could use to know and understand one another. Indeed, we might discover that we share a certain life-nature or certain life-needs. Nevertheless, it would ultimately be our relationship with the alien coupled with our imaginative capacities that would enable us to know and understand the alien's experience. It seems likely then that, over time, we would be able to empathize even with a space alien. Relevant to this thought experiment is Dominick LaCapra's rejection of Wittgenstein's claim that if a lion could speak, we would not understand the lion. LaCapra disputes the notion that animals "are beyond the embrace of empathy." LaCapra, *Understanding Others*, 61–62.

18 Empathy pushes back against the prevalent contemporary notion that only people who share the same sexual, gender, class, ethnic, and/or racial identity can truly know or understand one another.

19 See "Empathy versus Sympathy" in Chapter 3.

Bibliography

Abel, Theodore. "The Operation Called Verstehen." *American Journal of Sociology* 54 (1948): 211–218.

Agosta, Louis. *Empathy in the Context of Philosophy.* Basingstoke: Palgrave Macmillan, 2010.

Aird, David Mitchell. *Blackstone Economized: Being a Compendium of the Laws of England to the Present Time.* London: Longmans, Green, and Co., 1873.

Ankersmit, Frank R. *Sublime Historical Experience.* Stanford, CA: Stanford University Press, 2005.

Apel, Karl-Otto. "The Erklären-Verstehen Controversy in the Philosophy of the Natural and Human Sciences." In *Contemporary Philosophy: A New Survey*, edited by Guttorm Fløistad, 19–49. The Hague: Martinus Nijhoff, 1982.

Aschheim, Steven E. "The (Ambiguous) Political Economy of Empathy." In *Empathy and Its Limits*, edited by Aleida Assmann and Ines Detmers, 21–37. London and New York: Palgrave Macmillan, 2016.

Assmann, Aleida, and Ines Detmers. "Introduction." In *Empathy and Its Limits*, edited by Aleida Assmann and Ines Detmers, 1–17. London and New York: Palgrave Macmillan, 2016.

Assmann, Aleida, and Ines Detmers, eds. *Empathy and Its Limits.* London and New York: Palgrave Macmillan, 2016.

Bajohr, Frank. "Vom anti-jüdischen Konsens zum schlechten Gewissen: Die deutsche Gesellschaft und die Judenverfolgung, 1933–1945." In *Der Holocaust als offenes Geheimnis: Die Deutschen, die NS-Führung, und die Alliierten*, edited by Frank Bajohr and Dieter Pohl, 15–79. Munich: Beck, 2006.

Balter, Leon, and James H. Spencer. "Observation and Theory in Psychoanalysis: The Self Psychology of Heinz Kohut." *Psychoanalytic Quarterly* 60(1991): 361–395.

Basch, Michael. "Empathic Understanding: A Review of the Concept and Some Theoretical Considerations." *Journal of the American Psychoanalytic Association* 31(1983): 101–126.

Batson, C. Daniel. "These Things Called Empathy: Eight Related but Distinct Phenomena." In *The Social Neuroscience of Empathy*, edited by Jean Decety and William John Ickes, 3–15. Cambridge, MA: MIT Press, 2009.

Benjamin, Walter. *On the Concept of History.* Translated by Dennis Redmond. Gesammelte Schriften. Vol. I:2. Frankfurt: Suhrkamp, 1974.

Bergen, Doris L. *War and Genocide: A Concise History of the Holocaust.* Lanham, MD: Rowman & Littlefield, 2003.

Berlin, Isaiah. *Vico and Herder: Two Studies in the History of Ideas.* London: Hogarth, 1976.

Berlowitz, Shelley. "Unequal Equals: How Politics Can Block Empathy." In *Empathy and Its Limits*, edited by Aleida Assmann and Ines Detmers, 38–51. London and New York: Palgrave Macmillan, 2016.

Bevir, Mark. "Introduction: Historical Understanding and the Human Sciences." *Journal of the Philosophy of History* 1(2007): 259–270.

Bischof-Köhler, Doris. "Empathy and Self-Recognition in Phylogenetic and Ontogenetic Perspective." *Emotion Review* 4, no. 1(2012): 40–48.

Bolognini, Stefano. "Empathy and 'Empathism'." *International Journal of Psycho-Analysis* 78 (1997): 279–293.

Bos, Jacques. "Individuality and Interpretation in Nineteenth-Century German Historicism." In *Perspectives on Erklären and Verstehen*, edited by Uljana Feest, 207–220. Dordrecht: Springer, 2010.

Brady, Michael S. *Emotional Insight: The Epistemic Role of Emotional Experience.* Oxford: Oxford University Press, 2013.

Breithaupt, Fritz. *Die dunklen Seiten der Empathie.* Frankfurt: Suhrkamp, 2017.

Breithaupt, Fritz. "Empathy for Empathy's Sake: Aesthetics and Everyday Empathic Sadism." In *Empathy and Its Limits*, edited by Aleida Assmann and Ines Detmers, 151–165. London and New York: Palgrave Macmillan, 2016.

Breithaupt, Fritz. *Kulturen der Empathie.* Frankfurt: Suhrkamp, 2012.

Breithaupt, Fritz. "A Three-Person Model of Empathy." *Emotion Review* 4(2012): 84–91.

Brinton, Crane. *The Anatomy of Revolution.* New York: Vintage, 1965 (originally published 1938).

Browning, Christopher R. "German Memory, Judicial Interrogation, and Historical Reconstruction: Writing Perpetrator History from Postwar Testimony." In *Probing the Limits of Representation: Nazism and the "Final Solution"*, edited by Saul Friedländer, 22–36. Cambridge, MA: Harvard University Press, 1992.

Browning, Christopher R., and contributions by Jürgen Matthäus. *The Origins of the Final Solution: The Evolution of Nazi Jewish Policy, September 1939–March 1942.* Lincoln and Jerusalem: University of Nebraska Press and Yad Vashem, 2004.

Bubandt, Nils. "The Enemy's Point of View: Violence, Empathy, and the Ethnography of Fakes." *Cultural Anthropology* 24, no. 3(2009): 553–588.

Burckhardt, Jacob. *The Civilization of the Renaissance in Italy.* Translated by S. G. C. Middlemore. London and New York: Penguin, 1990.

Burckhardt, Jacob. *Reflections on History.* Translated by M. D. Hottinger, edited by Gottfried Dietze. Indianapolis: Liberty Classics, 1979.

Burckhardt, Jacob. *Weltgeschichtliche Betrachtungen.* 2nd edition, edited by Jakob Oeri. Berlin and Stuttgart: Spemann, 1910.

Burleigh, Michael. *The Third Reich: A New History.* New York: Hill and Wang, 2000.

Butterfield, Herbert. *History and Human Relations.* London: Collins, 1951.

Carr, David. "Narrative Explanation and Its Malcontents." *History and Theory* 47 (2008): 19–30.

Collingwood, R. G. *The Idea of History.* Oxford: Oxford University Press, 1956.

Confino, Alon. "From Psychohistory to Memory Studies: Or, How Some Germans Became Jews and Some Jews Nazis." In *History Flows through Us: Germany, the Holocaust, and the Importance of Empathy*, edited by Roger Frie, 17–30. London and New York: Routledge, 2018.

Confino, Alon. *Germany as a Culture of Remembrance: Promises and Limits of Writing History*. Chapel Hill: North Carolina University Press, 2006.

Confino, Alon. *A World without Jews: The Nazi Imagination from Persecution to Genocide*. New Haven, CT: Yale University Press, 2014.

Connelly, John, and Alan Costall. "R. G. Collingwood and the Idea of an Historical Psychology." *Theory and Psychology* 10(2000): 147–170.

Cooley, Charles H. *Human Nature and the Social Order*. New York: Schocken Books, 1964.

Cooley, Charles H. *Social Theory and Social Research*. New York: Henry Holt, 1930.

Cooley, Charles H. "The Roots of Social Knowledge." *American Journal of Sociology* 32, no. 1(1926): 59–79.

Coplan, Amy. "Understanding Empathy: Its Features and Effects." In *Empathy: Philosophical and Psychological Perspectives*, edited by Amy Coplan and Peter Goldie, 1–19. Oxford: Oxford University Press, 2011.

Coplan, Amy, and Peter Goldie. "Introduction." In *Empathy: Philosophical and Psychological Perspectives*, edited by Amy Coplan and Peter Goldie, ix–xlii. Oxford: Oxford University Press, 2011.

Cottrell, Leonard S. "The Analysis of Situational Fields in Social Psychology." *American Sociological Review* 7(1942): 370–382.

Cottrell, Leonard S. "Some Neglected Problems in Social Psychology." *American Sociological Review* 15(1950): 705–712.

Craig, Gordon. *Germany: 1866–1945*. Oxford: Oxford University Press, 1978.

Croce, Benedetto. *History: Its Theory and Practice*. Translated by Douglas Ainslie. New York: Russell and Russell, 1960.

D'Oro, Giuseppina. "Collingwood on Re-Enactment and the Identity of Thought." *Journal of the History of Philosophy* 38(2000): 87–101.

D'Oro, Giuseppina. "Collingwood, Psychologism and Internalism." *European Journal of Philosophy* 12(2004): 163–177.

D'Oro, Giuseppina. "Re-Enactment and Radical Interpretation." *History and Theory* 43(2004): 198–208.

Daniel, Ute. "Erfahrene Geschichte: Intervention über ein Thema Reinhart Kosellecks." In *Zwischen Sprache und Geschichte: Zum Werk Reinhart Kosellecks*, edited by Carsten Dutt and Reinhard Laube. Marbacher Schriften, 14–28. Göttingen: Wallstein, 2013.

Daniel, Ute. *Kompendium Kulturgeschichte: Theorien, Praxis, Schlüsselwörter*. Frankfurt: Suhrkamp, 2006.

Danto, Arthur C. *Analytical Philosophy of History*. Cambridge: Cambridge University Press, 1965.

Davis Jr., O. L., Elizabeth Anne Yeager, and Stuart J. Foster. *Historical Empathy and Perspective Taking in the Social Studies*. Lanham, MD: Rowman & Littlefield, 2001.

Davis, Mark H. *Empathy: A Social Psychological Approach*. Social Psychology Series. Boulder, CO: Westview, 1994.

De Vignemont, Frederique, and Pierre Jacob. "What Is It Like to Feel Another's Pain?" *Philosophy of Science* 79, no. 2(2012): 295–316.

De Vignemont, Frederique, and Tania Singer. "The Empathic Brain: How, When, Why?" *Trends in Cognitive Neuroscience* 10, no. 10(2006): 435–441.

Dean, Carolyn J. *The Fragility of Empathy after the Holocaust*. Ithaca: Cornell University Press, 2004.

Dean, Carolyn J. "History Writing, Numbness, and the Restoration of Dignity." *History of the Human Sciences* 17, no. 2–3(2004): 57–96.

Decety, Jean, and Claus Lamm. "Empathy versus Personal Distress: Recent Evidence from Social Neuroscience." In *The Social Neuroscience of Empathy*, edited by Jean Decety and William John Ickes, 199–213. Cambridge, MA: MIT Press, 2009.

Decety, Jean, and Andrew N. Metzoff. "Empathy, Imitation, and the Social Brain." In *Empathy: Philosophical and Psychological Perspectives*, edited by Amy Coplan and Peter Goldie, 58–81. Oxford: Oxford University Press, 2011.

Decety, Jean, Philip L. Jackson, and Eric Brunet. "The Cognitive Neuropsychology of Empathy." In *Empathy in Mental Illness*, edited by Tom F. D. Farrow and Peter W. R. Woodruff, 239–260. Cambridge: Cambridge University Press, 2007.

Demos, John. *Entertaining Satan: Witchcraft and the Culture of Early Modern New England*. New York and Oxford: Oxford University Press, 1982.

Demos, John. *A Little Commonwealth: Family Life in Plymouth Colony*. New York and Oxford: Oxford University Press, 1970.

Demos, John. *The Unredeemed Captive: A Family Story from Early America*. New York: Knopf, 1994.

Demos, John. "Using Self, Using History ...". *Journal of American History* 89, no. 1 (2002): 37–42.

Depraz, Natalie, and Diego Cosmelli. "Empathy and Openness: Practices of Inter-subjectivity at the Core of the Science of Consciousness." In *The Problem of Consciousness: New Essays in Phenomenological Philosophy of Mind*, edited by Evan Thompson, 163–203. Calgary: University of Calgary Press, 2003.

Dharamsi, Karim. "Re-Enacting in the Second Person." *Journal of the Philosophy of History* 5, no. 2(2011): 163–178.

Dilthey, Wilhelm. *The Formation of the Historical World in the Human Sciences*. Wilhelm Dilthey: Selected Works, edited by Rudolf A. Makkreel and Frithjof Rodi, vol. 3. Princeton, NJ: Princeton University Press, 2002.

Dilthey, Wilhelm. *Hermeneutics and the Study of History*. Wilhelm Dilthey: Selected Works, edited by Rudolf A. Makkreel and Frithjof Rodi, vol. 4. Princeton, NJ: Princeton University Press, 1996.

Dilthey, Wilhelm. *Introduction to the Human Sciences*. Wilhelm Dilthey: Selected Works, edited by Rudolf A. Makkreel and Frithjof Rodi, vol. 1. Princeton, NJ: Princeton University Press, 1989.

Dilthey, Wilhelm. *Introduction to the Human Sciences: An Attempt to Lay a Foundation for the Study of Society and History*, edited by Ramon J. Betanzos. London: Harvester Wheatsheaf, 1988.

Dilthey, Wilhelm. *Understanding the Human World*. Wilhelm Dilthey: Selected Works, edited by Rudolf A. Makkreel and Frithjof Rodi, vol. 2. Princeton, NJ: Princeton University Press, 2010.

Donagan, Alan. "The Verification of Historical Theses." *Philosophical Quarterly* 6, no. 24(1956): 193–208.

Dray, William. *History as Re-Enactment: R. G. Collingwood's Idea of History*. Oxford: Clarendon, 1999.

Dray, William. *Laws and Explanation in History*. Oxford: Clarendon, 1957.

Droysen, Johann Gustav. *Outline of the Principles of History (Grundriss der Geschichte)*. Boston: Ginn and Company, 1893.

Dymond, Rosalind F. "A Scale for the Measurement of Empathic Ability." *Journal of Consulting Psychology* 13, no. 2(1949): 127–133.

Edwards, Laura Hyatt. "A Brief Conceptual History of Einfühlung: 18th-Century Germany to Post-World War II U.S. Psychology." *History of Psychology* 16, no. 4 (2013): 269–281.

Eisenberg, Nancy, and Paul Miller. "Empathy, Sympathy, and Altruism: Empirical and Conceptual Links." In *Empathy and Its Development*, edited by Nancy Eisenberg and Janet Strayer, 292–316. Cambridge: Cambridge University Press, 1987.

Ermarth, Michael. *Wilhelm Dilthey: The Critique of Historical Reason*. Chicago, IL: University of Chicago Press, 1978.

Eustace, Nicole, Eugenia Lean, Julie Livingston, Jan Plomper, William Reddy, and Barbara Rosenwein. "AHR Conversation: The Historical Study of Emotions." *American Historical Review* 117, no. 5(2012): 1487–1531.

Evans, Richard J. *The Third Reich at War*. New York: Penguin, 2009.

Febvre, Lucien. *The Problem of Unbelief in the Sixteenth Century: The Religion of Rabelais*. Cambridge, MA: Harvard University Press, 1985.

Fliess, Robert. "The Metapsychology of the Analyst." *Psychoanalytic Quarterly* 11 (1942): 211–227.

Frevert, Ute. "Empathizing in the Theater of Horrors or Civilizing the Human Heart." In *Empathy and Its Limits*, edited by Aleida Assmann and Ines Detmers, 79–99. London and New York: Palgrave Macmillan, 2016.

Frie, Roger. "Psychoanalysis and History at the Crossroads: A Dialogue with Thomas Kohut." In *History Flows through Us: Germany, the Holocaust, and the Importance of Empathy*, edited by Roger Frie, 157–187. London and New York: Routledge, 2018.

Friedlander, Henry. *The Origins of Nazi Genocide: From Euthanasia to the Final Solution*. Chapel Hill: University of North Carolina Press, 1995.

Friedländer, Saul. *History and Psychoanalysis: An Inquiry into the Possibilities and Limits of Psychohistory*. Translated by Susan Suleiman. New York: Holmes and Meier, 1978.

Friedländer, Saul. "Introduction." In *Probing the Limits of Representation: Nazism and the "Final Solution"*, edited by Saul Friedländer, 1–21. Cambridge, MA: Harvard University Press, 1992.

Friedländer, Saul. *Reflections on Nazism: An Essay on Kitsch and Death*. Translated by Thomas Weyr. Bloomington: Indiana University Press, 1993.

Friedländer, Saul. "Trauma, Transference and 'Working through' in Writing the History of the 'Shoah'." *History and Memory* 4, no. 1(1992): 39–59.

Friedländer, Saul. *The Years of Extermination: Nazi Germany and the Jews, 1939–1945*. New York: HarperCollins, 2007.

Fritzsche, Peter. *Germans into Nazis*. Cambridge, MA: Harvard University Press, 1998.

Fritzsche, Peter. "Review: Did Weimar Fail?" *Journal of Modern History* 68, no. 3 (1996): 629–656.

Gadamer, Hans-Georg. *Truth and Method*. Translated by Joel Weinsheimer and Donald G. Marshall. Revised 2nd edition 2004. London: Bloomsbury, 2014.

Gallagher, Shaun. "Empathy, Simulation, and Narrative." *Scientific Context* 25, no. 3 (2011): 355–381.

Gallagher, Shaun, and Somogy Varga. "Social Constraints on the Direct Perception of Emotions and Intentions." *Topoi* 33, no. 1(2014): 185–199.

Gallese, Vittorio, Christian Keysers, and Giacomo Rizzolatti. "A Unifying View of the Basis of Social Cognition." *Trends in Cognitive Sciences* 8(2004): 396–403.

Gardiner, Patrick. "Interpretation in History: Collingwood and Historical Understanding." In *Verstehen and Humane Understanding*. Royal Institute of Philosophy Supplement 41, edited by Anthony O'Hear, 109–119. Cambridge: Cambridge University Press, 1996.

Gardiner, Patrick. *The Nature of Historical Explanation.* Oxford: Oxford University Press, 1961.

Gay, Peter. *Freud for Historians.* New York: Oxford University Press, 1985.

Geertz, Clifford. "'From the Native's Point of View': On the Nature of Anthropological Understanding." *Bulletin of the American Academy of Arts and Sciences* 28, no. 1(1974): 26–45.

Geis, Matthias, and Bernd Ulrich. "Wacht auf, verdammt!" *Die Zeit*, 14 February 2019.

Gerdes, Karen E. "Empathy, Sympathy, and Pity: 21st-Century Definitions and Implications for Practice and Research." *Journal of Social Service Research* 37, no. 3(2011): 230–241.

Gerlach, Christian. "Die Wannsee-Konferenz, das Schicksal der deutschen Juden und Hitlers politische Grundsatzentscheidung alle Juden zu ermorden." In *Krieg, Ernährung, Völkermord: Forschungen zur deutschen Vernichtungspolitik im Zweiten Weltkrieg*, edited by Christian Gerlach. Hamburg: Hamburger Edition, 1998.

Gerlach, Christian. "The Wannsee Conference, the Fate of German Jews, and Hitler's Decision in Principle to Exterminate All European Jews." *Journal of Modern History* 70, no. 4(1998): 759–812.

Ginzburg, Carlo. *Clues, Myths, and the Historical Method.* Translated by John Tedeschi and Anne C. Tedeschi. Baltimore, MD: Johns Hopkins University Press, 1989.

Gladstein, Gerald A. "The Historical Roots of Contemporary Empathy Research." *Journal of the History of the Behavioral Sciences* 20, no. 1(1984): 38–59.

Goldberg, Amos. "Empathy, Ethics, and Politics in Holocaust Historiography." In *Empathy and Its Limits*, edited by Aleida Assmann and Ines Detmers, 52–76. London and New York: Palgrave Macmillan, 2016.

Goldberg, Amos. "The Victim's Voice and Melodramatic Aesthetics in History." *History and Theory* 48(2009): 220–237.

Goldie, Peter. "Anti-Empathy." In *Empathy: Philosophical and Psychological Perspectives*, edited by Amy Coplan and Peter Goldie, 302–317. Oxford: Oxford University Press, 2011.

Goldie, Peter. "How We Think of Others' Emotions." *Mind and Language* 14, no. 4 (1999): 394–423.

Goldman, Alvin I. "Two Routes to Empathy: Insights from Cognitive Neuroscience." In *Empathy: Philosophical and Psychological Perspectives*, edited by Amy Coplan and Peter Goldie, 31–44. Oxford: Oxford University Press, 2011.

Goldman, Alvin I., and Vittorio Gallese. "Mirror Neurons and the Simulation Theory of Mind-Reading." *Trends in Cognitive Sciences* 12(1998): 493–501.

Grenville, John A. S. "Die 'Endlösung' und die 'Judenmischlinge' im Dritten Reich." In *Das Unrechtsregime: Internationale Forschung über den Nationalsozialismus*, edited by Werner Jochmann, Werner Johe, and Ursula Büttner, 91–121. Hamburg: Christians, 1986.

Gruner, Rolf. "Understanding in the Social Sciences and History." *Inquiry: An Interdisciplinary Journal of Philosophy* 10, no. 1–4(1967): 151–163.

Habermas, Jürgen. *Knowledge and Human Interests*. Translated by J. Shapiro. London: Heinemann, 1973.

Habermas, Jürgen. *On the Logic of the Social Sciences*. Translated by S. Nicholsen and J. Stark. Cambridge, MA: MIT Press, 1988.

Halpern, Jodi. *From Detached Concern to Empathy: Humanizing Medical Practice*. Oxford: Oxford University Press, 2001.

Haney, Kathleen. "Empathy and Otherness." *Journal of Philosophy* 4, no. 8(2009): 11–19.

Harrington, Austin. "Dilthey, Empathy and Verstehen A Contemporary Reappraisal." *European Journal of Social Theory* 4, no. 3(2001): 311–329.

Harrington, Austin. *Hermeneutic Dialogue and Social Science: A Critique of Gadamer and Habermas*. New York: Routledge, 2001.

Harris, William V. "History, Empathy and Emotions." *Antike und Abendland* 56(2010): 1–23.

Hausheer, Roger. "Three Major Originators of the Concept of Verstehen: Vico, Herder, Schleiermacher." In *Verstehen and Humane Understanding*. Royal Institute of Philosophy Supplement 41, edited by Anthony O'Hear, 47–72. Cambridge: Cambridge University Press, 1996.

Heal, Jane. *Mind, Reason, and Imagination*. Cambridge: Cambridge University Press, 2003.

Hempel, Carl G. "The Function of General Laws in History." *Journal of Philosophy* 39, no. 2(1942): 35–48.

Herf, Jeffrey. *Reactionary Modernism: Technology, Culture, and Politics in Weimar and the Third Reich*. Cambridge: Cambridge University Press, 1986.

Hickok, Gregory. *The Myth of Mirror Neurons: The Real Neuroscience of Communication and Cognition*. New York: Norton, 2014.

Hickok, Gregory, and Marc Hauser. "(Mis)Understanding Mirror Neurons." *Current Biology* 20, no. 14(2010): R593–594.

Himmler, Heinrich. "Speech of the Reichsführer SS at the Meeting of SS Major-Generals at Posen, October 4th, 1943, Document 1919-Ps." In *Nazi Conspiracy and Aggression*, edited by Office of United States Chief Counsel for Prosecution of Axis Criminality, 558–572. Washington, DC: United States Government Printing Office, 1946.

Hoffman, Martin L. "The Contribution of Empathy to Justice and Moral Judgment." In *Empathy and Its Development*, edited by Nancy Eisenberg and Janet Strayer, 47–80. Cambridge: Cambridge University Press, 1987.

Hoffman, Martin L. "Empathy, Role-Taking, Guilt, and the Development of Altruistic Motives." In *Moral Development and Behavior: Theory, Research, Social Issues*, edited by T. Lickona, 124–143. New York: Holt, Rinehart, and Winston, 1976.

Hoffman, Martin L. "Interaction of Affect and Cognition in Empathy." In *Emotions, Cognition, Behavior*, edited by C. E. Izard, J. Kagan, and R. B. Zajonc, 103–131. Cambridge: Cambridge University Press, 1984.

Hollan, Douglas. "Emerging Issues in the Cross-Cultural Study of Empathy." *Emotion Review* 4(2012): 70–78.

Hume, David. *Enquiries Concerning Human Understanding and Concerning the Principles of Morals*. 3rd edition. Oxford: Clarendon, 1975.

Hume, David. "On the Study of History." In *Essays: Moral, Political, and Literary*, edited by Eugene F. Miller, 563–568. Indianapolis: Liberty Fund, 1987.

Hume, David. "That Politics May Be Reduced to a Science." In *Essays: Moral, Political, and Literary*, edited by Eugene F. Miller, 14–31. Indianapolis: Liberty Fund, 1987.

Hume, David. *A Treatise of Human Nature*. edited by L. A. Selby-Bigge. 2nd edition. Oxford: Clarendon, 1978.

Hunt, Lynn. *Inventing Human Rights: A History*. New York: Norton, 2007.

Iggers, Georg G. *The German Conception of History: The National Tradition of Historical Thought from Herder to the Present*. Middletown, CT: Wesleyan University Press, 1968.

Jacquette, Dale. "Collingwood on Historical Authority and Historical Imagination." *Journal of the Philosophy of History* 3, no. 1(2009): 55–78.

Jay, Martin. *Songs of Experience: Modern American and European Variations on a Universal Theme*. Berkeley: University of California Press, 2005.

Jenkins, Keith. *Re-Thinking History*. London: Routledge, 2003.

Kaelber, Lutz, and Raimond Reiter, eds. *Kindermord und "Kinderfachabteilungen" im Nationalsozialismus: Gedenken und Forschung*. Hamburg: Peter Lang, 2011.

Kaplan, Thomas Pegelow. *The Language of Nazi Genocide: Linguistic Violence and the Struggle of Germans of Jewish Ancestry*. Cambridge: Cambridge University Press, 2011.

Kershaw, Ian. "Alltägliches und Ausseralltägliches: Ihre Bedeutung für die Volksmeinung, 1933–1939." In *Die Reihen fast geschlossen: Beiträge zur Geschichte des Alltags unterm Nationalsozialismus*, edited by Detlev Peukert and Jürgen Reulecke, 273–292. Wuppertal: Peter Hammer, 1981.

Kessel, Eberhard. "Rankes Idee der Universalhistorie." *Historische Zeitschrift* 178, no. 2(1954): 269–308.

Klee, Ernst. "'Euthanasie' im NS-Staat: Die 'Vernichtung lebensunwerten Lebens'." In *Die Zeit des Nationalsozialismus*, edited by Walter H. Pehle. Frankfurt: Fischer, 2009.

Knight, Robert. "Psychotherapy of an Adolescent Catatonic Schizophrenia with Mutism: A Study in Empathy and Establishing Contact." *Psychiatry* 9(1946): 323–339.

Kögler, Hans Herbert, and Karsten R. Stueber. "Introduction: Empathy, Simulation, and Interpretation in the Philosophy of Social Science." In *Empathy and Agency: The Problem of Understanding in the Social Sciences*, edited by Hans Herbert Kögler and Karsten Stueber, 1–61. Boulder, CO: Westview, 2000.

Köhler, Lotte. "Von der Freud'schen Psychoanalyse zur Selbstpsychologie Heinz Kohuts: Eine Einführung." In *Von der Selbsterhaltung zur Selbstachtung: Der geschichtlich bedingte Wandel psychoanalytischer Theorien und ihr Beitrag zum Verständnis historischer Entwicklungen*, edited by Hans Kilian and Lotte Köhler, 13–75. Giessen: Psychosozial-Verlag, 2013.

Kohut, Heinz. "Introspective, Empathy, and Psychoanalysis: An Examination of the Relationship between Mode of Observation and Theory." In *The Search for the Self: Selected Writings of Heinz Kohut: 1950–1978*, edited by Paul H. Ornstein, 205–232. London: Karnac, 2011.

Kohut, Heinz. "Introspection, Empathy, and the Semicircle of Mental Health." In *The Search for the Self: Selected Writings of Heinz Kohut: 1978–1981*, edited by Paul H. Ornstein, 537–568. London: Karnac, 2011.

Kohut, Heinz. "Letter to a Colleague." In *The Search for the Self: Selected Writings of Heinz Kohut: 1978–1981*, edited by Paul H. Ornstein, 580. London: Karnac, 2011.

Kohut, Heinz. "On Empathy." In *The Search for the Self: Selected Writings of Heinz Kohut: 1978–1981*, edited by Paul H. Ornstein, 525–535. London: Karnac, 2011.

Kohut, Thomas A. *A German Generation: An Experiential History of the Twentieth Century.* New Haven, CT: Yale University Press, 2012.

Kohut, Thomas A. "Psychohistory as History." *American Historical Review* 91, no. 2 (1986): 336.

Kohut, Thomas A. "Reflections on Empathy as a Mode of Observation in History." In *Sinngeschichten: Kulturgeschichtliche Beiträge für Ute Daniel,* edited by Christian Frey, Thomas Kubetzky, Klaus Latzel, Heidi Mehrkens, and Christoph Friedrich Webers, 190–197. Cologne: Böhlau, 2013.

Kohut, Thomas A. *Wilhelm II and the Germans: A Study in Leadership.* New York and Oxford: Oxford University Press, 1991.

Koselleck, Reinhart. *Futures Past: On the Semantics of Historical Time.* Translated by Keith Tribe. New York: Columbia University Press, 2004.

Koselleck, Reinhart. *Vergangene Zukunft: Zur Semantik geschichtlicher Zeiten.* Frankfurt: Suhrkamp, 1979.

LaCapra, Dominick. *History and Memory after Auschwitz.* Ithaca, NY: Cornell University Press, 1998.

LaCapra, Dominick. "History and Psychoanalysis." *Critical Inquiry* 13, no. 2(1987): 222–251.

LaCapra, Dominick. *History in Transit: Experience, Identity, Critical Theory.* Ithaca, NY: Cornell University Press, 2004.

LaCapra, Dominick. *Representing the Holocaust: History, Theory, Trauma.* Ithaca, NY: Cornell University Press, 1994.

LaCapra, Dominick. "Representing the Holocaust: Reflections on the Historians' Debate." In *Probing the Limits of Representation: Nazism and the Final Solution,* edited by Saul Friedländer, 108–127. Cambridge, MA: Harvard University Press, 1992.

LaCapra, Dominick. "Tropisms of Intellectual History." *Rethinking History* 8, no. 4 (2004): 499–529.

LaCapra, Dominick. *Understanding Others: Peoples, Animals, Pasts.* Ithaca, NY: Cornell University Press, 2018.

LaCapra, Dominick. *Writing History, Writing Trauma.* Baltimore, MD: Johns Hopkins University Press, 2001.

Lamm, Claus, C. Daniel Batson, and Jean Decety. "The Neural Substrate of Human Empathy: Effect of Perspective Taking and Cognitive Appraisal." *Journal of Cognitive Neuroscience* 19, no. 1(2007): 42–58.

Landsberg, Alison. "Memory, Empathy, and the Politics of Identification." *International Journal of Politics, Culture, and Society* 22, no. 2(2009): 221–229.

Lieber, Frederic William. "The Legacy of Empathy: History of a Psychological Concept." Dissertation, Indiana University, 1995.

Loewenberg, Peter. "Cultural History and Psychoanalysis." *Psychoanalysis and History* 9, no. 1(2007): 17–37.

Lunbeck, Elizabeth. *The Americanization of Narcissism.* Cambridge, MA: Harvard University Press, 2014.

Lunbeck, Elizabeth. "Empathy as a Psychoanalytic Mode of Observation: Between Sentiment and Science." In *Histories of Scientific Observation,* edited by Lorraine Daston and Elizabeth Lunbeck, 255–275. Chicago, IL: University of Chicago Press, 2011.

Maclean, Michael J. "Johann Gustav Droysen and the Development of Historical Hermeneutics." *History and Theory* 21, no. 3(1982): 347–365.

Maier, Charles S. *Recasting Bourgeois Europe: Stabilization in France, Germany and Italy in the Decade after World War I.* Princeton: Princeton University Press, 1975.

Maier, Charles S. *The Unmasterable Past: History, Holocaust, and German National Identity.* Cambridge, MA: Harvard University Press, 1988.

Makkreel, Rudolf A. *Dilthey: Philosopher of the Human Sciences.* Princeton, NJ: Princeton University Press, 1992.

Makkreel, Rudolf A. "How Is Empathy Related to Understanding?" In *Issues in Husserl's Ideas II*, edited by Thomas Nenon and Lester Embree. Contributions to Phenomenology, 199–212. Dordrecht: Springer, 1996.

Makkreel, Rudolf A., and Frithjof Rodi. "Introduction to Volume III." In *The Formation of the Historical World in the Human Sciences.* Wilhelm Dilthey: Selected Works, edited by Rudolf A. Makkreel and Frithjof Rodi. Princeton, NJ: Princeton University Press, 2002.

Mandelbaum, Maurice. *The Anatomy of Historical Knowledge.* Baltimore, MD: Johns Hopkins University Press, 1977.

Mandelbaum, Maurice. *The Problem of Historical Knowledge: An Answer to Relativism.* New York: Liveright, 1938.

Mead, George H. *Mind, Self, and Society: From the Standpoint of a Social Behaviorist.* Chicago, IL: University of Chicago Press, 1967.

Meyer, Beate. *"Jüdische Mischlinge": Rassenpolitik und Verfolgungserfahrung, 1933–1945.* Studien zur jüdischen Geschichte, vol. 6, edited by Monika Richarz and Ina Lorenz. Hamburg: Dölling und Galitz, 1999.

Mink, Louis O. "The Autonomy of Historical Understanding." *History and Theory* 5, no. 1(1966): 24–47.

Misgeld, Dieter. "On Gadamer's Hermeneutics." *Philosophy of the Social Sciences* 9, no. 2(1979): 221–239.

Müller, Philipp. "Understanding History: Hermeneutics and Source-Criticism in Historical Scholarship." In *Reading Primary Sources: The Interpretation of Texts from Nineteenth- and Twentieth-Century History*, edited by Miriam Dobson and Benjamin Ziemann. London and New York: Routledge, 2008.

Nagel, Ernest. *The Structure of Science: Problems in the Logic of Scientific Explanation.* New York: Routledge and Kegan Paul, 1961.

Noakes, Jeremy, and Geoffrey Pridham, eds. *Nazism 1919–1945: Volume 3. Foreign Policy, War and Racial Extermination: A Documentary Reader.* Exeter: University of Exeter Press, 1995.

Nowak, Magdalena. "The Complicated History of Einfühlung." *Argument* 1, no. 2 (2011): 301–326.

Nozick, Robert. *Philosophical Explanations.* Cambridge, MA: Harvard University Press, 1981.

Nussbaum, Martha C. *Upheavals of Thought: The Intelligence of Emotions.* Cambridge: Cambridge University Press, 2001.

O'Hear, Anthony, ed. *Verstehen and Humane Understanding.* Royal Institute of Philosophy Supplement 41. Cambridge: Cambridge University Press, 1996.

Oakes, Guy. "Introductory Essay." In *Roscher and Knies: The Logical Problems of Historical Economics*, edited by Guy Oakes, 1–49. New York: Free Press, 1975.

Oliver, Sophie. "The Aesth-Ethics of Empathy: Bakhtin and the Return to Self as an Ethical Act." In *Empathy and Its Limits*, edited by Aleida Assmann and Ines Detmers, 166–186. London and New York: Palgrave Macmillan, 2016.

Orange, Donna M. "Experiential History: Understanding Backwards." In *History Flows through Us: Germany, the Holocaust, and the Importance of Empathy*, edited by Roger Frie, 49–60. London and New York: Routledge, 2018.

Pigman, George W. "Freud and the History of Empathy." *International Journal of Psycho-Analysis* 76(1995): 237–256.

Poland, Warren. "Clinician's Corner: The Limits of Empathy." *American Imago* 64 (2007): 87–93.

Popper, Karl R. *The Open Society and Its Enemies*. Vol. 2, London: Routledge and Sons, 1945.

Pulzer, Peter. *Germany, 1870–1945: Politics, State Formation, and War*. Oxford and New York: Oxford University Press, 1997.

Retz, Tyson. *Empathy and History: Historical Understanding in Re-Enactment, Hermeneutics and Education*. Making Sense of History, edited by Stefan Berger. New York and Oxford: Berghahn, 2018.

Roper, Lyndal. *Oedipus and the Devil: Witchcraft, Sexuality and Religion in Early Modern Europe*. London and New York: Routledge, 1994.

Roper, Michael. "The Unconscious Work of History." *Cultural and Social History* 11, no. 2(2014): 169–193.

Roseman, Mark. *The Wannsee Conference and the Final Solution*. New York: Metropolitan, 2002.

Sandis, Constantine. "A Just Medium: Empathy and Detachment in Historical Understanding." *Journal of the Philosophy of History* 5, no. 2(2011): 179–200.

Scheler, Max. *The Nature of Sympathy*. Translated by Peter Heath. London: Routledge and Kegan Paul, 1954.

Schwaber, Evelyne A. "Empathy: A Mode of Analytic Listening." *Psychoanalytic Inquiry* 1, no. 3(1981): 357–392.

Scott, Joan W. "The Evidence of Experience." *Critical Inquiry* 17, no. 4(1991): 773–797.

Scriven, Michael. "Truisms as the Grounds for Historical Explanations." In *Theories of History*, edited by Patrick Gardiner, 443–475. Glencoe, NY: Free Press of Glencoe, 1964.

Shapiro, Edward R. *Finding a Place to Stand: Developing Self-Reflective Institutions, Leaders, and Citizens*. Bicester: Phoenix, 2020.

Sherman, Nancy. "Empathy and Imagination." *Midwest Studies In Philosophy* 22, no. 1(1998): 82–119.

Shum, Peter. "Avoiding Circularities on the Empathic Path to Transcendental Intersubjectivity." *Topoi* 33, no. 1(2014): 143–156.

Simmel, Georg. "Vom Wesen des historischen Verstehens." In *Gesamtausgabe*, edited by Gregor Fitzi and Otthein Rammstedt, 151–179. Frankfurt: Suhrkamp, 1999.

Simmel, Georg. *The Problems of the Philosophy of History*. Translated by Guy Oakes. New York: Free Press, 1977.

Smith, Adam. *The Theory of Moral Sentiments*. edited by Knud Haakonssen. Cambridge: Cambridge University Press, 2002.

Spencer, James H., and Leon Balter. "Psychoanalytic Observation." *Journal of the American Psychoanalytic Association* 38, no. 2(1990): 393–421.

Stein, Edith. *On the Problem of Empathy*. Translated by Waltraut Stein. The Hague: Martinus Nijhoff, 1970.

Stoltzfus, Nathan. *Resistance of the Heart: Intermarriage and the Rosenstrasse Protest in Nazi Germany*. New York: Norton, 1996.

Strayer, Janet. "Affective and Cognitive Perspectives on Empathy." In *Empathy and Its Development*, edited by Nancy Eisenberg and Janet Strayer, 218–244. Cambridge: Cambridge University Press, 1987.

Stueber, Karsten. "Empathy." In *Stanford Encyclopedia of Philosophy*, edited by Edward Zalta. Palo Alto, CA: Stanford University Press, 2014.

Stueber, Karsten. "Empathy." In *Stanford Encyclopedia of Philosophy*, edited by Edward Zalta. Palo Alto, CA: Stanford University Press, 2019.

Stueber, Karsten. "Intentionalism, Intentional Realism, and Empathy." *Journal of the Philosophy of History* 3, no. 3(2009): 290–307.

Stueber, Karsten. "Reasons, Generalizations, Empathy, and Narratives: The Epistemic Structure of Action Explanation." *History and Theory* 47, no. 1(2008): 31–43.

Stueber, Karsten. "Understanding Versus Explanation? How to Think About the Distinction between the Human and the Natural Sciences." *Inquiry: An Interdisciplinary Journal of Philosophy* 55, no. 1(2012): 17–32.

Stueber, Karsten. *Rediscovering Empathy: Agency, Folk Psychology, and the Human Sciences*. Cambridge, MA: MIT Press, 2006.

Taylor, Barbara. "Historical Subjectivity." In *Psyche and History*, edited by Sally Alexander and Barbara Taylor, 195–210. Basingstoke: Palgrave Macmillan, 2012.

Thompson, Evan. *Mind in Life: Biology, Phenomenology, and the Sciences of Mind*. Cambridge, MA: Belknap Press of Harvard University Press, 2007.

Throop, C. Jason. "On the Problem of Empathy: The Case of Yap, Federated States of Micronesia." *Ethos* 36, no. 4(2008): 402–426.

Tompkins, Silvan. "Affects: Primary Motives of Man." *Humanitas* 3, no. 3(1968): 321–345.

Turner, Stephen. "Collingwood and Weber vs. Mink: History after the Cognitive Turn." *Journal of the Philosophy of History* 5, no. 2(2011): 230–260.

Vaage, Margarethe Bruun. "Fiction Film and the Varieties of Empathic Engagement." *Midwest Studies in Philosophy* 34(2010): 158–179.

van Baaren, Rick B., Jean Decety, Ap Dijksterhuis, Andries van der Leij, and Matthijs L. Leeuwen. "Being Imitated: Consequences of Nonconsciously Showing Empathy". In *The Social Neuroscience of Empathy*, edited by Jean Decety and William John Ickes, 31–42. Cambridge, MA: MIT Press, 2009.

Vico, Giambattista. *On the Most Ancient Wisdom of the Italians: Drawn out from the Origins of the Latin Language*. Translated by Jason Taylor. New Haven, CT and London: Yale University Press, 2010.

Vico, Giambattista. *The New Science of Giambattista Vico: Abridged Translation of the Third Edition (1744)*, edited by Thomas Goddard Bergin and Max Harold Fisch. Ithaca, NY: Cornell University Press, 1970.

Vielmetter, Georg. "The Theory of Holistic Simulation: Beyond Interpretivism and Postempiricism." In *Empathy and Agency: The Problem of Understanding in the Social Sciences*, edited by Hans Herbert Kögler and Karsten Stueber, 83–102. Boulder, CO: Westview, 2000.

von Moltke, Johannes. "Sympathy for the Devil: Cinema, History, and the Politics of Emotion." *New German Critique* 34(2007): 17–44.

von Ranke, Leopold. "On the Character of Historical Science (a Manuscript of the 1830s)." Translated by Wilma A. Iggers and Konrad von Moltke. In *The Theory and Practice of History*, edited by Georg G. Iggers and Konrad von Moltke, 33–46. Indianapolis: Bobbs-Merrill, 1973.

von Ranke, Leopold. *Englische Geschichte*. Sämtliche Werke, vol. 2. Leipzig: Duncker und Humblot, 1880.

Walsh, William Henry. *An Introduction to the Philosophy of History*. London: Hutchinson's University Library, 1951.

Walter, Henrik. "Social Cognitive Neuroscience of Empathy: Concepts, Circuits, and Genes." *Emotion Review* 4, no. 1(2012): 9–17.

Watson, Jeanne C., and Leslie S. Greenberg. "Empathic Resonance: A Neuroscience Perspective." In *The Social Neuroscience of Empathy*, edited by Jean Decety and William Ickes, 125–137. Cambridge, MA: MIT Press, 2009.

Weber, Max. "Critical Studies in the Logic of the Cultural Sciences." In *The Methodology of the Social Sciences*, edited by Edward A. Shils and Henry A. Finch, 113–188. New York: Free Press, 1977.

Weber, Max. *Economy and Society: An Outline of Interpretive Sociology*, edited by Guenther Roth and Claus Wittich. Vol. 1. Berkeley: University of California Press, 1978.

Weber, Max. "'Objectivity' in Social Science and Social Policy." In *The Methodology of the Social Sciences*, edited by Edward A. Shils and Henry A. Finch, 49–112. New York: Free Press, 1977.

Weber, Max. *Roscher and Knies: The Logical Problems of Historical Economics*. Translated by Guy Oakes. New York: Free Press, 1975.

Weitz, Eric D. *Weimar Germany: Promise and Tragedy: New and Expanded Edition*. Princeton, NJ: Princeton University Press, 2013.

White, Morton. *Foundations of Historical Knowledge*. New York: Harper Torchbooks, 1965.

Winch, Peter. *The Idea of a Social Science and Its Relation to Philosophy*. London: Routledge and Kegan Paul, 1970 (originally published 1958).

Winch, Peter. "Understanding a Primitive Society." *American Philosophical Quarterly* 1, no. 4(1964): 307–324.

Winkler, Heinrich August. "Mehr Revolution wagen?" *Die Zeit*, 21 February 2019.

Winter, Jay. "From Sympathy to Empathy: Trajectories of Rights in the Twentieth Century." In *Empathy and Its Limits*, edited by Aleida Assmann and Ines Detmers, 100–114. London and New York: Palgrave Macmillan, 2016.

Wispé, Lauren. "The Distinction between Sympathy and Empathy: To Call Forth a Concept, a Word Is Needed." *Journal of Personality and Social Psychology* 50 (1986): 314–321.

Wispé, Lauren. "History of the Concept of Empathy." In *Empathy and Its Development*, edited by Nancy Eisenberg and Janet Strayer. Cambridge Studies in Social and Emotional Development, 17–37. New York: Cambridge University Press, 1987.

Wolin, Richard. *The Seduction of Unreason: The Intellectual Romance with Fascism from Nietzsche to Postmodernism*. Princeton, NJ: Princeton University Press, 2004.

Wollheim, Richard. *The Thread of Life*. New Haven, CT: Yale University Press, 1984.

Yahil, Leni. *The Holocaust: The Fate of European Jewry, 1932–1945*. Translated by Ina Friedman and Haya Galai. New York and Oxford: Oxford University Press, 1990.

Zahavi, Dan. "Empathy and Mirroring: Husserl and Gallese." In *Life, Subjectivity, and Art: Essays in Honor of Rudolf Bernet*, edited by Roland Breeur and Ullrich Melle, 217–254. Dordrecht: Springer, 2012.

Zahavi, Dan. "Empathy and Other-Directed Intentionality." *Topoi* 33, no. 1(2014): 129–142.

Zahavi, Dan. "Simulation, Projection, and Empathy." *Conscious Cognition* 17(2008): 514–522.

Zahavi, Dan. *Subjectivity and Selfhood.* Cambridge, MA: MIT Press, 2005.

Zahavi, Dan, and Søren Overgaard. "Empathy without Isomorphism: A Phenomenological Account." In *Empathy: From Bench to Bedside*, edited by Jean Decety, 3–20. Cambridge, MA: MIT Press, 2012.

Zaki, Jamil, and Kevin Ochsner. "The Neuroscience of Empathy: Progress, Pitfalls and Promise." *Nature Neuroscience* 15, no. 5(2012): 675–680.

Index